Introduction to H
for Interpreters and Translators

Introduction to Healthcare for Interpreters and Translators

Ineke H.M. Crezee

Auckland University of Technology

with illustrations by

Jenny Jiang

with contributions by

Maureen Kearney, Dana Lui and Dr. Linda Hand

John Benjamins Publishing Company

Amsterdam / Philadelphia

The paper used in this publication meets the minimum requirements of the American National Standard for Information Sciences – Permanence of Paper for Printed Library Materials, ANSI z39.48-1984.

Library of Congress Cataloging-in-Publication Data

Crezee, Ineke.
Introduction to Healthcare for Interpreters and Translators / Ineke H.M. Crezee ; with illustrations by
    Jenny Jiang ; with contributions by Maureen Kearney, Dana Lui, and Dr. Linda Hand.
    pages cm.
     Includes bibliographical references and index.
  1. Medicine-Translating. 2. Health facilities--Translating services. 3. Translating and interpreting.
    I. Kearney, Maureen. II. Lui, Dana. III. Hand, Linda. IV. Title.
R119.5.C74   2013
362.1--dc23   2013021516
ISBN 978 90 272 1205 4 (Hb; alk. paper) / ISBN 978 90 272 1206 1 (Pb; alk. paper)
ISBN 978 90 272 7150 1 (Eb)

John Benjamins Publishing Company • P.O. Box 36224 • 1020 ME Amsterdam • The Netherlands
John Benjamins North America • P.O. Box 27519 • Philadelphia PA 19118-0519 • USA

Table of contents

Table of illustrations

List of tables

Author's notes

This book is intended, first and foremost, as a guide for all those who are working as or wishing to work as interpreters or translators in healthcare settings, but who have not had any formal training as health professionals. Health interpreter trainers may also find this book useful as a course text for programmes aimed at preparing interpreters for work in the healthcare setting. There is no point in simply learning medical terminology lists or surfing the internet without a good basic understanding of health and healthcare. The workings of the body are very complicated but will be explained only in very broad terms in relevant chapters, so as to enable the interpreter to have a good general understanding of what doctors and other health professionals are talking about when they explain the patient's condition to the patient or the patient's relatives. This publication is intended to give health interpreters who do not have a professional health care background some very basic insights into the health system, as well as anatomy, physiology and common disorders. The field of medicine may be compared to a magical onion: researchers keep unpeeling further and further layers of previously unknown details, however the aim of this book is, first and foremost, to enable health care interpreters to do their job with a better knowledge of the subject area. Secondly, the book aims to provide interpreters with a good basis for ongoing self- and professional development. For this reason, language has been kept fairly plain throughout the book and information has been restricted to main points, to avoid losing readers in a jungle of details.

The blue print for this book was based on feedback from students in one of the author's health interpreting courses. Students said they wanted a three part book that would firstly give a brief introduction to health interpreting, followed by an overview of various settings and finishing with a number of chapters dedicated to health specialties. They wanted the overview of the various settings to incorporate questions commonly asked by health professionals. Students requested that the final part of the book be organized by health specialty. Students asked that each chapter in the final part be named by specialty (e.g. Orthopedics) and organized so as to optimize preparation for assignments. Accordingly, each chapter in Part III of this book will start with an overview of anatomy and physiology of a particular body system. This will be followed by a brief look at the Latin and Greek roots which are the building blocks of much of the terminology to do with particular body systems. Health interpreters will be able to go to relevant chapters prior to an interpreting assignment, to re-familiarize themselves with anatomy, physiology, Latin and Greek roots and most common conditions, investigations and treatment options. Users should feel free to use this book as a glossary, and write terminology in their own language next to the English terms.

This work will be equally useful to health translators, since both interpreters and translators need to be thoroughly familiar with a setting in order to 'interpret' it. Health translators working on medical reports will be able to find commonly used abbreviations. Translators who have been asked to translate health information material into community languages will be able to gain a good basic overview of related background information.

This book will not discuss general aspects of interpreting or translation in great detail. Interested readers are referred to the excellent publications by Scimone and Ginori (1995), Shlesinger (1995), Pöchhacker and Shlesinger (2007), Gile (1995), Gentile, Ozolins and Vasalikakos (1996), and Hale (2004, 2007) for thorough studies on the main issues in community and legal interpreting and the need for pre-service training (Hale 2007). Pöchhacker and Shlesinger (2007) address discourse in healthcare interpreting, while issues in healthcare interpreting settings across countries are discussed in (Valero-Garcés & Martin 2008).

Care has been taken to provide information which may prove useful to interpreters in a wide range of English speaking countries. Those interpreting for new migrants or refugees from a range of countries are referred to the excellent work on specific health risks in different regions of the world by Kemp and Rasbridge (2004), and on traditional cultural values and crosscultural communication by Jackson (2006) and Camplin-Welch (2007).

The author is under no illusion that this book will be so comprehensive as to cover the entire range of areas interpreters may come across when working in health care settings. With the continuing developments in the fields of technology, biophysics, biochemistry and integrative medicine, healthcare delivery will see the introduction of ever changing procedures, tests, and approaches to treatment. There is no doubt that publications like the current one will need to be updated fairly regularly to keep abreast of new procedures and changes in the use of terminology.

The author also wishes to stress that the present publication contains some anecdotal evidence relating to ethical conflicts in healthcare settings. Such anecdotes were commonly shared by experienced interpreters who wished to remain anonymous.

This book is intended for an international readership, and every effort has been made to ensure the contents reflect the general healthcare setting in a range of countries as current at the time of writing. US spelling has been followed throughout. This means that words originating from the Greek words containing 'αι', which are spelled with 'ae' in the UK tradition, have been spelled with 'e' instead. An example would be hematology (rather than haematology) and pediatrics (rather than paediatrics). Labour has been spelled as labor. Where possible alternative spellings have been included in the index.

The author has attempted to avoid jargon. As an example the word 'investigations' has been used throughout rather than the word workup, and similarly the term 'blood tests' has been used rather than blood work.

The author welcomes any suggestions or comments!

Ineke Crezee, February 2013
Affiliation: Auckland University of Technology, Faculty of Culture and Society, Auckland, New Zealand.

Disclaimer

"Nothing in this book should be construed as personal advice or diagnosis, and must not be used in this manner. The information provided about conditions is general in nature. This information does not cover all possible uses, actions, precautions, side-effects, or interactions of medicines, or medical procedures. The information in this book should not be considered as complete and does not cover all diseases, ailments, physical conditions, or their treatment. Any decision regarding treatment and medication for medical conditions should be made with the advice and consultation of a qualified health care professional."

Acknowledgments

This publication is dedicated to my parents, who lived the concept of ongoing education and sharing knowledge. They never failed to support me, even when I could not make up my mind as to what I wanted to be: translator, interpreter, English scholar, health professional or interpreter and translator educator. If in the end, I have turned out to be a little bit of everything, it is thanks to them. My thanks must also go to my brother, Dr Hans Crezee, who works as a Principal Investigator at the University of Amsterdam Academic Medical Centre, and to my colleagues at the Auckland University of Technology, in particular Annette Sachtleben and Deborah MacRae. Annette very kindly edited my responses to the suggested revisions. Deborah spent many hours on a close reading of the book, to ensure consistency of layout and content and acted as a sounding board during many of our long road runs together. Thanks must also go to our wonderful librarian Shahzad Ghahreman for for his assistance with all relevant resources.

I am indebted to Maureen Kearney (RN, RM) and Dana Lui (RN, RM, NP) for their valuable contributions, and to Dr Linda Hand for her specialized contribution about interpreting for Speech Therapists. I also want to thank Dr Minsi Xu, Dr Hans Crezee, Dr Ronald Goedeke, Viola Ziolkowska (graduate of Gdansk Medical School) and Sue McCulloch, for assisting me in keeping up-to-date with new advances in medicine and healthcare.

I am very grateful to my Australian colleagues Sandra Hale, Uldis Ozolins and Annamaria Arnall for their enthusiasm and support. I am delighted that Sandra Hale, author of many groundbreaking books and articles on interpreting, very graciously consented to write a foreword to the book.

I would also like to thank Cynthia Roat, Terry Mirande, Marjory Bancroft, Katharine Allen, Maria Gonzalez Davies, Jan Cambridge, Teruko Asano, Deborah Miyashita and the late Miriam Shlesinger for their collegial encouragement.

I want to thank Vladimir Madjar and Jane Visserman for sharing their experience with me, and also experienced interpreters Cyril Young, Slavitsa Madjar, Slavica Radovic, Zoreh Karimi, Norah and Ahmed Aklil for their insightful comments. I am also indebted to Dr Sabinc Fenton who had the great foresight to set up the very first health interpreting course in New Zealand in 1990. Sabine invited me to 'look after' the health specific aspects, thus allowing me to combine my passion for health with my love of language, translation and interpreting.

I am very grateful to my interpreting students, who gave me the idea for this book, and who told me exactly what they wanted in a book of this nature.

Many thanks to Jenny for taking up the challenge to produce very clear illustrations for this book, based on my own rather less professional ones.

I appreciate the time and care taken by the reviewers who went through the book with great care and attention and who came up with a number of truly excellent suggestions, which I have tried to implement in detail.

Last but not least, I want to thank my husband Paul Tetteroo, for his caring level-headed advice and support throughout.

Foreword

As interpreting and translation educators and practitioners we are privileged to meet interesting people from different professional, educational and ethnic backgrounds with a wealth of knowledge about language and culture and about life in general. The people we interpret for and the students we teach are usually our inspiration to do better. We learn from them and they learn from us. As practitioners, we are constantly confronted with new topics, new settings, new language and new challenges. The interdisciplinarity of our work leads to constant gaps in our knowledge and skills and as educators we feel the responsibility to do something about filling those gaps. One way is to conduct research to find answers, another is to disseminate our new acquired knowledge in the form of teaching resources. This book is an example of the latter. Written by a health professional, practicing interpreter and educator, *Introduction to Healthcare for Interpreters and Translators* is an easily accessible, practical guide for students and practicing healthcare interpreters. Ineke Crezee's motivation for writing this useful resource came from her own students who specifically asked for a book of this kind.

Interpreters do not work in isolation. They work in specific settings with their own cultures, organizational practices, institutional goals, participant roles, and context-specific discourses. In order for interpreters to be able to interpret accurately, they must first understand the context in which they are working, the content they are to interpret, the discourse strategies used by the different participants and the discipline specific terminology. This book aims to provide guidance on many of those context specific issues. It describes different health settings, hospital procedures and health care interactions; explains the roles of primary care providers, nursing, medical and other hospital staff; provides easy to understand descriptions of anatomy and the different biological systems, complemented with figures and pictures; presents samples and explanations of typical illnesses and conditions, diagnoses, tests, medical procedures, treatments and medications; and descriptions of common equipment used in hospitals. The book also provides a section on the language and discourse of health and medicine, firstly by presenting an overview of its Greek and Latin origins, followed by glossaries of terms with clear definitions and lists of typical medical and other health related questions.

The book complements the content pertaining to the healthcare context and setting with anecdotes from practicing interpreters and practical advice from the author as educator. Continuous reference to the work of interpreters and their ethical obligations is made throughout in a didactic way to make relevant links to the work of interpreters and at times translators.

Practising interpreters and interpreting students will be able to achieve the author's goal of increasing their knowledge of the medical field and apply it to the improvement of their practice by using this book as a practical guide. *Introduction to Healthcare for Interpreters and Translators* is a welcome addition to the training resources available.

Sandra Hale
Professor of Interpreting and Translation
School of Humanities and Languages
University of New South Wales, Australia

PART I

Interpreting

Chapter 1

Introduction

1. How to use this book

This book contains 28 chapters, divided into three separate parts. Part I provides a brief introduction to healthcare interpreting, while Part II provides an overview of a range of healthcare settings. Part III offers a brief overview of the main body systems, conditions and disorders, investigations and treatments, organized around the body as a framework. Some items may of necessity be mentioned under different headings, however it is hoped that this will strengthen understanding. Each chapter will be completed by a summary of the main points, to assist learning and understanding. Health interpreter educators may want to use this book as a course text, while health interpreters may want to use the book as a reference, checking briefly on anatomy, terminology and most commonly encountered conditions before leaving to interpret in a certain setting.

As mentioned under the author's notes, this work will be equally useful to health translators, since they too need to be thoroughly familiar with healthcare settings and terminology in order to successfully carry out translation assignments (Gonzalez-Davies 1998). Sections of this book will concentrate on health interpreters and issues they may face in practice, including the pressures which result from being in the setting, at close quarters to both health professionals and healthcare users. Translators will not usually find themselves in the actual setting, but will still need to possess a good basic knowledge of healthcare and medical terminology to carry out their assignments. Translators will find these described in Parts II and III of this book, whilst cultural issues relevant to both translators and interpreters will be described in Chapter 3.

This chapter and the next will focus mainly on the development of the interpreting profession and the demand for healthcare interpreters. The wide range of studies in the area of health interpreting will be touched upon only very briefly, the reader being referred to other publications for further reading. The chapter will also touch on teaching health interpreting, since health interpreter educators may wish to use the book as a course text.

2. Development of the interpreting profession

Before discussing specific aspects associated with healthcare interpreting, some thought needs to be given to the development of the interpreting profession in general. Interpreting is probably one of the oldest professions in the world, the presence of interpreters being mentioned in the Bible when Joseph talks to his brothers through an interpreter (Genesis 29–50). Interpreters are also mentioned by Roman and Greek historians including Cicero, Plutarch and Herodotes (Hermann 2002; Mair 2011).

In contrast to translation theory, which has been discussed in detail by a considerable number of authors from the Classical period to the current time, interpreting studies have only claimed the attention of theorists, linguists and educators much more recently. We might surmise from this that perhaps the services of interpreters have long been taken for granted and not been given much thought. It might also be assumed that, for a long time, interpreters were merely viewed as bilingual individuals who were incidentally called upon to use their linguistic skills on certain occasions (i.e. commercial or military). Such examples include Malinche, who acted as interpreter (and more) to Hernán Cortes (Mair 2011), and Tupaia, the Tahitian, who, while engaged as a pilot and navigator, also acted as an interpreter for Captain Cook when visiting New Zealand. For centuries too, the demand for interpreters may not have been that obvious, as the residents of many countries sought to use one 'common language' (or *lingua franca*) for the purpose of communicating with speakers of other languages. In this way, Latin was long used as the lingua franca by scientists and statesmen from a wide range of European countries. The Renaissance and the advent of nationalist movements in many European countries was reflected in the resurgence of a feeling of national identity and a renewed interest in and emphasis on national languages. The influence of Latin (and Greek) in medical terminology remained, however, and as a result, those engaged in healthcare interpreting between English and other languages need to acquire a good knowledge of Latin and Greek roots, affixes and suffixes.

3. The demand for interpreters around the world

From the early part of the 20th century, there has been an increasing demand for interpreters worldwide. After the First World War, interpreters were employed during lengthy international negotiations over the terms of the Treaty of Versailles. After World War II, interpreters were needed for proceedings such as the Nuremberg War Crime Trials, which were attended by participants from a wide range of countries. In more recent times, civil wars, unrest and fighting in various *hot spots* around the world have led to an increase in the number of refugees settling in new countries, while globalization has led to international trade and organizations such as the European Common Market, the United Nations and World Health Organization. These changes have brought with them an ever growing demand and need for interpreters and translators.

Migrants, in particular, bring great diversity to countries like the United States (US), the United Kingdom (UK) Canada, Australia and New Zealand (NZ). Gill et al. (Gill, Shankar, Quirke & Freemantle 2009) suggest that linguistic diversity is such that in the UK interpreting services need to cater to the needs of almost 300 different community languages, excluding dialects. Gill et al. estimate that interpreting services might be needed during some 2,520,885 general practice consultations per year.

In the US, 20% of the population speak a language other than English at home (US Census Bureau 2011), with approximately 47 million people speaking a language other than English (Swabey & Nicodemus 2011) and more than 24 million residents unable to speak English fluently (U.S. Census Bureau). The first US telephone interpreting service was offered in 1981, with many others following. Today courts and hospitals in the US make extensive use of face-to-face, telephone and video interpreters. Phelan (2001) offers a good overview of the services and range of training programmes offered.

In Australia in the 1970s, the influx of migrants (from a wide variety of cultural, ethnic, religious and linguistic backgrounds) led to an increased and ongoing demand for interpreters who were able to work in various community contexts, including health, legal and public service settings. An accreditation system was set up for the identification of different skill levels and for the accreditation of individual translators and interpreters who were able to work at these differing levels. A National Accreditation Authority for Translators and Interpreters (NAATI) was set up (Chesher 1997), which remains involved in training, accreditation and certification of translators and interpreters to this day. Hale (2007, 2012) argues that interpreters need specialized pre-service training to work in special settings such as the legal and medical contexts. The author wholeheartedly agrees, and would argue that, likewise, there is no doubt that healthcare interpreters need specialized training to enable them to work in health-related settings.

In the late 1980s, NZ faced controversy surrounding a large cervical cancer research project involving many women who did not have English as their first language (Coney 1998). The subsequent findings of the committee of inquiry concluded that trained interpreters should be used in interactions with patients from non-English speaking backgrounds (NESB). Subsequently, the need to use trained interpreters where practicable was included in the 1996 Health and Disability Act. New Zealand society has since become increasingly multilingual and multicultural (Crezee 2009a, 2009b), with services reportedly catering for up to 190 different community languages, including Moon, Chin, Karen and Xhosa. LanguageLine, the New Zealand government telephone interpreting services, catered for 43 languages at the time of writing.

4. Health interpreting studies

Today, the need for interpreters is acknowledged around the world, with interpreting being increasingly recognized as a profession in its own right. This has led to widespread discussion of the ethics and standards of the profession, a debate which is reflected in the literature.

Since the 1980s there has been an increasing number of studies associated with interpreting in public service settings, in particular those related to health and justice. Hale (2007) provides an excellent summary of such studies. Of special interest to healthcare interpreting studies is 'the loss of crucial information in the medical encounter mediated by unprofessional interpreters' (Hale 2007, p. 200), This is also discussed in studies by Vasquez and Javier (1991) and Cambridge (1999). There is no doubt that the use of untrained interpreters can have a considerable impact on the communication between health professionals and patients. The various Codes of Ethics developed for interpreters (see Hale 2007, for an overview) therefore tend to focus not only on ethical conduct during the interpreting session, but also on the need for ongoing professional development and education and the necessity to decline interpreting assignments which the interpreter should reasonably know to be beyond his or her area of competence. Many studies have therefore focused on issues relating to the interpreter's role and the interpreters' impact on interactions between health professionals and patients (Athorp & Downing 1996; Wädensjö 1998; Cambridge 1999; Bolden 2000; Meyer et al. 2003; Flores, Barton Laws & Mayo 2003; Flores 2005, 2006; Tellechea Sanchez 2005) and on ethical dilemmas (Kaufert & Putsch 1997; Angelelli 2004; Mason 2004; Hale 2005; Clifford 2005; Rudvin 2004, 2007). In New Zealand, Gray, Stubbe and Hilders (2012) developed a toolkit for the use of interpreters in general practice. In Australia Napier, Major and Johnston have developed a medical terminology sign bank for signed language (AUSLAN interpreters). See also Major, Napier, Ferrara and Johnston (2012), Napier, Major & Ferrara (2011) and Johnston and Napier (2010). Other areas related to health interpreting (education) and translation have been explored by Bancroft 2013; Crezee, Jülich and Hayward (forthcoming); Ferner and Liu 2009; Fischbach 1998; Holt, Crezee and Rasalingam 2003; Meyer 2001; Napier 2010, 2011; O'Neill 1991; Pöchhacker 2004; Roat 1999a, 1999b, 2000; Roberts-Smith, Frey and Bessel-Browne 1990; Roy 2000, 2002, Stewart 1995.

Several researchers have commented on the lack of empirical studies as to what goes on in interpreter-mediated health encounters (Angelelli 2008; Chen 2003; Swabey & Nicodemus 2011). This is most likely due to the fact that such studies would include a complex process involving ethics approval and consent from all those involved in such encounters: health professionals, interpreters and patients. Thus studies aimed at protecting a patient's right to effective communication (and protection from potential breaches of the interpreters' code of ethics) often appear to fall at the first hurdle, namely that of obtaining the approval of ethics committees who are equally intent on protecting patient rights. This apparent paradox still looks to be some way from being revolved. This is primarily due to the fact that arguably only large scale studies into interpreter-mediated encounters would yield the statistically significant findings needed to gain real insights into health interpreting practice. However, large scale studies are typically less likely to gain ethics approval, than small scale studies, where the latter might allow the researcher more control over variables. In the case of clinical studies, ethics approval is usually obtained because the perceived benefits are seen to outweigh possible objections. Quality interpreting research may be said to be comparable to clinical studies in terms of their importance on patient outcomes.

5.   Teaching healthcare interpreting

One challenge faced at the author's university is training interpreters in languages that the lecturers may not be familiar with, because of the ongoing demand in an ever changing range of community languages (Crezee & Sachtleben 2012). A second challenge is to teach health interpreting in such a way, that students feel empowered and ready to develop further in practice, as lifelong learners. Health is a huge and complex area: the more layers you unpeel, the more are revealed underneath. The challenge is to give aspiring student health interpreters enough information to empower them, setting them off on a path of effective lifelong development, without confusing and undermining them.

Learning starts with a good text book. Student feedback on what they wanted in a course book has resulted in the book before you now. The challenges of preparing students for interpreting in healthcare comprise:

- reducing the virtual Mount Everest of Latin, Greek and complex science, to a seemingly surmountable 'molehill';
- allowing students to practise interpreting whilst also getting immediate feedback on their performance, as that is effective and powerful (something the author learnt from a friend who trains football referees);
- familiarizing and preparing students for the ethical dilemmas they will face in practice.

The author would advise educators to keep thinking of how they can make the learning experience better still, not being afraid to draw on personal experiences as a health professional and/or interpreter in telling helpful anecdotes. Miming, drawing cartoons and stories are very powerful and consolidate the 'drier' points of learning.

The author strongly believes that healthcare interpreting needs to be taught following a situated learning model (Gonzalez Davies 2004) where learning is partly co-constructed, especially in team and pair work. Teaching should center on:

- theoretical knowledge of healthcare settings and terminology,
- theoretical and practical knowledge of the professional code of conduct, and
- providing semi-authentic simulated opportunities for interpreting practice, also using videoclips.

In some cases, the lecturer may be both a practising health interpreter and health professional. In other cases, the teaching team may consist of an experienced interpreter plus an experienced health professional.

Care should be taken to choose a health professional who has the ability and skill to explain the necessary information clearly, without overwhelming the students with too much detail, as this will merely lead to confusion. The knowledge base provided should prepare student interpreters for the knowledge required to accurately and comfortably interpret between health professionals and patients.

Sessions should involve a presentation, interspersed with videoclips showing patients in hospitals during related doctor-patient interviews and/or undergoing certain procedures.

Watching videoclips will serve to give student interpreters the feeling of being 'right there' in the hospital room. This simulated presence in the healthcare setting may help give student interpreters the feeling that they are being induced into the Community of Practice of practising healthcare interpreters (Lave 1990, 1991, 1996; Lave & Wenger 1991). Once they are practicing interpreters, they will repeat this experience in real life, and this will consolidate their knowledge of healthcare settings, allowing them to develop as healthcare interpreters.

Medical equipment such as real angiography catheters, nebulizer masks, stents, inhalers, peak flow meters should be passed around the class. It is much easier to interpret the word 'catheter' when you have held a real one in your hands. Such realia can be obtained from healthcare settings, e.g. when a pack has been opened by accident and the catheter can no longer be used as it is no longer sterile.

Induction into the professional code of conduct and into interpreting practice should be led by an experienced healthcare interpreter. Interpreting practice may involve students working in pairs or in triads, reading out scripts in English and LOTE (Language Other than English). In this way, student A can act as a the health professional, reading out the script for that role in English. Student B can act as the patient, doing a sight translation from English into LOTE while Student C does not have a script, but has to interpret what he or she hears. This practice enables *immediate feedback* from Students A and B on word choice and interpreting competence. In the author's experience, students find this type of practice thoroughly enjoyable and effective (Crezee & Sachtleben, in progress).

The author and her colleagues utilize Blackboard Collaborate Voice Authoring® technology in the computer lab, where students record their responses to pre-recorded interpreting dialogues. This technology also allows student interpreters to get their 'language buddies' or family members at home or anywhere in the world to listen to their interpreting practice and give them language-specific feedback.

Other valuable practice may take the form of field trips. As an example the author took her student interpreters off campus to practise interpreting with Speech Language Therapists (SLTs)*, some of whom spoke the same Language Other Than English (LOTE) as the students. Students and SLTs spent hours practising interpreter-mediated real life scenarios, with some playing the role of interfering parents, incompetent interpreters, four-year old children with speech problems, or stroke victims. The students were there for three hours and when it was time to stop, nobody wanted to stop. It was a real buzz, and not hard to organize.

*Post-graduate students who were already qualified SLTs

Summary of main points

This chapter has identified three possible categories of readership for this book:

– healthcare interpreters
– health translators
– health interpreter educators

This chapter has touched on the development of the interpreting profession and the increasing demand for healthcare interpreters. It has also briefly touched on the range of publications in the area of health interpreting as well as on the challenges involved in health interpreter education.

Chapter 2

Interpreting in healthcare settings

This chapter will touch on some of the challenges faced by professionals interpreting in healthcare settings, and will move from there to an overview of what skills, abilities and knowledge health interpreters need to possess. Health interpreter training should address all these areas to allow (student) interpreters to develop the knowledge and capabilities required.

1.   Interpreting in healthcare settings

There is a great demand for trained and competent interpreters in healthcare settings. Unfortunately, all too often, staff on the ward may feel tempted to utilize the services of the so-called BYO (Bring-Your-Own) interpreters. Alternatively, they may ask anyone who happens to speak the patient's language, be this a visitor, an orderly, or a cleaner, to act as interpreter. This may happen because ward staff are in a hurry, for instance because the patient has to go to the Operating Room for a lifesaving operation, and there is no time to lose. In most cases, however, the real reason for not using a trained interpreter may be that staff, who are often monolingual, have a poor understanding of what is involved in interpreting, e.g. linguistic skills, cultural knowledge, interpreting techniques, code of ethics, or of the risks of using untrained interpreters in healthcare settings. Sometimes the cost of bringing in a trained healthcare interpreter also comes into play.

Most countries have a health interpreting system in place, which may involve *on site* (face-to-face) interpreting, telephone interpreting or interpreting via videoconferencing (e.g. the My Accessible Real Time Trusted Interpreter (MARTI) system in the US) or video remote interpreting (VRI). So let us have a look at what is involved in healthcare interpreting and what qualities a good healthcare interpreter needs to possess.

2.   Different healthcare systems

Most countries have healthcare systems offering healthcare at the primary and secondary care level. Differences between countries are mainly due to differences in historical development and funding. The healthcare systems in former Commonwealth countries (like Canada, Australia and New Zealand) tend to be quite similar to that which operates in the UK, being mainly publicly funded. The healthcare system in the US, in contrast, is still primarily funded and operated by private entities.

In the early days of most healthcare systems, patients were only seen when they were ill, with little or no emphasis placed on disease prevention. This is sometimes referred to as the *ambulance at the bottom of the cliff* system. More recently, healthcare emphasis has moved to include illness prevention. Preventive care involves education, screening and preventive measures. These may include such things as breast cancer and cervical cancer screening programmes and diabetes educators. Chapters 5 through to 8 will provide some information on both primary care and hospital care settings.

3. Accuracy

Accuracy has been a problematic concept in interpreting and translation over the centuries (Venuti 2000; Pöchhäcker & Shlesinger 2002) and the discussion is still evolving. Hale (1996, 2004, 2007) has provided an excellent overview of the discussion, which includes the very important pragmatic aspects of communication. Hale states that 'the interpreter's very difficult role is to understand the intention of the utterance and portray it as faithfully as possible in the other language (Hale 2008, p. 115). Morris (1999, as cited in Hale 2008) with reference to court interpreting, asserts that interpreting involves 'gaining an understanding of the intentions of the original-language speaker and attempting to convey the illocutionary force of the original utterance' adding that this 'understanding will be to some extent a personal, i.e. a subjective one'. Hale agrees that while it may not be possible to ever be sure about the intention behind other people's utterances, it is possible for the interpreter 'to be faithful to their own interpretation of the original utterance' as that is the best they can be expected to do (Hale 2008, p. 115).

In most cases, healthcare interpreters will be involved in situations where *information needs to be exchanged*. See also Wadensjö (1998, 2002), Meyer (2000, 2003) and Tebble (1998, 2004) for just some of the discussion on the discourse analysis of such interviews). Such exchanges may include:

- the healthcare professional trying to elicit information from the patient or client by asking questions, e.g. when taking a patient's history or when trying to assess the patient's condition after surgery or other forms of treatment.
- The healthcare professional giving the patient instructions which are essential for preventing complications and for managing the patient's condition, e.g. the healthcare professional may tell the patient what to watch out for after a head injury, or may instruct a patient with diabetes about lifestyle changes, which are essential to prevent further complications.

- The healthcare professional giving information about a procedure for which he requires the patient's Informed Consent. In this situation, the patient may be asking for further information in relation to the proposed benefits of the procedure, as well as its side-effects, risks and any possible alternatives.
- The patient may also ask for information, e.g. about the disorder, the disease process, further treatment options and medications.
- Alternatively, the interpreter may be needed in a *counselling* situation. Here, the interview between the client and the health professional or counsellor will revolve not so much around an exchange of information, as around an expression of feelings and emotions on the part of the client, and an understanding of these on the part of the professional.

It is clear that, in order to interpret accurately, a healthcare interpreter needs a good knowledge and understanding of anatomy and physiology of the main body systems, most common diseases and/or disorders, assessments and treatment methods, including pre-operative instructions. Interpreters should be familiar with informed consent procedures, and with commonly used healthcare terminology, including their Latin and Greek roots, prefixes and suffixes. Health interpreters also need to be familiar with idiomatic language. In some countries, health professionals like to use idiomatic expressions in order to make the patient feel at ease, not realizing that non-native speakers may not have learned such expressions (Crezee & Grant 2013). Similarly, patients may use everyday expressions to describe their symptoms and interpreters need to understand these in order to interpret them accurately. For example, Spanish speaking interpreters need to be familiar with a wide range of expressions used in the many different Spanish speaking countries.

If the interpreter does not interpret information accurately, the consequences may be disastrous. The author was told about a NZ based interpreter who had rendered the words 'major surgery' as 'a small operation'. The family had signed the consent form, believing the procedure to be a minor one. When the child ended up in the Intensive Care Unit after surgery, they expressed shock and a feeling of distrust towards the doctor who had given them this 'false' information.

Accuracy is similarly important in history taking. Most of the studies reviewed by Stewart (1995) demonstrated a correlation between effective physician-patient communication and improved patient health outcomes. Health professionals are very much aware of the fact that people who cannot express the history of their complaints, are at risk of not having their underlying disorders fully diagnosed. An incorrect diagnosis may lead to either an inappropriate course of treatment or to the patient being discharged in error. This may lead to frequent re-admissions or detoriation in the patient's condition.

Migrants or visitors from other countries, who do not speak English (well enough), may not be able to express exactly how they came to be in the condition they are in, what their family history or social background is – in other words, they may be unable to give the healthcare professionals the exact information needed in order to reach the correct diagnosis and to institute the most appropriate treatment. Therefore the role of a trained interpreter who is very familiar with health terminology, anatomy and physiology cannot be underestimated. Interpreters who do not know the difference between heartburn, heart failure, a heart attack or cardiac arrest, cannot interpret such terms accurately and this may cause significant problems for patients and health professionals. See Chapters 18 and 26 for more information on the differences between these conditions.

To summarize: In order to interpret accurately and appropriately, healthcare interpreters need to have a very wide knowledge base. They need to be familiar with the healthcare system in both their current country of residence and their country of origin. This familiarity should include at least the following:

i.   Organization and procedures in the healthcare system of the client's country of origin, today and in the past, and organization and procedures in the healthcare system of the host country.

    Sometimes healthcare interpreters may find it difficult to keep abreast of developments in the healthcare system in the clients' or their own countries of origin, for instance because they cannot return there for fear of (political) prosecution. Sometimes it is the client who simply does not understand the organization of the healthcare system, even if it is interpreted into the healthcare terminology currently used in their country of origin. The author once acted as interpreter for an elderly woman who had never previously been admitted to hospital in NZ and who had been away from the Netherlands for the past 40 years. This client was not familiar with either Dutch or NZ healthcare terminology and did not understand the plain Dutch word for *epidural anesthesia*.

ii. Various professionals involved in the healthcare system of the client's country of origin and various professionals involved in the healthcare system of the host country.

    Healthcare professionals involved in the healthcare system, may be known by names which may sound similar, but which often indicate completely different roles. In the US junior doctors who have recently completed Medical training may be referred to as *interns*, whilst in NZ, *interns* are medical students. Similarly, in some parts of the US, Advanced Nurse Practitioners may carry out some of the roles typically associated with Primary Physicians, by providing primary care and prescribing some medications. The issue of correctly understanding and interpreting the titles of various health professionals becomes even more important in Informed Consent situations, where it may be very important for the client to know whether it is Mr Johnson, the Surgical Specialist or Dr Johnson the Senior Surgical *Registrar* who is going to carry out a procedure.

iii. Appointment and referral system in the client's country of origin and appointment and referral system in the host country.

One might presume that all countries have a system whereby the client sees his or her primary physician first and is then referred on to either the outpatients' clinic, the hospital or to a private specialist. In practice, however, there are enormous differences in appointment and referral systems, also dependent on the way in which the healthcare system is funded. In some countries, patients do not have a primary physician, but are in the habit of self-diagnosing and subsequently self-referring to the specialist they think they need to see. This may lead to unrealistic expectations of any other healthcare system they may find themselves in.

iv. Informed Consent forms and their implications as legal documents.

The 'Informed Consent' or 'Agreement to Treatment' form is a legal document. It protects both the patient and the healthcare professional. The patient cannot undergo any procedure without having been fully informed of the reasons why the procedure is necessary, the expected outcomes, the risks and benefits, possible side-effects, any alternatives and the qualifications and experience of the person(s) performing the procedure. The Informed Consent procedure protects the professional in that, if things do not work out as expected during the procedure, the professional can state that the patient was aware of the possible risks before he or she agreed to the procedure.

v. Common pre-and post-operative procedures and instructions.

The interpreter must have a sound understanding of common pre-operative procedures and instructions in order to be able to interpret these accurately. 'Nil by mouth from midnight' means just that: *no food, no drink, no smoking*.

It is extremely useful if the interpreter has a good understanding of what is involved in common pre-operative tests such as an ECG or Chest X-Ray. This is particularly true for languages which do not have a direct equivalent for words such as *gastroscopy* or even *vertebrae*. Some interpreters always find themselves having to paraphrase words, as traditionally, their languages do not have words for vertebrae, bipolar disorder, laparotomy or pre-medication. Similarly, those interpreting into Signed Languages may find themselves developing a new sign for a term they have not previously encountered. The need to paraphrase medical terms requires a very good understanding of the concepts involved.

4. Understanding common responses to bad news

Interpreters should also be aware that patients may resort to different coping strategies when they are admitted to hospital or when they are coping with bad news. The hospital environment has an uncanny way of stripping patients of their normal social status and turning them into a 'case' in pyjamas. In hospital, company directors look exactly the same as the cleaner in the next bed. Some patients feel threatened and may resort to some kind of coping strategy. As a result, some patients may get abusive, in what seems an attempt to regain some sort of control over others, if only by annoying them. In other cases, patients and relatives may get abusive and sometimes even aggressive towards staff because they are genuinely worried about themselves or their loved ones, and want to ensure that the health professionals try their very best to help them.

Dr Elizabeth Kübler-Ross (1969; Kübler-Ross & Kessler 2008), a world famous physician, spent hours listening to people who were trying to come to terms with their impending death. She described the following **five stages of grief**:

> **Denial** – 'No! It's not true!' 'You must have mixed up the test results! It must be somebody else!'
>
> **Anger** – 'Why me?' 'It's not fair! I have always lived such a healthy life!' 'I am too young to die!'
>
> **Bargaining** – 'What if I give up smoking now?' 'What if I try this new wonder diet?' 'What if I see a faith healer?' 'What if I go to church every week from now on...' and so on.
>
> **Depression** – the patient may be withdrawn and refuse to speak.
>
> **Acceptance/Introspection** – the patient may accept that he or she is going to die, but may only wish to speak to those closest to him or her; many patients will choose whom they want to talk to or say good-bye to.

It is important to realize, however, that not everybody ends up accepting their loss. Occasionally people keep returning to earlier phases, such as anger and denial. In addition, the word 'loss' should not be used solely to refer to 'life and death' situations. Loss may mean the loss of fertility, moving to a different ward or losing a limb.

Another situation which may pose problems for the doctor and/or interpreter later on is where the patient goes 'into denial' upon being told that he has cancer and that this must be operated on straight-away. Let us say that a woman is told that she has breast cancer. The specialist explains the situation to her and says that surgery is the best option. The woman gives her consent for surgery, with the interpreter interpreting exactly all the woman's questions and all the explanations given by the doctor. After surgery, the woman is horrified to find that one breast has been removed and maintains that she was never told that she had breast cancer.

The phenomenon of denial of bad news may serve to emphasize, once again, the importance of full and accurate interpretation. Only in doing so, will the interpreter ensure that no accusations of 'inaccurate rendition of the message' will ensue. Health professionals involved may realise that the woman's statements are probably due to denial, this being one of the most common responses to 'bad news'.

Health professionals learn about the five stages of grief during their training, and **so should interpreters**. Interpreters should be aware of the reasons why clients may respond to certain information in a certain manner, and should use this understanding to help them remain 'cool, calm and collected'.

Obviously interpreters should not admonish patients who get angry with a health practitioner when confronted with 'bad news'. They should not take it personally when the patient denies that he has ever been told about the cancer in his prostate. They should not try and get the depressed person to talk.

It is important that interpreters understand and respect people's individual responses to loss. It is also important that they acknowledge that the professionals also understands the various stages of grieving and that they leave it to the professional to deal with the situation.

5. Cultural liaison

Interpreting is not a matter of language alone (Hale 1996, 2004, 2007; Rudvin 2007). The patient's cultural background also needs to be understood and taken into account. In some cultures it may be inappropriate for a woman to discuss gynecological problems such as 'spotting' or 'vaginal blood loss after intercourse' with a male interpreter present. Given such blood loss may be an indication of cancer, the woman's unwillingness to discuss such symptoms may have serious consequences. *Patient preferences as to the interpreter's gender should be respected.* Similarly, in some cultures, it may not be acceptable for patients to question the doctor, while in others it may be usual practice for patients to be extremely assertive. In some countries, again, the words 'We cannot do anything further' may equate to a demand for payment of additional fees. Even if the interpreter interprets such words appropriately, a culture-specific misunderstanding may arise, and the interpreter may need to act as a cultural liaison and resolve the resulting communication breakdown.

We usually assume our own cultural beliefs to be 'normal' and we may therefore also assume that everyone else will (or should) share these beliefs.

Most people almost automatically fall back on their traditional cultural beliefs when their health is failing. It seems natural for humans to return to what they know best when they find themselves in a situation which they perceive to be threatening. Patients from particular ethnic communities may call in faith healers when told that they have a terminal illness. Some patients may insist on a traditional diet in accordance with the principles of *yin* and *yang* when faced with a particular disorder at a particular time of year.

Healthcare interpreters need to be aware of their own cultural backgrounds and of cultural beliefs held in the patients' community in relation to health, diet, 'patient' behaviour and attitudes towards illness and disease (Helman 1991). This will enable them to brief healthcare professionals on a range of cultural attitudes in relation to health and to also recognize the differences and similarities between those beliefs and beliefs often held by people in the host country.

Cultural differences may also affect non-verbal behaviour (e.g. eye-contact, facial expressions, physical distance, touching, gestures, posture), the use of politeness formulas; tone of voice; loudness of delivery; rhythm, and a whole range of other paralinguistic factors. These will be discussed in more detail in Chapter 3.

6.   Interpreters' Codes of Ethics

Each of the various professional bodies of interpreters across different countries have their own Code of Ethics. Examples are the Code of Ethics of the National Council for Interpreting in Health Care (NCICH) in the US and Canada, the Code of Ethics of the UK Institute of Interpreters, the Code of Ethics of the Australian Institute of Interpreters and Translators (AUSIT) which is also endorsed by the New Zealand Society of Translators and Interpreters (NZSTI). Sign Language Interpreters' Associations also have their own specific Codes of Ethics. Weblinks to the websites of these professional bodies may be found in the reference section. When comparing the various Codes the similarities are immediately apparent. It is essential that healthcare interpreters adhere to such ethical guidelines, as they are often present in situations which may in themselves be potentially embarrassing and difficult for the clients. See Hale (2007) for a discussion of various aspects of ethical guidelines for interpreters.

Professional healthcare interpreters understand the need for complete confidentiality. They do not go around telling others within their community that Miss X has had a termination of pregnancy, that Mr Y is considering having a vasectomy, or that Mrs Z has bowel cancer.

The interpreter's attitude has to be one where his or her mind 'goes blank' as soon as he or she leaves the room where the interpreting assignment has taken place. Interpreters who maintain strict confidentiality enjoy all-round respect and trust.

Untrained, non-professional interpreters are not bound by the Interpreters' Code of Ethics and do not feel obliged to keep things 'in confidence'.

Healthcare practitioners employing untrained interpreters need to be aware of the fact that the untrained interpreter may censor and/or leave out information. Such interpreters may distort what is being said simply because they do not understand the medical condition and/or medical terminology, carrying on regardless and incorrectly interpreting information, because they do not want to lose face. In addition, untrained interpreters may censor the information given to the patient by the health professional, because the interpreter does not want the patient to know what is wrong with him/her. In some cultures, too, it is taboo to mention words such as cancer. Many of the author's former interpreting students recount having come under pressure from family members who would ask them not to interpret words like cancer, because the family did not want their (elderly) relatives to be given this bad news. One interpreting student once told the author that she would be inclined to interpret the words 'lung cancer' as 'chest infection' because of a cultural taboo on cancer in her home country.

Professional interpreters, however, are bound by their Code of Ethics to interpret what the patient is told. Professional interpreters should either disclose a conflict of interest or turn down an assignment in a given situation where they would not be able to remain completely unbiased or impartial, for whatever reason. So, by engaging professional interpreters, health professionals can be assured that the interpreter will be accurate and impartial. There is no such guarantee with BYO (Bring-Your-Own) interpreters or other untrained 'language aides'.

In brief, health professionals should not use untrained interpreters because untrained interpreters are not bound by a professional Code of Ethics. This means that they may (amongst other things):

- not maintain accuracy (see Chapter 2), but leave out things they do not understand, change information or add information *they* feel should have been included;
- not maintain strict confidentiality;
- not maintain impartiality: they may be tempted to take sides with either party (the client or the professional) and 'interpret' what they want the other party to hear, rather than what was really said;
- not disclose any possible conflict of interest (including any personal connections with the patient);
- offer advice to the client, which may include giving the client the answers to a test the client is taking (e.g. when they are interpreting for someone who is taking their driver's licence test!);
- not be able to provide the healthcare practitioner with cultural background information, as they may not be aware of, or able to elucidate, differences between their own culture and that of the host country;
- not be able to brief the professional on the 'triangle of communication' and the need to use the 'first person singular';
- not be able to use the correct interpreting technique or to explain to both client and professional about the various interpreting techniques which can be used.

7.   Duty of Care

Occasionally difficult situations may arise where the interpreter is 'torn between' the ethical conduct guidelines, specifically the duty to maintain complete confidentiality and another obligation called 'duty of care'. Duty of care means that the interpreter must speak out if he or she is aware of situations which could endanger the patient's life, but situations he or she knows the health professionals are not aware of. It will be obvious that interpreters may find it difficult to reconcile the concept of Duty of Care with ethical guidelines relating to confidentiality and impartiality. In general, the author's personal feeling is that the interpreter needs to weigh up whether there is in fact a serious risk to the patient's life if the interpreter does not speak up. Issues relating to Duty of Care and how this can be reconciled with the various interpreters' Codes of Conduct deserve much wider and more indepth discussion. Hale (2007) offers an excellent discussion of various Codes of Conduct.

8.   Triangle of communication

Trained healthcare interpreters are able to explain to both patient and professional the best seating arrangements. They know that the main flow of conversation and communication should be between the professional and the client. They are also able to instruct the professional and the client as to the different interpreting modes, such as simultaneous or consecutive interpreting. Once all parties in the three-way communication are aware of the 'ground rules', the interpreter will do his or her job almost imperceptibly, thus enabling a natural flow of conversation and exchange of information between the professional and the client.

Untrained interpreters may unconsciously 'side' with either the client or the professional,. As a result, either the client or the professional may feel uncomfortable and excluded.

In addition, *untrained* interpreters do not use the 'first person' when they are interpreting, which interpreting theorists agree is the best approach (Scimone & Ginori 1995; Tebble 1998; Hale 2004, 2007). Bot (2005, 2007) has observed that interpreters may on occasion use the third person singular possibly to distance or protect themselves from what they are interpreting. Untrained interpreters may therefore say things like: 'He says his name was Samuel Smith and he says he is glad he saw him before he went back to his house'. This method of 'interpreting' leads to a lot of confusion – with nobody quite sure who 'he', 'his' and 'him' refer to. Confusion is, of course, the opposite of accuracy.

Trained interpreters interpret accurately what the professional or the client has said, no matter how strange it may seem to them to say things like: 'I am 84 and

I have 3 sons and 21 grandchildren' or 'I can hear voices coming out of the handle-
bars of my bicycle.'

9. Note-taking

Trained interpreters are able to take notes which enable them to interpret what has
been said completely and accurately. They will include dates, numbers, names, names
of conditions, lab results, and so on, in their notes. Often, our short-term memory
cannot cope with details such as numbers and dates, and note-taking skills are an
essential tool in storing and retrieving important information such as the dates of the
client's 'last menstrual period', blood-pressure readings, and instructions relating to
the taking of medication.

In addition to being competent note-takers, trained interpreters will tell the client
or the professional if they could not hear part of what was said, or if they are not
familiar with the terminology used. As a result, the trained interpreter can maintain
a high degree of accuracy and completeness. Those interested in techniques, memory
training and notetaking should read the short introduction by Scimone and Signori
(1995) on these issues. They may also follow some of the notetaking practices used
by doctors and nurses when it comes to commonly used abbreviations such as IV
abs (intravenous antibiotics), Hy (history), on P/E (on physical examination), Ty
(treatment), and SOB (shortness of breath). This book includes commonly used abbreviations wherever appropriate.

10. Terminology

It is essential that healthcare interpreters possess not only an excellent knowledge of
everyday expressions and idioms but also specific knowledge of terminology.

A knowledge of everyday expressions is important because health professionals
often 'switch' to everyday language in an attempt to make themselves more readily
understood. The effect may be more confusing, however, if the interpreter is not
familiar with everyday idioms such as 'How're your waterworks?' and 'Is that how you
got your crook back?' The author once heard an obstetrician refer to *mastitis* (breast
infection) as 'arthritis of the breast'. Since arthritis refers to an inflammation of a joint,
the author found this very confusing.

It is also essential that the interpreter has a very good knowledge of healthcare
terminology. The author has regularly encountered healthcare professionals who
maintained that the interpreter does not need to know 'too much' about healthcare.
On the contrary, the basic rule is that *you simply cannot interpret what you do not*

understand. Healthcare interpreters should make every effort to gain a good basic understanding of healthcare terminology and to keep building on their knowledge base. They need to be familiar with existing resources. In most countries health services put out excellent resource material and with the advent of the internet, much information is easily accessible. However, once again, without a good basic knowledge of healthcare terminology, it may be difficult to fully utilize such material. This book offers a brief chapter on medical terminology (Chapter 4) as well as lists of commonly used medical terminology in other relevant chapters.

Summary of main points

This chapter has touched on some of the many challenges faced by professionals interpreting in healthcare settings; it has also provided an overview of the skills, abilities and knowledge competent health interpreters need to possess.

Chapter 3

A word about culture

1. Culture

What is culture? Anthropologists and other writers have produced a wide range of definitions of culture. In 1871, anthropologist E. B. Tylor defined culture as: 'That complex whole which includes knowledge, belief, art, morals, law, custom and other capabilities and habits acquired by man as a member of society' (1871, p. 1). Keesing (1981, p. 518) defines culture as 'systems of shared ideas, systems of concepts and rules and meanings that underlie and are expressed in the way that humans live.' Helman (1990, p. 2) argues that culture consists of

> 'a set of guidelines (both explicit and implicit) which individuals inherit as members of a particular society, and which tells them how to view the world, how to experience it emotionally, and how to behave in it in relation to other people, to supernatural forces or gods, and to the natural environment. It also provides them with a way of transmitting these guidelines to the next generation – by the use of symbols, language, art and ritual'.

This chapter will limit itself to two important aspects of culture in relation to the work of the healthcare interpreter:

– aspects of communication that may be influenced by cultural beliefs
– cultural beliefs in relation to health, i.e. attitudes towards sickness and health, behaviour, diet

2. Cultural influence on spoken communication

People with a certain cultural set of 'communication rules', may misunderstand the communication attempts of speakers who regard as normal an entirely different set of 'communication rules'. This applies to users of different spoken languages as well as to users of signed languages. Sign language interpreters need to be very familiar with Deaf culture (cf. Meador & Zazove (2005)).

Culture influences communication in a large number of ways, including content, manner of delivery and pragmatics, (van Dijk 1977; Candlin 2003; Candlin & Gotti 2004a; Candlin & Gotti 2004b; Hale 1996, 2004, 2007; Hofstede 2003;

Scollon & Scollon 2001; Bowe & Martin 2007; Dysart-Gale 2007; Tate & Turner 2003). Cultural impact on message content may pertain to levels of explicitness and implicitness, levels of directness, acceptability of topics, and the taboo nature of certain topics (usually topics relating to sex or death). Cultural and crosslinguistic influences on the way the message is delivered may include both nonverbal and paralinguistic aspects of communication.

Nonverbal aspects of communication include, but are not restricted to posture, physical proximity, gaze, eye-contact, facial expression, gestures and even style of dressing (Grice 1975; Searle 1969, 1975).

Eye contact – in some cultures women should not look a man in the eye when talking to him as they can find themselves being misunderstood.

Physical closeness – speakers from some cultures move up very close to the person they are talking to and may find it very offensive if the other person moves back to gain more physical space for themselves.

Physical contact – in some cultures, it is acceptable to touch the person you are talking to, in other cultures it is definitely not okay and may be misinterpreted completely.

Facial expressions – sometimes facial expressions, such as smiles, can be totally misinterpreted by speakers from other cultures. A Laotian interpreter once told me how he had interpreted for two refugees at a refugee camp in Thailand. As they recounted their harrowing journey, they kept smiling. Afterwards the UNHCR official told him he was shocked by their account, but could not believe they had smiled right through, and was therefore wondering whether they were telling the truth. The interpreter told him that in the refugees culture it would have been very impolite to impose anger or sadness on the person they were talking to. By smiling they tried to ensure that the other person would not be negatively affected by their story. Needless to say, most native speakers of English would interpret a smile as a sign of happiness, not of anger, shyness or sadness.

Hand gestures – these may be misinterpreted as well: the author once beckoned to a Taiwanese friend in the Northern European way, with the fingers pointing upwards, not downwards. He replied that he was 'not a dog'. In many cultures, people hold their fingers downwards when beckoning others.

Cultural attitudes also dictate paralinguistic aspects of communication, including volume or loudness, tone, pitch, speech rhythms, speed of delivery, pausing before responding, sentence stress, intonation and flow. Volume or loudness are but one aspect of the way in which a spoken message is delivered. Different cultures harbour different ideas on 'loudness'. In some cultures speaking in a very low voice is a way of expressing respect towards the person you are addressing. In other cultures, this might be interpreted as a sign of shyness, and may even be received with irritation. When the way in which a message is uttered is interpreted in a way completely opposite to what was intended, cultural breakdown results. Other aspects of speech which may be misinterpreted might include the natural speech rhythms or speed of delivery. The natural speech rhythms which occur in some languages may be received by speakers of other languages as whining or monotonous. The speed with which a message is delivered may also be misinterpreted by speakers of other languages. Recipients might think: "They speak too fast – they must be very nervous or upset", when that rate of delivery may be common among speakers of that language.

For the speakers of some languages, pausing before responding is a sign that the question is taken seriously and given some thought. To speakers from other cultures, however, these long pauses may convey hesitation and be a sign that the speaker does not know what to say.

Stress-timed languages such as English, emphasize the key words through stress, however this may be interpreted as rude by speakers of some cultures. Similarly, speakers of certain languages habitually speak in a very loud voice, which may be perceived as either rude or aggressive by people not familiar with that language.

In short, paralinguistic features may play a considerable role in the way a spoken message is interpreted by the listener, especially if the listener does not share the speaker's cultural background.

3. Implications for interpreting

Before embarking on an interpreting job, interpreters need to ask themselves some of the following questions:

– How may speakers from this cultural background express respect in the way they deliver a spoken message, in their facial expressions, body posture and so on?
– How may these speakers generally express respect when it comes to the way they deliver a spoken message, their facial expressions, body posture and so on?
– How may these native speakers express anger?
– Are there any gestures, body postures or facial expressions used by speakers from this cultural background which may be misinterpreted by health professionals from a different background and vice versa?

Being aware of these differences will help interpreters become aware of the pitfalls of cross-cultural communication between people from their own cultural background and native speakers of English. Interpreters should always bear in mind that their own interpretation of such pitfalls may also be subjective and that every speaker is a unique individual.

4. Culture and health

With regards to health, Helman (1990) describes in some detail how members of different societies use different cultural definitions of anatomy and physiology. Cultural beliefs with regard to anatomy govern beliefs, not only to do with desirable body size and how to clothe and decorate the body, but also with the body's inner structure and with how the body functions. Cultural beliefs include concepts of balance and imbalance. The belief system of *yin* and *yang* is quite well known, with *yin* representing that which is 'dark, moist, watery and female', and *yang* representing that which is 'hot, fiery, and male' (Helman 1990: 20).

The World Health Organization (WHO) provides a good definition of health, defining it as 'a state of complete physical, mental and social well-being and not merely the absence of disease or infirmity' (WHO 1948). Cultural beliefs also influence our attitudes towards important areas of our lives, such as marriage and relationships, family relationships, child-rearing practices, education and, very importantly, health.

Even people who emigrated to another country many years ago, and who feel that they have assimilated to their new country in many areas of their lives, may return to their original cultural attitudes when faced with ill health.

South East Asian mothers giving birth in hospital, may be told to have a shower straight after birth, in the interests of hygiene and to prevent perinatal infection. In practice, however, many of these women refuse, as they remember what their mothers and grandmothers told them about the dangers of getting wind (or *fong*) into their bones by stepping under the shower.

The extent to which immigrants continue to adhere to their own traditional practices and beliefs in the area of health, depends on a lot of different factors: length of time spent in their new country, age, educational background and so on. In this way, a Chinese woman doctor, may well shower after childbirth, as her traditional beliefs have been replaced by the medical knowledge she has gained in the course of training.

So what are some of these traditional beliefs regarding health, and how can they constitute a problem for the Healthcare Interpreter?

5. Cultural beliefs pertaining to health and their implications for the interpreter

Our attitudes towards health issues may be deeply influenced by cultural beliefs, which we have had passed down from our mothers and their mothers before them.

An interpreter needs to be aware of both traditional ideas around health and illness held by clients and of approaches advocated in the healthcare system they are working in. This way, the interpreter can provide cultural background information if a complete breakdown of communication threatens. See also Rudvin (2004, 2007) and Dysart-Gale (2007) for a discussion of how interpreters negotiate cultural and linguistic aspects of the interpreting process in relation to their professional roles.

The culture of the hospital system in countries like the US, Canada, the UK, Australia and NZ is largely medico-scientific in nature. This means that spirits and malicious spells are not seen as a cause of illness. In addition, it means that natural remedies are not considered useful unless scientific research has proven otherwise. Those who have been educated within the healthcare system of the aforementioned countries usually have the same confidence in scientific evidence and may have little patience with patients who have faith in witch doctors and unproven herbal remedies. This can lead to a fair amount of cultural misunderstanding with patients and hospital staff possibly getting upset at the obviously incorrect beliefs of the other party.

5.1   Sickness and disease (or medical condition)

What is sickness? Obviously, we should be able to define sickness as the absence of health. Yet, what may be defined as a sickness by one person or one culture, may not be seen as such by another person at all. In a culture where the common cold is extremely common, people suffering a cold are not considered to be sick. If they take sick leave 'just because they have a cold', this will be frowned upon.

For many people having a medical condition does not equate with being sick. Something the medical professional might diagnose as a disease or disorder, may not be seen in the same light by the patient at all. Often the patient will not consider himself to be ill if he does not feel 'ill'. Such patients may only return to the doctor when the disease is in such an advanced stage that it has become incurable or has resulted in serious complications.

A good example of different cultural attitudes towards 'sickness' and 'disease' is diabetes. In countries such as NZ, some of the problems with diabetes arise from the patients' cultural perspectives. Thus some patients who have been diagnosed with diabetes and who have been told to take their medications, change their lifestyles and more specifically their diets, do not consider themselves to be sick at all. Unfortunately, these patients may well disregard their condition and only return to hospital when they 'feel sick'. By that stage they may have end-stage renal failure or gangrene.

5.2   Patient behaviour

In some cultures, patients are supposed to behave as patients. They have to lie in bed, refuse to do anything for themselves, cry out in pain and so on. This type of behaviour can be greeted with extreme annoyance by care givers from other cultural backgrounds, who have been taught to grin and bear it and to 'carry on' regardless.

Many hospital staff will encourage patients to mobilize and do things for themselves, as this has been proven to reduce the risk of many complications such as bedsores, contractures, chest infections and thrombosis. This type of approach reflects 'medico-scientific' ideas and may be greeted with dismay by patients who have always been taught that sick people should stay in bed and not exert themselves.

The cultural misunderstanding which results can easily lead to non-compliance. A patient who has been told that he has diabetes and needs to exercise, may well disregard his doctor's admonitions and spend most of his time lying in bed or sitting in a chair, because that sort of behaviour befits an 'ill' person.

5.3   Cultural attitudes towards pain

Pain behaviour can be another obstacle to effective communication. Patients from some cultures express the fact that they are in pain by yelling, shouting and moaning, whereas people from other cultural backgrounds may have learned to grit their teeth and 'suffer in silence'. The latter might well view the former as 'moaners' and treat them with disdain. A Muslim friend in the Netherlands once told me that it is important to show others how sick you are, because by doing so you enable them to perform a good deed by coming to see you in hospital and bringing you food and gifts.

5.4   Causes of sickness

Medical professionals tend to look for scientific causes for illness and disease. Research is undertaken to find out the causes of those illnesses whose origins remain unknown. The underlying principles of treatment will also be based on scientific evidence. Patients may come from cultures where illnesses are believed to be caused by evil spirits. Sometimes, people believe that an adversary has put a spell on them. It seems logical to them that the only treatment in that case is to 'undo' the spell or to invoke other spirits to counter the attack on their health. The author remembers NZ doctors and nurses being very much taken aback when a patient with melanoma was taken out of hospital by his family in order to be taken to a faith healer from his ethnic community.

Similarly, some people in Indochina may still practise 'mother roasting' to help dry up the woman's vaginal discharge after childbirth. One interpreter told the author how fire-fighters in Wellington, NZ, were called in to a suspected house-fire, with smoke coming out of the window of an apartment. When they entered the apartment, they found a woman lying on a bed. Under the bed were a few smoldering coals, put there to help dry up the woman's discharge after childbirth.

Many of these beliefs apply to the behaviour of pregnant women. Some Cook Islands women have been known to refuse to wear the ID bracelet, (or anything circular around their bodies, including rings and belts) for fear it may cause their babies to be born with their cords around their necks.

5.5   Diets in sickness and health

Many deep-rooted cultural beliefs come to the fore when it comes to what we choose to eat in sickness and health (Helman 1990).

It is no coincidence that many visitors can be seen carrying in pots and pans when visiting relatives in hospital. In NZ elderly Maori patients who refuse all the hospital food that is set in front of them, may well perk up at the sight of 'pork and puha' (a type of leafy green vegetable).

Chinese patients often prefer rice gruel above all else. It is well-documented that Indo-Chinese patients often follow the philosophy of Yin and Yang. (Adams & Osgood 1973). To them, sickness is the result of ill-balance and the diet needs to be chosen in such a way that this balance is restored. Interestingly, Indo-Chinese patients will often follow a different diet if they catch a cold in winter than if they catch a cold in summer. The only food they can eat all year round is rice, as rice is neutral and will therefore not cause any imbalances.

The belief in special diets for certain conditions and special remedies for certain ailments can be so strong that patients will adhere to these above all else. Sometimes the effect can be detrimental or interfere with medically prescribed treatments. After childbirth or heavy periods, Chinese women are traditionally given a special strengthening soup, containing special herbs which are said to make the body strong again. Interestingly, according to some hospital sources, the ginger and sesame oil in the food traditionally eaten by new mothers pass into the breast milk and may make their baby's jaundice worse, as the ginger specifically is thought to interfere with the breakdown of *bilirubin* in the baby's body. I was told that some obstetricians simply tell these mothers to just stop breast-feeding, saying that the breast milk will make the baby's jaundice worse, without explaining that the reason lies in the ethnically varied food.

5.6   The role of the interpreter as a Cultural Liaison

It is often said that the interpreter's role is to bridge any communication gap that might exist. As we have seen, cultural attitudes may affect communication between people from different cultural backgrounds in a variety of ways.

Patients may not comply with the doctor's instructions if these go against their own cultural beliefs. New mothers from South East Asian countries may not have the prescribed shower after birth if they believe it can give them *fong* (wind). They may feel quite taken aback, and may not want to say 'No' directly, as it would be impolite to do this to a person in a position of authority, such as a medical doctor.

People with diabetes may not get fit and exercise if they firmly believe that a 'sick' person should stay in bed. They may not understand the apparent contradiction between the doctor telling them that they have a medical condition and the prescribed lifestyle. They may respond by simply not complying with instructions.

It is the interpreter's role to be conscious of situations where different cultural attitudes towards sickness and health may potentially lead to communication breakdown and non-compliance. Interpreters needs to be aware of any cultural beliefs the patient may hold. They also need to be aware of the hospital culture in the country they are working in, and of the scientific approach followed by the health professionals.

Interpreters should be aware of all these, without stereotyping. Some anesthetists may be fully convinced of the benefits of acupuncture and even practise it themselves. Some new immigrants may have trained as doctors in their home countries and share the scientific approach to health and illness. Every patient is shaped by his or her own life-experiences, personal upbringing and family background, professional development and time spent in the new country of residence.

Ideally, interpreters should have the opportunity to discuss different cultural backgrounds during the pre-briefing session with the professional, or alternatively, during the de-briefing session following the interpreting assignment. Unfortunately, briefing and debriefing often do not take place in practice, although mental health professionals appear more willing to spend time with interpreters before or after assignments. Once the health professionals become aware of the impact of cultural beliefs in relation to sickness and health, they may start to value the interpreter's cultural knowledge more (Crezee 2003).

Finally, cultural beliefs may cause severe communication breakdown during interpreting assignments. The nature of cultural attitudes is such that we all think our own are the norm and should be or are shared by everyone else. For this reason, people are often not aware that the other party in the interview may approach health issues in an entirely different way. According to anecdotal evidence, a woman in an Australian hospital was told that she had an incurable illness and that nothing more could be done. In her country this meant that the doctor would 'pull out all the stops' as long as the patient paid a higher fee. When her husband pulled out his wallet, the doctor got upset and said: "No, you don't understand. Money doesn't enter into it. There is nothing more I can do." The man then pulled out more banknotes while both he and the doctor got increasingly upset. Had an interpreter been present, they might have been able to prevent this breakdown in communication by explaining cultural differences to both parties. When interpreters do this, they should put up their hand and ask permission to provide some cultural background information. They need to state that this will be a subjective statement and that each individual is unique, before proceeding to make a general statement. They will need to repeat any cultural background information provided in both languages. This way both the patient and the professional will know what was said and will be able to express their agreement or disagreement if need be.

Interested readers are advised to read Battle (2002), Angelelli (2004), Tellechea Sánchez (2005); Hale (2005, 2007); Rudvin (2004, 2007); Pym, Shlesinger and Jettmarová (2006). Bowe and Martin (2007); Dysart-Gale (2007); Lee, Lansbury and Sullivan (2005); Lim, Mortensen, Feng, Ryu and Cui (2012) and other authors for some of the extensive debate on cross-cultural communication involving interpreters in health settings.

Summary of main points

This chapter has touched on some of the impacts culture may have on interpreter-mediated crosscultural communication in healthcare settings, including:

– cultural aspects of communication
– cultural beliefs relating to health and illness and their impact on the interpreter

---

Chapter 4

Medical terminology

(Student) interpreters preparing to work in healthcare settings using English as one of their working language, will in fact need to acquire some basic knowledge of two additional languages: Latin and Greek. There are a number of excellent books available on medical terminology (Walker, Wood & Nicol 2013; Chabner 2011; Thierer & Breitbard 2006; Prendergast 1991) however, no book on healthcare interpreting would be complete without a brief section on medical terminology.

This chapter will provide a very brief introduction to the historical background of why these two languages are still reflected in healthcare terminology today, followed by an overview of basic Latin and Greek roots, suffixes and affixes. Each chapter in Part Three will include a brief list of Latin and Greek roots (Muller & Thiel 1969; Muller & Renkema 1970) used in a particular field of medicine. For this reason, the current chapter will restrict itself to a general overview only.

1. History of medical terminology in the Western world

Medical traditions developed in various civilizations around the world, including Mesopotamia (ca. 3500 BC), Egypt (ca. 3000 BC), India (ca. 2500 BC) and China (ca. 1600 BC) (Pourahmad 2010). It is likely that there was some contact between the various civilizations resulting in the sharing of certain health-related beliefs. Translations of health-related writings have played a major role in the spread of health-related beliefs to other cultures as documented by McMorrow (1998); Van Hoof (1998a, 1998b); Segura (1998) and many others.

Ancient Greek doctors were very skilled at diagnosing as evidenced by the continued use of Greek words denoting certain medical conditions: the term *diabetes mellitus* (literally: flowing through-sweet as honey) is but one example. The Ancient Romans liked to employ Greek doctors and many of these, including a famous physician known as Claudius Galen, travelled to and worked in Rome. In the 1st century BC, a Roman nobleman called Cornelius Celsus (53BC-7AD) recorded all that was then known about Greek and Roman medicine in a huge encyclopedia called *De Medicina* (about medicine).

The invasion of Spain by the Moors (718AD) also introduced into Spain what Segura (1998) calls 'a treasure cove of medical and scientific knowledge' from other countries, including Greece. The establishment of the Toledo School of Translators by Archbishop Raimundus (1125–1152) brought about the translation and dissemination of a wealth of scientific works, including medical writings (Segura 1998). In the Middle Ages, a small group of doctors formed an influential medical school in Salerno (Italy), revisiting the teachings of Greek physicians such as Hippocrates and Galen. Medical schools all over Europe followed suit and Latin and Greek terminology is used by medical scientists to this day.

Even though Latin (L) and Greek (Gk) are distinct languages, roots from either language will be presented in this chapter without indicating their linguistic origins.

Overall, terms of Greek origins can often be recognized because they may include the English spelling conventions for the following Greek letters: χ (ch) as in *brachy* (short); θ (th) as in *pathology* (study of illness); φ (ph) as in *angiography* (blood vessel imaging), ψ (ps) as in *psychology* (study of the mind) and υ (y) as in *hysterectomy* (removal of the womb) and αι (ae) as in *gynaecologist*.

2. Spelling and pronunciation

In the US spelling convention, Greek words which were originally written with 'ae' or 'oe' in English, are written with an 'e', whereas in most former Commonwealth countries, these words are still spelled with 'ae' or 'oe'. Thus, in the US we write *gynecologist, anesthetist* and *edema*, whereas in the UK spelling these are spelled as *gynaecologist, anaesthetist* and *oedema*. US spelling conventions have been followed throughout this book and in the corresponding index.

Word stress and pronunciation varies between health professionals and also between countries. As an example, the word *alveoli* (small air sacs in the lungs) is pronounced by some professionals as 'al-VEE-oh-leye', whereas others may pronounce it as 'al-vee-OH-leye'. See the Reference section for websites and books providing guidance as to the pronunciation of medical terms.

3. Latin and Greek elements in medical terms

Latin and Greek medical terms often contain a combination of elements from either language. Thus, the word *mammo-graphy* contains a form of the word *mamma* (breast) and the Greek *graphein* (to write). Alternatively terms may consist wholly of terms originating from either Latin or Greek. Often, both elements originating from either Latin or Greek may still exist side by side. As an example, the Greek words *ops* and *ophtalmos* (eye), are both used in various medical terms (e.g. *optic* nerve, *ophthalmologist*), alongside terms which contain forms derived from the Latin word *oculus* (eye).

Where medical terms consist of more than one root, a combining form may be inserted in between roots, but only if the second root starts with a consonant. The combining form is usually an 'o', used as a linking vowel. Examples are found in Table 4.1.

Table 4.1. Some examples of combining form in medical terminology

First root	Combining form	Second root	Combination
Arthr	–	-itis	arthritis
arthr-	o	-scopy	arthroscopy
psych-	o	-logy	psychology
cyst-	–	-itis	cystitis
cyst-	o	-scopy	cystoscopy

4. Common combinations

Medical terms can be a combination of

– Word root + word root
– Word root + suffix
– Prefix + word root + suffix
– Prefix + word root + suffix
– Word root + linking vowel*+ word root (*usually 'o')

4.1 Common word roots

The most common roots used in medical terms are

– Body parts – these come first within the medical term (see Table 4.2)
– Nouns denoting what is done to these body parts, or what is wrong with these body parts – these nouns usually come last within the medical term, e.g. *-algia* in the term *myalgia* (muscle-pain).
– Nouns denoting body parts + preposition + verb, e.g. gastr-ec-tomy (stomach-out-cut).
– Prefixes providing information about position, size, colour or number of the roots that follow them.

Table 4.2. Common nouns denoting body parts

Noun	Meaning	Adjective	Example
abdomen	belly	abdominal	abdominal fat
adip(o)	fat	adipous; adipose	adipose tissue
aden(o)	gland	adeno-	adenocarcinoma
caud(o)	tail	caudal	caudal anesthesia
cephal(o)	head	cephalic	cephalic presentation
cervic(o)	neck	cervical	cervical vertebra
chondr(o)	cartilage	chondr(o)	chondrosarcoma
cranio	skull	cranial	cranial nerves
dors(o)	back	dorsal	dorsal root
inguino	groin	inguinal	inguinal hernia
lumb(o)	lower back	lumbar	lumbar spine
mamm(o)	breast	mammary	mammary glands
mast	breast	–	mastectomy
my(o)	muscle	–	myalgia
neur(o)	nerve	neural	neural system
o(o) or ov(o)	egg	–	oophorectomy
oste(o)	bone	–	osteoarthritis
sarco	flesh	–	sarcal
spin(o)	spine	spinal	spinal nerves
thorac(o)	chest	thoracic	thoracic surgery
ventr(o)	belly	ventral	ventral surfaces
vertebr(o)	vertebrae; spinal column	vertebral	vertebral column
viscer(o)	internal organ	visceral	visceral fat

Examples of the various possible combinations will be given in separate tables below.

4.2   Common procedure nouns and verbs

As indicated above, often 'body part nouns' are followed by verbs or nouns denoting what is happening with the body part. Some common procedure nouns and verbs are given in the table below. Please note that these procedure nouns and verbs will come in last position in the medical terms. Examples of the resulting medical terms may be found in the third column in the table below. Table 4.3 provides information about terms containing nouns and verbs which describe what is happening to the body parts concerned.

Table 4.3. Nouns and verbs describing conditions or procedures

Procedure nouns/verbs	Approximate meaning of verb	Examples	Meaning
–ec-tomy	– cutting out	mastectomy; hysterectomy	surgical removal of the breast; surgical removal of the womb
–emia	– in the blood	uremia	urea in the blood
–gram	– result of imaging	angiogram	blood vessel imaging/recording (visible result of the procedure)
–graphy	– process of imaging	angiography	blood vessel imaging/recording (the procedure)
–itis	– inflammation of	arthritis	inflammation of the joint
–logy	study; have knowledge of	neurology	study of nerves
–plasty	– repair	angioplasty	blood vessel repair
–scopy	– looking	gastroscopy; arthroscopy	looking inside the stomach; looking inside the joint
–tomy; (o) tomy	– cutting	gastrotomy	operation on the stomach

5. Common prefixes

Prefixes were often originally prepositions denoting **a position in the body**, e.g. epi (on top), para- (alongside), sub- or hypo- (both meaning 'under'). Prefixes may also provide information about a state (e.g. overactive, underactive, abnormal). See Table 4.4 for some examples.

Table 4.4. Prefixes relating to position in the body

Prefix	Meaning of prefix	Examples	Meaning
ab	away from	abductor	leading away from
ad	towards	adductor	leading towards
ante	before (g)	antenatal	before birth
bi	two	biceps	twoheaded (muscle)
anter(o)	front	anterior	at the front; front
epi	on top of	epidural	on top of the dura
endo	inside	endoscopy	looking inside
intra	in between	intracostal	between the ribs
para	alongside	parathyroid	alongside the thyroid
peri	around	perinatal	around birth

(Continued)

Table 4.4. Prefixes relating to position in the body (Continued)

Prefix	Meaning of prefix	Examples	Meaning
post	after	postnatal	after birth
pre	before (l)	prenatal	before birth
poster(o)	behind; back	posterior	at the back; behind
inter	between	interpersonal	between people
meta	beyond; after;	metastasis	secondary growth; secondary spread (of cancer)

Other prefixes say something about the size, state, number or colour. A small sample of these have been represented in Table 4.5.

Table 4.5. Prefixes relating to size, state, number or colour

Prefix	Meaning of prefix	Examples	Meaning
a	no	aphasia	no speech
neo	new	neoplasia	new growth (cancer)
dys	abnormal	dysfunctional; dysmenorrhea	not functioning normally; abnormal menstrual periods
macr(o) (g)	large	macroscopic	visible to the naked eye
micr(o) (l)	small	microscopic	visible only using a microscope
poly (g)	many	polyuria	[passing] a lot of urine
olig(o) (g)	few	oliguria	not [passing] much urine
megal(o) (g)	large	megacolon	abnormally enlarged colon
erythr(o)	red	erythrocyte	red [blood] cell
leuk(o)	white	leukemia	'white blood'
cyan(o)	blue	cyanosis	having a bluish colour
melan(o)	black	melanoma	black swelling
hyper	higher; over-	hyperglycemia; hyperactive	high blood sugar level; overactive
hypo	underneath; below	hypoglycemia	low blood sugar level
sub	underneath; below	subnormal	lower than normal
super	higher; over-	superjacent	lying (just) above
uni	one	unilateral	on one side
ambi	both	ambilateral	on both sides

6. Suffixes

These are often adjectival forms such as -al, -ic, -ist, and -iac (e.g. celiac; hypochondriac) but may also originate from nouns such as oma (tumor), scopy (looking). Table 4.6 shows some common roots related to illness. In medical terminology, these roots are usually preceded by a noun denoting which body part is affected. Some authors describe these roots as suffixes, because they usually appear in word final position.

Table 4.6. Some common roots denoting illness – usually appearing in word final position

Procedure nouns/verbs	Meaning of verb	Examples	Meaning
-algia	- pain	my-algia	muscle ache
-patho	- disease	neuropathy	nerve-disease
-rrhaphy	suturing a gap or defect	angiorrhaphy	suturing a blood vessel
-megaly	enlargedness	cardiomegaly	enlarged heart
-rrhea	flow	dysmenorrhea	difficult or painful menstruation
-rrhage	burst	hemorrhage	leeding heavily
-troph(o)	growth; development	hypertrophy	overly developed; grown larger than normal
-blast	developing cell	leukoblast	immature leukocyte, still developing
-cyte	cell	leukocyte	white (blood) cell
-gen(esis)	producing	antigen	producing antibodies
-iasis	state of	candidiasis	state of candida (yeast infection)
-lysis	breakdown; destruction	hemolysis	breakdown of blood cells
-oma	tumor; swelling	adenoma; haematoma	fat (tissue) tumor; swelling consisting of blood
-plasia	formation	(hip) dysplasia	abnormal formation (of hip)
-plasm	result of formation	neoplasm	new growth (cancer)
-osis	abnormal condition	thrombosis	abnormal condition involving blood clots

Summary of main points

Latin and Greek roots often relate to

- body parts
- position in the body
- illness or condition
- number, size or colour

Within medical terms, the body part often comes first, followed by a root or suffix which describes what is happening with the body part in question.

PART II

Interpreting in healthcare settings

Chapter 5

Primary physicians and General Practitioners

This chapter aims to provide interpreters in English speaking countries with a brief introduction to primary care in their setting. As stated in Chapter 2, differences between countries mainly relate to the way in which healthcare is funded. In 1946 the UK introduced the National Health Service (NHS), a system based on the approach that publicly funded and good quality healthcare should be available to everyone, regardless of income. The NHS pays for services provided by general practitioners (primary care) and specialists, inpatient and outpatient hospital services, the cost of medication, dental care, mental healthcare, assistance with learning disabilities and rehabilitation services. Similar systems operate in former Commonwealth countries such as Canada, Australia and NZ.

At the time of writing, US primary and secondary (see below) healthcare services were predominantly offered by private providers and patients mostly paid for this care with the aid of health insurance plans (Sultz & Young 2006). Some healthcare programmes (e.g. Medicare, Medicaid and the Veterans Health Administration) are provided by the public sector.

1. Primary care providers

In most countries, primary care is generally provided at a local community level whilst secondary care is mostly provided by specialist doctors, either in public or private hospitals. Primary care doctors specialize in general medicine and family medicine.

Depending on the country, primary care doctors may be referred to as primary (care) physicians (US, Canada), Family Physicians (US, Canada), General Practitioners (UK, Australia, NZ), primary doctors (Australia) or family doctors (UK, Australia, NZ). In the US and most other countries, all those wanting to practise as primary care physicians have to complete a supervised training period as medical residents first (see page 62). For convenience sake, general practitioners and primary care physicians will hereafter be referred to as GPs/PPs.

In most US states, patients receive primary care from either a PP or from Advanced Nurse Practitioners (ANPs), depending on the State, whilst secondary care is usually provided by privately funded hospitals. Outpatient services may be provided by privately owned entities or hospitals, and occasionally by other entities.

In the UK primary care is provided by GPs, nurses, and physiotherapists, whilst publicly funded hospitals provide secondary care which includes both outpatient and inpatient services. In the UK, Australia and NZ, GPs generally serve as the *gatekeepers* to the healthcare system. In other words, patients with non-urgent health problems generally need to see their GP, before they can access other services in the healthcare system.

Typically patients see their primary care doctor every time they want medical advice about a new health issue or for family planning and vaccinations. They also see their primary care doctor for treatment and follow-up of ongoing health conditions such as high blood pressure, diabetes, asthma and chronic obstructive lung disorders.

2. History taking

When a patient comes in for a visit, the primary care doctor will ask what current problem the patient has come in with. Questions may include the following:

- What is the problem you have come to see me with today?
- Are you in any pain? If so, what is the pain like? (Note it is important to accurately interpret the nature of the pain, see *Pain* below).
- Are you experiencing any abnormal sensations:
    - Is there any tingling or pins and needles? Any numbness?
    - Any pain or discomfort anywhere in your body?
- Do you have a fever or have you had a fever?
- Did you take your temperature? When and what was it?
- Are other people in the house or in the family sick as well?
- Are other people in the house or in the family (or at school) sick with the same symptoms?
- Have you had any change in appetite?
- Have you developed a dislike or aversion to any particular foods?
- Have you lost weight? Gained weight?
- Have you got a sore throat?
- Do you have to cough?
- Do you bring up any phlegm (spit)? What does it look like?
- Do you have a runny nose? What does the discharge look like?
- Do you have an earache/sore ear? Is there any discharge from your ear?
- Do you feel nauseated? Do you have to vomit?
- How are your bowel motions?

- Do you move your bowels regularly?
- Do you get diarrhea?
- Are your stools formed/soft/loose/watery?
- Do you have irritable bowels?

3. Pain

The doctor may ask the following questions about pain:

- Where is the pain?
- What sets it off? What brings on the pain? What triggers the pain?
- Does the pain shoot down your leg or up your shoulder?
- Does the pain spread or radiate anywhere?
- Is there anything that relieves the pain?
- Does your … feel irritated/tender or sore?

It is important to establish and accurately interpret the precise nature of the pain. Pain can be described as:

- a dull ache
- niggling or nagging
- a stitch
- superficial or deep-seated
- stinging
- pressing or dragging
- severe – excruciating, unbearable, intolerable, patient is in agony
- slight/mild/moderate
- heavy – crushing, like a belt is tightened round the chest
- like a knife – sharp/stabbing/piercing/cutting
- pulsating – coming and going like a pulse
- pounding/throbbing – beating or drumming
- hot – like a burning or searing sensation

4. New patients

When seeing a new patient, the primary care doctor will take the person's history first, including family; social; medical and surgical and obstetric.

The family history will focus on illnesses which may 'run in families' or be hereditary or imply that the individual concerned may have a predisposition (i.e. a tendency or higher than average chance) for developing a certain condition.

Some of the most commonly asked questions would be is there a family history of:

- allergies (e.g. eczema, hives, hay fever, rhinitis/runny nose, conjunctivitis/watery eyes) or asthma
- epilepsy
- diabetes
- high blood pressure (hypertension)
- certain cancers (such as breast cancer)
- kidney disease

The social history will focus on factors which can contribute to good health or directly, or indirectly, to health problems. Some major factors would be smoking, and drinking (alcohol), but stresses related to relationship problems or problems at work are also seen as factors which may lead to health problems. The doctor will ask questions which aim to elicit this sort of information. Some questions are quite sensitive. Questions as to how many cigarettes the individual smokes or how many units of alcohol he or she drinks per day or per week do not always get an honest response, but the health professional usually makes allowances for this.

Commonly asked questions in relation to the patient's social history would include:

- Do you smoke? If so, how much do you smoke?
- If you have stopped smoking now, how much did you use to smoke and when did you stop smoking?
- Do you drink alcohol?
- How much alcohol do you drink and how often?
- If you have stopped drinking now, how much did you use to drink and for how long?
- Do you use drugs (hard drugs/soft drugs)?
- What type of drugs do you use? (cocaine, heroin, cannabis/marijuana, ecstasy/MDMA, pseudoephedrine, amphetamines, prescription painkillers)
- How often do you take them and in what dosage?
- Are you currently employed?
- Are you experiencing any stresses at work? What kind of stresses?
- Are you experiencing any stresses at home? What kind of stresses?
- Are you experiencing any stresses in your relationship? What kind of stresses?
- What is your home situation like?
- Do you live
    - in your own home
    - in rental accommodation
    - in a trailer or caravan
    - with other people as a boarder

- how many people live in your house?
- do any of them smoke?
- do you have support at home? (i.e. people who are willing and able to help you and or look after you)

The medical history may encompass questions about any previous medical problems, which may include:

- heart disease (angina pectoris/chest pain; heart attack; heart failure)
- diabetes (insulin-dependent or non-insulin dependent)
- circulation problems (thrombosis; bleeding; narrowing of the arteries)
- digestive (ulcers; constipation; diarrhea; wind)
- lungs (tuberculosis; asthma; pneumonia; bronchitis; chronic obstructive lung disease).

The surgical history will focus on past surgery, what this was (or where) and when. This may include procedures such as:

- total hip replacement
- appendectomy ("Have you had your appendix out")
- terminations of pregnancy (this is the medical term for the lay word 'abortion')
- laparoscopy (minor operation where the surgeon looks inside the abdomen through a fiber optic tube called a scope)

Obstetric history questions focus on previous pregnancies or miscarriages/terminations of pregnancy. These are discussed in detail in Chapters 11 and 27.

The primary care doctor may also ask questions concerning the patient's mental health. Such questions may include:

- How have you been feeling in yourself?
- Has your appetite changed? Have you lost appetite? Are you eating more than before?
- Have you been feeling down?
- Are you experiencing any stresses at the moment? Are you able to sleep?
- Do you hear voices in your head?
- Have you ever been admitted to a Psychiatric Ward/Acute Assessment Unit/ Psychiatric Hospital?
- When and what for?
- Are you currently on any medication?

Once again, it is important that interpreters not only interpret exactly what the patient says but also interpret and relay questions to the patient accurately. In order to do so the interpreter needs to be familiar with currently used medical and healthcare terminology in both languages. In addition, the interpreter needs to be aware of the healthcare systems in both countries. The interpreter also needs to be aware of the cultural differences and different cultural attitudes towards health problems so as to be able to inform the professional of these if necessary.

5. Physical examination

In order to reach a provisional diagnosis, the primary care doctor will examine the patient and perform certain checks including:

– *Pulse*: The doctor may say '*I will take your pulse*'; This may enable the doctor to tell if the pulse is weak or strong (heart is beating weakly or strongly, blood pressure is low or high), if the pulse is slow or fast, regular or irregular.
– *Blood pressure*: The doctor may say: '*I will take your blood pressure; your blood pressure is up (higher than normal)/high/low*'. If the blood pressure is 120/80, 120 is the systolic blood pressure, while 80 refers to the refers to the diastolic blood pressure. The doctor may ask certain questions in relation to the person's blood pressure. Some of these might be:
    – Do you smoke? How much/how often do you smoke?
    – Do you drink a lot of coffee/strong tea? How much coffee/tea do you drink in a day?
    – How much salt do you take in your food?
    – What medication are you on at the moment? (This includes asthma inhalers)
    – Have you lost a lot of blood/do you have very heavy periods?
    – Is there a family history of kidney problems?
    – Do you feel faint when you get up suddenly?
    – Do you feel any pressure/tightness in your head?
– *Auscultation:* The doctor may use his stethoscope to listen to the person's chest or abdomen. He or she may listen for abnormal breathing sounds or abnormal heart sounds, or for signs that the bowels are working.
    Auscultation of the lungs: The doctor will tell the patient to '*take a deep breath*' and listen to the breath sounds.
    Auscultation of the heart: the doctor may count the heart rate by placing a stethoscope at the base of the heart. This may enable the doctor to tell if there are any problems such as heart murmurs (abnormal heart sounds) or irregular heart beat
– *Percussion:* This involves the doctor tapping the patient's chest and abdomen – listening for 'dull' and 'hollow' sounds. This does not usually require any interpreting.

– *Palpation:* This involves the doctor feeling for normal/abnormal '*lumps and bumps*'. The doctor may feel the lymph nodes or lymph glands (in the neck or groin) to see if they are enlarged. They may also feel the liver. Often the doctor will ask questions such as '*Does it hurt if I press here?*'

6. Tests

Some tests may be performed at the primary care doctor's rooms, whilst others are carried out elsewhere. Patients may be given a lab form and told to report to the nearest laboratory for blood tests, or to go to the nearest Radiographer's Rooms for X-Rays or Ultrasound scans.

Tests still done by primary care doctors include:

– Cervical smear tests
– Blood glucose tests – to test the amount of sugar in the patient's bloodstream
– Urine tests – checked for sugar, protein, ketones
– Peak Flow Test – to test the amount of air a patient with asthma is able to breathe out
– Electrocardiogram (ECG or EKG) – to record the electrical activity of the heart

Other common tests which the primary care doctor may order and give the patient a referral form for include:

– *Chest X-Ray* – an X-Ray of the chest to examine the structures of the organs in the chest (heart, lungs, windpipe, diaphragm)
– *Ultrasound scan of the abdomen* – a scan using high-frequency sound waves. Some gel is placed on the abdomen and the sensor is moved around to examine organs in the abdomen. Patients may need to have a full bladder, depending on the instructions they are given prior to the ultrasound.
– *Blood tests.* Commonly ordered blood tests would include:
    – Full Blood Count; especially Hemoglobin (see glossary),
    – White blood cells (see glossary) and platelets (see glossary)
    – Urea and Electrolytes
    – Thyroxin and TSH levels – to test the amount of thyroid and thyroid stimulating hormone in the blood
    – Liver function tests – to see if the liver is working normally
    – Cholesterol test – see page 212
    – Erythrocyte Sedimentation Rate (ESR) – a blood test mainly used to check if there is any inflammation process going on in the body
    – Urine tests – some urine tests may be performed by the primary care doctor, e.g. pregnancy tests; tests which show sugar or protein, the presence of which can be tested by using a simple dipstick

7. Immunization schedule

Parents who wish to have their children immunized may go to their primary care physician who will examine the child first to ensure that it is in a fit state to be immunized. The vaccinations themselves are usually given by the doctor's nurse. Parents are instructed to contact the doctor if the child becomes unwell following the vaccination.

8. Health education

The primary care doctor has an important role to play in the area of health education. They can explain medical conditions to the patient and also give instructions and advice on how to control the medical condition; how to deal with warning signs; what diet to follow; what exercise to undertake (if any), and where to go for specialist advice. The primary care doctor will also explain what referrals are possible and which associations offer further help and advice.

It is important that the interpreter conveys instructions and advice very carefully and accurately. Interpreters may wish to provide the primary care doctor with information on the patient's cultural background where appropriate.

9. Referrals

On the basis of his/her findings the primary care doctor may reach a provisional diagnosis and decide to either

- treat and observe the patient himself/herself. In which case the patient will be sent home with a prescription and instructions and the patient may be asked to come back for a follow-up visit
- refer the patient to other health professionals more specialized in a particular area. In this case the patient may be referred to
    - a surgical outpatient clinic if the doctor suspects that the patient's problem may (eventually) require surgery
    - a medical specialist clinic or medical outpatient clinic
    - the hospital's Emergency Room or Emergency Department
    - to other health professionals out in the community. In most instances patients will be referred to the district nurse for a first assessment and the district nurse will then liaise with other professionals in the area of community health as required, e.g. community social workers; community occupational therapists; community physiotherapists.

In the US some specialist doctors will accept patients who have self-referred. In the UK, Australia and NZ specialists will usually want a *letter of referral* from the patient's doctor (or from another specialist).

It will be clear from this chapter that primary care doctors such as GPs and PPs have a good all-round knowledge of medicine, and may often reach a provisional diagnosis, but will refer patients onto specialist doctors for further investigation and treatment when necessary.

10. Some notes for interpreters and translators

The interpreter should always wait for the patient's answer and not answer 'Yes' or 'No' as in the case of the interpreter who was interpreting for a pregnant woman. The midwife said: '*Do you have a pain in your abdomen?*' to which the interpreter hurriedly replied '*Yes, yes, yes*', without relaying the question to the patient. The woman was rushed to the delivery suite where another interpreter was called in. With the aid of this second interpreter, who did relay all questions faithfully to the patient, it was established that the woman was not in premature labor, as it was first assumed, but merely experienced a burning sensation whenever she was passing urine, because she did, in fact, have a urinary tract infection.

When asked '*Do you drink alcohol?*' the word *alcohol* itself may give rise to confusion. Nurses at a public hospital tuberculosis clinic in New Zealand were told by interpreters that patients from some cultural and linguistic backgrounds did not consider *beer* to be alcohol. Consequently, many of the patients who were told not to drink any alcohol with their anti-tuberculosis medication still drank beer, in the mistaken belief that that was not really alcohol. For this reason, some of the interpreters decided to render the word '*alcohol*' as '*alcohol and beer*'.

As to the number of cigarettes the person actually smokes, even if the interpreter knows that the person smokes two packs a day, he or she will have to interpret whatever the client says. Questions relating to employment are mainly intended to find out if the patient is stressed or depressed or going through financial difficulties. The patient may be unemployed or may have been made redundant. Loss of work can lead to the patient going through the various stages of the grieving process (see Chapter 2). Long periods of unemployment may leave some patients depressed.

Accommodation can also be a major factor in health outcomes. Overcrowded housing situations may lead to children picking up bacterial and viral infections from others in the house. Families may have to sleep on moldy mattresses in draughty caravans, trailer homes or garages. Many may be subjected to passive smoking by inhaling second-hand smoke exhaled by others in the house. Smoking (active or passive) has been linked to childhood asthma, cot death and lung cancer, so these are important questions.

Summary of main points

This chapter has looked at Primary physicians and General Practitioners including:

– history taking (medical, surgical, family, social, mental health)
– physical examination
– common investigations

Chapter 6

Outpatient Clinics and specialist clinics

Most people will see their primary care physician or other primary care provider first when suffering from ill health. In many cases, their provider will examine, diagnose and treat the patient. However, if the doctor feels that the patient's condition is outside their area of specialty, or the patients' condition is unstable or not improving, or the doctor feels that another (differential) diagnosis may be possible the doctor may refer patients to either an Outpatient Clinic or to a specialist clinic (or private specialist).

In this chapter, the word Outpatient Clinic will be used to refer to a place in which outpatients are given medical treatment or advice, often connected to a (public) hospital. The word Specialist clinics will be used to refer to a similar place, run by doctors who specialize in a particular area (specialty). Outpatients visit such clinics for consultations, examinations and investigations provided by specialist doctors (or by those training to be specialists). Outpatient Clinics may also provide follow-up care to people with chronic conditions such as diabetes or chronic obstructive lung disorders. Before referring patients, the primary doctor may discuss their condition with the appropriate person (public hospital or private specialist) and give the patient a letter of referral. This letter will briefly outline the patient's previous history and the history of his current condition.

Seeing a private specialist or visiting a privately funded outpatient facility has advantages in that patients get to be seen by a highly experienced doctor immediately and, mostly, do not have to wait that long for an appointment. Some patients find they cannot afford the specialist's fees or that their health insurer will not cover them.

In some countries, public hospitals may provide Outpatient Clinics for every specialty or special field in medicine, depending on the size of the population they are serving. Small town hospitals may only have a General Outpatient Clinic, while slightly larger hospitals may have a Surgical Outpatient Clinic and a Medical Outpatient Clinic. Large general hospitals in big cities, may provide a whole range of outpatient services, including clinics for patients with endocrinological problems or urological problems. Surgical clinics offer both presurgical (investigating the patient before surgery) and postsurgical (monitoring the patient's condition after surgery) services, while medical clinics focus on assessing and monitoring patients whose conditions are managed without surgery.

1. Outpatient Clinics

What follows is a brief list of more common outpatients' clinics in countries with publicly funded healthcare:

Antenatal/Prenatal	Women are referred here for check-up visits during pregnancy.
Gynecological	Women are referred here if their doctor thinks they may need specialist consultations for gynecological problems. Sometimes the hospital may have a special *colposcopy* clinic, where specialists perform colposcopies (looking at the cervix/vagina).
Neurological	Patients are referred here if their doctor suspects they may problems affecting the Central Nervous System or peripheral nervous system.
Cardiological	Patients are referred here if their doctor suspects they may have a problem with their heart, e.g. coronary artery disease, heart valve problems or rhythm problems, pre-operative and post-operative assessment of the heart and Holter monitoring (monitoring heart rate and sometimes also blood pressure over a longer period).
Orthopedic	GPs/PPs will refer their patients here if they suspect they might have a problem to do with their bones or joints (e.g. osteo-arthritis of the hip joint, possibly needing a total hip replacement). Many patients who have fractured (broken) a bone, go here for follow-up visits.
Urological	Patients are referred to the urologist for problems such as prostate problems, recurring urinary tract infections, and so on.
Endocrinological	Patients are referred here with problems of the hormone producing system, including problems such as hyperthyroidism (an overactive thyroid gland), diabetes and the like.
Sexual Health	Patients are referred here for education about sexual health, how to avoid sexually transmitted diseases, and for treatment of sexually transmitted diseases (STDs).
Family Planning	Couples who wish to conceive or those who do not wish to conceive can go to the Family Planning Clinic for advice on contraception, fertility and so on.
Dental	Patients are referred here with major and acute problems concerning their teeth.
Plastic Surgical	Burns patients can be referred to the plastic surgical clinic for surgical repair of badly scarred areas on their bodies (e.g. due to burns); patients can also be referred here for treatment of skin

cancers, repair of nerves, tendons and skin, or correction of cleft palate or protruding ears.

Renal   This is a special clinic for people who have kidney problems. Some patients may have end-stage renal failure and will need to go on dialysis.

Some Outpatient Clinics aim to provide medical checkups and assistance for people with chronic conditions such as diabetes or asthma. This may include the following:

Incontinence Clinic   Special 'Incontinence' nurses teach patients about bladder control or may do urodynamics (measurements to do with the working of the bladder).

Diabetes Clinic   Here patients can consult special diabetes nurses who can teach them how to inject insulin and how to do their own blood sugar readings; in addition, there are special dietitians who can offer special dietary advice.

Eye clinic   Here patients go with eye complaints.

Asthma Clinic   Asthma patients or parents of children with asthma can come here for monitoring, control and advice.

Colostomy Clinic   Special 'stoma' nurses advise patients on how to look after their colostomy (when the bowel has been brought to the surface of the skin as a temporary or permanent measure), how to change bags, what diet to keep, and so on.

Oxygen Clinic   This clinic coordinates and monitors patients in the community who are dependent on oxygen. These patients are provided with oxygen concentrators and oxygen supplies.

2.   Staff at the outpatients or specialist clinics

Staff at outpatient or specialist clinics will vary from one country or state to another, but in general includes Registered Nurses and Specialist doctors. Clinics may also employ medical technicians, healthcare assistants and *Resident Medical Officers* (called *Registrars* in some countries) training to become specialists.

3.   Procedure at Outpatients Clinics or specialist clinics

The patient may have been to see his primary care doctor or the patient may have been to either the hospital or the outpatients' clinic before, and may have been asked to return for a follow-up appointment.

After reporting to the clinic, the patient's weight may be checked. Usually medical staff will want to know the patient's weight for three main reasons:

–   Weight gain may be a sign that the patient has regained his/her appetite, which can be a sign of recovery. Conversely, weight loss may be a sign that the patient has lost appetite and may be deteriorating.
–   Weight gain may be a sign that the patient has too much fluid on board (retaining fluid in his/her body). For this reason weight gain is checked in patients who are pregnant, or patients with heart or kidney problems, amongst other things.
–   Doctors use the person's body weight to calculate the doses of medication that they need to receive. A tiny little woman might be easily 'overdosed' if she received the drug dose prescribed for a much taller and heavier woman. She might possibly experience more side effects.

In addition to weight the patients history will be documented and physical examinations and commonly performed tests may be performed (much the same as that for the procedure followed by the primary care provider).

The following procedures may also be carried out at outpatient service facilities:

Imaging: This may include X-Rays; MRI scanning; CT scanning; PET scanning; Ultrasound scanning; Doppler Tests.

Investigative procedures: These may include bronchoscopy, colonoscopy, colposcopy, gastroscopy; eye examinations; lung function testing, hearing testing and many others.

For more information on specific areas of medicine and common disorders and treatment methods, please refer to the relevant chapters.

4.   Some notes for interpreters and translators

The word clinic may be difficult to translate. In some languages the word 'clinic' is just another word for (small) hospital.

There are countries in which the concept of Outpatients Clinics does not exist. In some countries, people 'self-diagnose' their problems to a large extent and go straight to a private specialist without any referral from a primary care provider. Alternatively, patients may self-diagnose and then visit a chemist store or pharmacy to buy what *they* think they need (such as antibiotics). Some countries do not have a system where primary healthcare is provided by GPs/PPs and so the whole concept of primary care physicians referring patients on to Outpatient Clinics may be difficult to convey.

The word outpatients too, may give rise to misunderstanding. In simple terms, an outpatient is a person who comes from home, has a history taken, undergoes an examination or test, and is then either sent home (with or without a follow-up appointment). The word outpatient implies that the patient is not admitted to hospital. As soon as the outpatient is admitted to hospital he or she becomes an inpatient.

An inpatient is a patient who is admitted to hospital under a certain medical team and who stays at least overnight. The medical team in question assumes responsibility for the patient's treatment and discharges him or her back to the care of the primary care provider when treatment has been completed.

A 'day-stay patient' is a patient who comes to stay in hospital for the express purpose of undergoing specific procedure on that day without staying overnight.

In those countries where outpatient clinics are part of the publicly funded system, patients (and interpreters) may have to wait quite a while in the waiting room before they can go in to see the specialist. Interpreters should take this into account when booking interpreting assignments. In these countries, patients are usually seen by a specialist in training, not by the specialist themself. The doctor who sees them may have to discuss their case with the specialist, all of which adds to the amount of time patient (and interpreter) have to spend in the clinic. If it is decided that the patient needs further treatment in the public hospital, the patient may have to go on a (long) waiting list before he can have this treatment.

Summary of main points

This chapter has looked at Outpatient and Specialist Clinics including:

- different specialties (medical, surgical, family, social, mental health)
- health professionals involved
- procedures and common investigations

Chapter 7

Hospitals

Very often interpreters are first called in when the patient has been admitted or is in the process of being admitted to hospital (private or public). Due to differences between countries and states, and ongoing changes within the various healthcare systems, information in this chapter will be very general,. Every hospital has its own culture and its own way of doing things. However, in most English speaking countries the hospital system can trace its historical roots to Britain. Some commentators (cf. Risse 1999; Wall, n.d.) describe the broad underpinnings of hospital cultures in countries within North-Western Europe and North America as follows:

– the isolation of the sick – Dating back to the isolation of ill people in Medieval Europe, in hospitals (literally: guest houses), looked after by religious 'brothers and sisters' (monks and nuns);
– the medico-scientific approach – Diagnosis and treatment are based on scientific evidence, (cultural beliefs are not taken into account);
– the patient-oriented approach – Medical staff are focused on the individual patient, rather than on the patient's family.

It needs to be stressed that internationally hospitals can be expected to be uniform and consistent in core matters such as standards of care and professional ethics of medical and nursing staff. The three aspects listed above can result in cross-cultural issues which may affect the interpreter and will therefore be discussed in some more detail below.

1. The isolation of the sick

Peculiar, perhaps, to western culture is the tendency to isolate sick people in hospitals, where they are looked after by health professionals. As Helman states, (1990, p. 70), 'Patients are removed from the continuous emotional support of family and community and cared for by healers whom they may never have seen before'. In most western countries, people accompany their loved ones to hospitals, stay only during visiting hours, two visitors at a time and then depart, trusting that their loved ones will be well looked after by those whose job it is to do so. Nurses expect family members to come in to visit only during visiting hours, so as not to disturb the nurses in doing their job in caring for the patients.

The tendency to isolate sick people in hospitals, and to leave them to the care of professionals, may not be found in all countries. New immigrants from many areas around the world may feel that leaving a sick relative in hospital, without being there for them, is socially unacceptable. Anybody who left their old parents all by themselves in hospital overnight would be branded a 'bad' child. For this reason, relatives may request to be allowed to stay with patients in order to look after them. Such requests may be misunderstood in healthcare systems where the isolation of the sick is the accepted norm.

2.   The medico-scientific approach

In most western countries, the diagnosis of 'disease' is based on scientific evidence. The word medico-scientific also means that it is medical staff who prescribe treatment on the basis of scientific evidence. As explained in Chapter 3, sometimes patients' attitudes may be based on different cultural and religious belief systems and this may lead to conflict and mutual misunderstanding and mistrust. Immigrant patients may self-diagnose illness and self-treat their conditions. The diagnosis they reach will be based on their own belief system as to how the body functions. Similarly, the remedies they choose may be based on scientifically unproven popular beliefs and folk remedies (Helman 1990; Jackson 2006; Camplin-Welch 2007). If the initial remedies do not have the desired effect, sick people may seek help from a wide range of alternative healers such as herbalists, faith healers, clairvoyants and shamans. Often, medical help is only sought as a last resort.

Cases of patients receiving a diagnosis and then leaving the hospital to try alternative healers have been known. In some unfortunate cases, patients have then returned to hospital when alternative treatments have failed. Interpreters may find that they have to act as cultural liaisons in cases where hospital staff find it difficult to understand the various cultural and popular beliefs that motivate patients to seek unproven alternative treatment based on deep-seated cultural beliefs.

3.   The patient-oriented approach

In most Western societies (cf. Hofstede 1980) it is the patient who is told that they have a certain condition. The doctor will explain treatment options so as to enable the patient to make a decision on these treatment options and will obtain the patient's agreement (Informed Consent) before embarking on any operations or potentially harmful procedures.

This is in contrast with accepted procedure in some other societies where the patient may be the last to know what is wrong and what is going to happen as family members may have decided what is best for the patient. One Pacific Island support worker reported the case of the young woman who needed radical surgery to give her a real chance of surviving her cancer. Her family were outraged and insisted that she seek help and advice from a faith healer. The woman had to literally 'go into hiding' from her family in order to have the treatment she wanted.

Situations such as these may give rise to conflict and misunderstanding and may lead to relatives putting pressure on the interpreter asking that he not interpret the real diagnosis. According to anecdotal evidence this is a recurrent occurrence for interpreters in New Zealand. Relatives should approach medical staff through the interpreter, rather than asking interpreters to breach the interpreters' Code of Ethics.

4. Hospital staff

In certain areas of the hospital, it may be difficult to differentiate between nursing staff, medical staff and technical support staff as all may be wearing '*blues*' or '*greens*' or even everyday clothing. In this case the interpreter should pay specific attention to name badges in order to know who he or she is dealing with. In most wards, the contact person for the interpreter may be the Ward Clerk or Receptionist.

5. Nursing staff

Hospital nursing staff may include the following groups of nurses:

Enrolled Nurses	Enrolled Nurses (ENs) may still be found in Australia and the UK. They have had shorter training than Registered Nurses (RNs) and usually work under the supervision of RNs.
Registered Nurses	In the UK, interpreters may come across the following four groups of RNs:

- –   RNA (Registered Nurse Adult)
- –   RNC (Registered Nurse Child)
- –   RNMH (Registered Nurse Mental Health)
- –   RNLD (Registered Nurse Learning Disabilities)

The UK also has Nurse Practitioners, who often work in child health or acute medicine.

Interpreters in the US may work with a range of nursing staff, varying from Registered Nurses (RNs) and Nurse Practitioners (NPs) to Advanced Practice Registered Nurses (APRNs). The scope of practice of these practitioners is determined by the Nurse Practice Act of the state in which RNs or NPs and ANPs are licensed.

Nurse Practitioners	Nurse practitioners (NPs) hold a minimum of a Bachelor's degree, plus a Master's degree or Postgraduate qualification. Their role is often similar to that of medical staff, which means that they may be allowed to prescribe medication and to refer or admit patients to hospital. The scope of the Nurse Practitioner role often depends on current legislation and regulations in the various states or countries. NPs often work in child health (US, UK), acute medicine (UK) or primary healthcare (US, Canada).
Midwives	Midwives are health practitioners trained to guide women during pregnancy, as well as during and after childbirth. Different countries and states have different training programmes and different legislation around midwives' scope of practice.

6. Medical staff

Interpreters may come across medical students (who have not graduated from Medical School as yet) or medical doctors (ranging from newly qualified to specializing or qualified specialists).

In the US and Canada newly qualified medical doctors undertake 3–8 years training as a resident, the duration of training depending on their chosen specialty.

In the UK, medical doctors undertake a two-year foundation programme after graduation, during which time they are referred to as Foundation House Officers. After completing this foundation programme they get a position as Registrars, doctors who are training to be specialists.

In Australia, newly qualified doctors undertake one year of supervised practice after graduating, during which time they are referred to as interns. Those training to be specialists, do two years as a Resident Medical Officer (RMO), followed by a position as a Registrar.

Similarly, in NZ, new graduates undertake one or two years of supervised practice as Junior Doctors after graduating followed by a position as a Registrar for those wishing to train in a specific specialty.

Interpreters need to be aware of the word intern, as in New Zealand Trainee Interns, are in fact in their last year of Medical School.

7. Specialists

Specialists are physicians who have developed a specialist knowledge in a specialist area over many years of supervised training in a particular specialty (special area of medicine) and who have been recognized as a specialist by members of a specific college of specialist physicians (e.g. the Royal College of Surgeons).

In some countries (including the UK and NZ), specialists working in public hospitals are referred to as consultants and some surgical specialists like to be addressed as Mr, rather than Dr. In this case the 'Mister' indicates the high degree of specialty they have achieved.

8.   Other hospital staff

Admitting Clerk	The Admitting Clerk is based in the Admitting Department or at the Front Desk. This clerk ensures that the necessary information required for admission is collected and entered. The Admitting Clerk may also ask for proof that the patient is a Permanent Resident or Citizen or has health insurance.
Chaplain	Most hospitals have designated chaplains, usually representing the Catholic faith and major Protestant denominations. Chaplains are available for a range of spiritual needs and support. They are on call.
Orderlies	Men or women who mainly carry out 'fetch and carry' duties. Apart from those orderlies who are designated as 'Special Orderlies', most orderlies have no direct patient contact. Orderlies transport goods and equipment around the hospital and have certain designated functions with regards to emergency and disaster situations.
Ward Clerk	The Ward Clerk may also be referred to by other titles. The Ward Clerk usually does not have much contact with the patient, but fulfills mainly clerical duties, which may include calling in an interpreter. The Ward Clerk ensures that patient notes are processed correctly, although these days most patient records are completely electronic. In addition, the Ward Clerk makes appointments, arranges ambulances and other travel arrangements.

9.   Other healthcare staff

Dietitian	Hospital meals are prepared by the Dietary Department for all patients. However, dietitians ensure that specific patients receive special individually 'designed' meals in relation to their medical condition.

Lactation Consultant	Usually a Nurse or Midwife with special responsibility for breast-feeding mothers.
Occupational Therapist or (OT)	A health professional trained to help people to carry out the Activities of Daily Living (ADL), including work activities and self-care activities such as washing, bathing, showering, dressing/undressing, preparing drinks or food and toileting. OTs are also involved with providing adaptations such as orthotics, ramps for wheelchairs, handrails and the like. OTs working in the community may advise on the installation of toilet heighteners, bath planks, wheelchair ramps and support bars on walls.
Pharmacist	The hospital pharmacist checks which drugs are in stock and monitors patients' drug charts and ward drug supplies.
Physical therapist	Also known as a Physio or Physiotherapist, these health professionals are trained to assist with mobilization following surgery or serious medical event (such as stroke). They may also be called in to assist with deep-breathing exercises following surgery.
Speech therapist	Professional involved in treating people who have problems with normal oral communication, usually following some physiological event such as a stroke or head injury. Also called Speech Language Therapist or Speech Pathologist. See also Chapter 14.
Social Worker	Specially trained professional who assists people who have social, domestic and financial problems as a result of their condition or disability.

10. Hospital procedures

Hospital procedures can be baffling and confusing to any and everyone who comes to hospital for the first time, but particularly so for people who are new to the country as a whole. Hospital procedures vary from country to country and from hospital to hospital. In addition every department, or ward, may also have its own procedures. This book will only present a very general outline of commonly used procedures.

11. Admissions

11.1 Types – acute and booked

An acute admission is the result of a sudden and unexpected referral, necessitating immediate admission to the hospital. Usually, the primary care provider will ring the hospital and speak to the registrar or resident about the patient and arrange for the patient to go to the hospital. Occasionally, a patient may have had an appointment at the Outpatients' Clinic and may have been found to be very ill. In this case, the patient may be admitted from the Outpatients' Clinic. Alternatively, patients may be brought in by ambulance (Emergency Services).

If the hospital has an Emergency Department, the patient may need to go there first to be stabilized. Stabilizing involves ensuring that the patient's condition does not get any worse.

An acute admission can be very stressful for both the interpreter, the patient and his or her family. In acute admission cases the interpreter may be called in to interpret at odd hours. They may be woken from sleep and may not be feeling quite alert and awake upon arrival in the hospital, yet be required to interpret all information with great accuracy. In addition the patient and his/her family may be very stressed and emotional, which may make it difficult for the interpreter to concentrate and/or remain calm. Furthermore the interpreter may not have time or opportunity to prepare for the assignment, or for any terminology that may crop up, and there may be very little background information available on the patient and the patient's condition.

It is essential, however, that the interpreter interpret all questions to the patient or the patient's family very accurately. In some cases the interpreter may note that the medical staff is not getting the complete message because they do not understand specific non-verbal cues, which may mean that they are not able to reach an accurate diagnosis. It is important, in such cases, that the interpreter also serves as a cultural liaison by clarifying certain non-verbal expressions to the health professional.

In the case of a booked admission, the patient has been told beforehand to report to the hospital for a certain procedure or investigation on a certain date.

On the whole, booked admissions are less stressful to both interpreter and patient. The interpreter may be told beforehand where the admission will take place and for what reason and therefore typically has time to prepare for the interview. Likewise the patient may be more prepared for the admission and may be less stressed.

12. Admission process

Upon arrival in the ward one of the nursing staff will show the patient where their bed is and where to put clothes and other personal belongings. Some ward procedures may be explained and the patient may be shown the layout of the ward. After this, the nursing staff will do some baseline recordings for comparison purposes (e.g. weight, height, blood pressure, temperature, respiratory/breathing rate and heart rate/pulse). Additional baseline recordings may be done, such as a peak flow reading, an electro-cardiogram (ECG) or a blood glucose reading, depending on the type of ward and the condition of the patient. The nurse will record these findings in a chart.

The nurse may then proceed to take a nursing history. These questions typically focus on the patient's mental and physical state. It is important for nursing staff to know whether the patient is fully aware of the reason for his admission, how they feels about it, whether they have other concerns or stresses in their life (such as worries about employment, benefits, young children at home, relationship problems), the presence or absence of support people, religious or cultural beliefs, and any special needs and or habits. The nurse will also ask the patient whether they can still cope with the Activities of Daily Living, such as cooking, doing the household chores, gardening, and so on.

If the patient is in possession of money and other valuables, the hospital provides safekeeping facilities. Usually the hospital will not accept responsibility for valuables stolen while the patient is in hospital. Valuables can be given to a nurse to be locked away in the 'valuables cupboard'. In this case a description of the valuables is written into the valuables book and the patient is given a receipt. The patient needs to keep the receipt and hand it in to reclaim the valuables.

When the nurse has finished taking the nursing history, a medical staff member may come to admit the patient. It may be confusing to hear the same term admitting used again. This means that the medical staff identifies the problem that the patient 'is presenting with' and decides on the treatment.

For the patient, this means that the same questions are repeated again, but they are now written up in the medical records and will constitute the basis for medical treatment or further investigations. The medical staff member will take the patient's history and do a physical examination. In some wards, such as the Ear, Nose and Throat ward, this may be followed by a checkup in an examination room, especially equipped for this purpose. Similarly, women who are admitted to an acute assessment ward for gynecological or obstetric problems will undergo a speculum examination, or an ultrasound scan, or even an emergency colposcopy. Please refer to the chapters in Part III for investigations and tests in relation to specific health conditions.

13. Most important rooms (from the patient's perspective)

Day Room	This room is intended for patients to spend some time to relax and talk to other patients, to read magazines or watch TV. It is often also used by visitors. The day room usually contains sofas and the like and a television set.
Drug Cupboard	Storage area for ward drugs which are replenished by the Pharmacy.
Interview Room	A room which contains the necessary equipment for medical staff to examine patients or to talk to patients about their diagnosis and prognosis.

Nurses' station	This is the central area where nurses keep patient records. Medical staff may also be found here, writing up patient notes.
Patient's room	Can be a single, double room or may be a ward containing four or more beds. The patient's room will generally contain a bedside locker or bed-side table on wheels, a few chairs and a wardrobe. The toilets and showers usually have to be shared with other patients. Some rooms will contain a toilet chair also referred to as a commode.
Sterile Room or Treatment Room	Where medication and equipment are kept.
Sluice Room or Utility Room	This room contains a sterilizer for used bedpans and (urinary) bottles. There are also facilities for rinsing, washing and storing bowls for bed-washes or bed-sponges. In some wards, toilet chairs or commodes are stored in the sluice room. This room may also have a washing machine (for soiled linen) and a dryer.
Valuables Cabinet	Patients can have their valuables (gold rings, watches, money) locked away in the valuables cupboard. This is a good idea especially when the patient is confused or has to take off all his/her valuables because the patient has to go to theatre.
Expression Room	This room will contain equipment such as electrical breast pumps or expression pumps, which will enable mothers to express breast milk for their babies. It usually contains sterilizing equipment and sterilizing solutions such as 'Milton' (a Sodium Hypochlorite solution).
Milk Room	This room will contain refrigerators which are filled with (named and dated) bottles containing expressed breast milk (also referred to as *raw* breast milk).
Nursery	Found in maternity wards, a special room where babies spend their days/nights. The nursery will be kept at an agreeable temperature and may contain equipment for bathing and changing babies.

14. Discharge

Once the patient has completed their stay in hospital, the medical staff will decide on a discharge date and mode. Most commonly patients are discharged home with follow-up by their primary care doctor or provider. Sometime there may be follow-up by staff at the relevant Outpatients' Clinic or patients may be given a referral for the District Nursing Service.

Interpreters may be needed to interpret specific discharge instructions to medication, diet, follow-up and activities of daily living. Some patients may be advised to avoid certain activities of daily living (such as heavy lifting, vacuum cleaning or sexual intercourse) for a certain period of time. Obviously such instructions will need to be interpreted accurately to avoid putting the patient's health in jeopardy. Clarification of different cultural attitudes may be of great importance at this stage. In some cultures, for example, the idea of being told that you are ill and that you have to exercise, may well be considered to be incompatible. The interpreter may need to act as a cultural liaison and clarify this to the health professionals concerned, interpreting any clarification s/he provides in the patient's language also. Once alerted to any possible issues, the health professional may then be able to address this with the patient.

15. Rehabilition

Rehabilitation is an important part of medical care – both in the hospital setting and in the community. Rehabilitation has been defined as the process of restoring 'personal autonomy in those aspects of daily living considered most relevant by patients or service users and their family carers' (Sinclair & Dickinson 1998, p. 27). In general, rehabilitation focuses mainly on restoring a person's physical (and psychological) independence, well-being and quality of life. This section will also touch on Geriatrics, because it is common for older patients to need (long-term) rehabilitation relating to chronic conditions (e.g. lung emphysema), neurological consequences of stroke or after surgery.

Interpreters may work with health professionals who are assisting patients with recovery after heart attacks (cardiological rehabilitation) and strokes or spinal cord injuries (neurological rehabilitation), to those working with patients suffering from long-term disabilities or or recovering from cancer surgery or. Braddom (2011) provides an excellent overview of rehabilitative care in a wide range of settings.

Interpreting for rehabilitation therapists and geriatricians centers mostly on an accurate exchange of information. The health professional will usually start by assessing what the client's needs are and what the client is still able and willing to do. Once the therapist has made this assessment, he will proceed with a treatment plan, which he will want to discuss with the client and/or the client's family.

16. Health professionals

Geriatrician – medical specialists specializing in the health of older adults.

Occupational therapist – health professional who helps people to improve their ability to perform tasks in their daily living and working environments; the abbreviation OT is often used to refer to this profession. See also Hammell (2009).

Physical therapist or Physiotherapist – Health professional who has completed a studies in the treatment of muscular disorders – see also Chapters 7 and 22.

Speech (Language) Therapist – see also Chapter 14.

Podiatrist – US: medical professional specializing in the medical assessment and treatment of disorders relating to foot, ankle and lower leg, including foot and ankle surgery. Their medical title may be abbreviated as DPM – Doctor of Podiatric Medicine. *NB* Outside of the US, the term podiatrist usually refers to an allied health professional who specializes in the assessment and treatment of disorders of foot, ankle and lower leg.

Nutritionist – provides guidance on nutrition and diet.

Dietitian – Registered or Licensed dietitians provide guidance on diets and nutrition.

Geriatric Nurse – Registered Nurse specialized in nursing elderly patients.

17. Physical therapy

Physical therapists have completed a programme of studies in the treatment of muscular disorders and may assist clients with a range of treatment options, following an assessment. Rehabilitation physical therapy usually involves exercises to improve the client's range of motion (ROM), teaching the client to walk with a walking aid (crutches, walker) or teaching the client how to use a wheelchair and transfer from wheelchair to bed, toilet or even to a motor vehicle. Other treatment options may include exercises; electrical stimulation; massage; taping and bandaging or applying heat or cold (ice).

The physical therapist may give the client instructions on certain exercises and may ask the client if they experience any pain whilst carrying out particular movements. The physical therapist may ask the client to flex (bend) or extend (stretch). Instead of using these words, the physiotherapist may say things like '*Curl up your toes*', '*Make a fist*', '*Grab my hand and squeeze as hard as you can*'.

18. Occupational therapy

Occupational Therapists may work with clients in hospitals, nursing homes or in the wider community. Their aim is to help people to improve their ability to perform tasks in their daily living and working environments (activities of daily living. Where occupational therapists work with people in their own homes, they may recommend that equipment and aids be installed, to help their clients cope with the activities of daily living, abbreviated as (ADL. Equipment may include ramps so the client can get in/out of his house by wheelchair, raised toilet seats, bath boards, shower seats, antislip mats, handrails.

19. Some notes for interpreters and translators

It is important that all questions and answers are interpreted accurately, as information given may influence the care given to the patient e.g. nurses will often liaise with other health professionals, such as house surgeons, dietitians, district nurses, counselors, psychiatric registrars, diabetes nurse specialists and physiotherapists. In addition when the patient is discharged (allowed to go home) the nursing staff will write a district nurse referral and it is important that this contains all the necessary information to ensure that appropriate care can be continued.

The author will end with a brief note about surgical wards as opposed to medical wards. She has noticed that many health interpreting students are not familiar with the double meaning of the word medical. In hospitals, the word medical is often used to denote the opposite of surgical. Surgical treatment involves surgery, whereas medical treatment involves non-surgical treatment methods, such as medication, observation, exercise, bed-rest, and the like. Note the word ward may present a problem in itself, in that it can refer to a whole nursing department or a multi-bed room within a department.

Summary of main points

This chapter has looked at hospital settings, including:

- admission and discharge procedures
- health professionals involved in medical care, nursing and allied care and rehabilitation.

Chapter 8

Emergency Departments or ERs

The Emergency Department (ED) may also be referred to as Casualty or as Accident and Emergency Department (A & E), or the Emergency Room (ER). Some hospitals have been accredited as Trauma Centers, which means they have highly specialized trauma staff, diagnostic equipment and special trauma surgeons. Such hospitals usually have a helipad where helicopters carrying seriously injured patients can land.

Interpreting in the ED may present a real challenge to the interpreter. One of the factors which may make interpreting in the ED a challenge is that accuracy is essential, yet the interpreter may have been called in urgently with little or no preparation time. The best advice that may be given to the interpreter is to interpret both the doctor's questions and the patient's responses exactly and to ask for clarification whenever something is not quite clear. Furthermore the interpreter may be faced with situations where there have been terrible accidents, instances of domestic violence or acute medical situations. There may be gross injuries, visible blood loss, a very stressed and very ill patient, surrounded by equally stressed relatives (and staff). In addition the interpreter's services may be required when the doctor tells friends and relatives that the patient has died. The doctor may use phrases such as '*He has passed on*' and '*There was nothing more we could do*' or '*We tried everything we could*' or '*It was very quick*'.

The ED can be full of tension and stress. In spite of all this, the interpreter should try and remain cool, calm and collected, so as to be able to interpret information accurately. The level of accuracy will go a long way to helping the medical staff obtain a clear picture of what has happened, and this in turn will help them reach a correct diagnosis. ***Once the correct diagnosis has been reached, appropriate treatment can be started.*** If correct information is not obtained, or is incorrectly relayed through the interpreter, the consequences may be very unfortunate.

This chapter will list some common reasons for admission to the Emergency Department, as well as some of the most commonly asked questions. Common procedures and investigations have also been included. What follows, first of all, is a list of some commonly encountered staff in the Emergency Department, listed here in alphabetical order.

1.   Emergency Department staff

The first point of contact in ED will be the person at the front desk:

Clerk Emergency Department
or Admitting Clerk   Not a medical person. The clerk 'checks' the patient by
                               asking them why they have come in and whether they are
                               eligible for treatment. Eligibility for treatment may depend
                               on the person's insurance status or on whether the person is
                               a citizen or permanent resident of the country. The clerk will
                               also check whether the patient has been admitted before and
                               may check the person's medical records and eligibility for
                               treatment. Many countries now also keep electronic patient
                               records. Names may need to be spelled out. Interpreters for
                               languages using non Latin scripts (e.g. Russian, Chinese,
                               Korean, Arabic, Hindi) should be careful when transcribing
                               the patient's name as there may be several systems in use
                               and the patient himself may have used a different transcrip-
                               tion during an earlier admission.
                               The clerk will call the Registered Nurse if he/she thinks
                               that the patient needs immediate medical attention (e.g.
                               chest pain, shortness of breath, bleeding, or unconscious-
                               ness). The clerk will also give the patient their Identification
                               bracelet, usually in the form of a wristband with the patient's
                               name and hospital number on it.

Emergency Room
Imaging specialists   Staff trained in carrying out imaging such as MRI or CT
                               scanning.

Orderly   Aide or ward assistant who help healthcare staff in a variety
                               of ways e.g. fetch and carry patients to the ward or to the
                               X-Ray department; take blood specimens to the laboratory.

Junior Doctor,
Foundation Medical Officer
or Intern   Doctor undertaking their first professional experience in the
                               hospital system. Junior doctors answer to the Registrars or
                               Residents (see below) and often check with the latter when
                               in doubt.

Radiographers   People who are specially trained in working X-Ray equip-
                               ment. They often come to the ED with portable X-Ray
                               equipment to take X-Rays of patients who are too ill to be
                               taken to the X-Ray department.

Registered Nurse	In Emergency Department this will be a nurse with experience in triage (sorting out who needs attention first) and observation. It may also be a special Trauma Nurse.
Registrar or *Resident or Resident medical Office*	Senior doctor who has undergone a the minimum period of required post-graduate experience as a Foundation Medical Officer, Junior doctor or Intern (titles and duration of training vary per country) and who has been accepted for further study towards a specialization in a particular medical field. The Registrar or Resident answers to the Consultant or Specialist. Please refer to Chapter 7, page 62 for more detail.
Security Guard	The security guard may often be seen in the ED as tempers may rise and some of the patients or their friends and relatives may be drunk and cause a disturbance. They often man the front desk after hours, regulating entry by visitors and others to the hospital's facilities.
Technicians	Are now employed by many ED and ER to carry out technical duties to provide basic life support. Technicians are also called *Techs* or *Techies*.
Trauma Team	Many hospitals have a special team of doctors and nurses who specialise in dealing with trauma patients. This will include a *Trauma Specialist or Traumatologist* (a doctor specialized in Trauma Medicine).

2.   Emergency Department areas

Ambulance Bay	Where ambulance officers (paramedics) load or unload their patients, usually with the aid of stretchers.
Cubicles	Within the triage area, patients are kept in separate cubicles – small spaces with a bed and some equipment such as oxygen. Cubicles are separated from other cubicles by either a wall or a curtain.
Front Desk	Counter manned by the Admitting Clerk and possibly also by security guards. All those who present to ED need to report here first. *This is also where interpreters would present themselves.*
Heli pad (or helicopter pad)	A large open space where the Emergency Services Helicopter can land.

Observation Ward *(or Holding Ward)*	Some patients are given medication and then observed for some time, until the medical staff have decided whether they should be discharged home or transferred to one of the wards.
Resus room	Resus is an abbreviation for resuscitation which literally means 'bringing back to life'. In the ED, seriously ill patients are taken straight into resus, where they are either stabilized (doctors make sure that the patient does not get any worse) or resuscitated (doctors make sure that the patient stays alive or comes back to life). The process of 'resuscitation' may include *cardiac massage* plus administering breaths/oxygen (CPR), administering fluids, blood and medication to the patient, and perhaps defibrillating the patient's heart to restore normal heart rhythm and placing the patient on a ventilator or respirator (breathing machine).
Triage area	Triage refers to the process of sorting out who needs treatment first and/or who is most likely to survive without immediate treatment. Assessment takes place based on the kind of illness or injury, how serious it is, and whether the hospital has the facilities to treat the problem. If hospital staff have established that they do not have the facilities to treat the patient, the patient may be transferred to another hospital which does have those facilities. Patients may be transferred by ambulance or by helicopter.
Waiting room	Area outside of the ED proper where patients with less acute medical or surgical problems sit and wait. Once the patient is called in, they go to the Triage area for assessment first.

3. Emergency Department admission

Patients may be taken to the ED or ER by ambulance, often following a distress call or telephone call to the *Emergency Services* (911 in Canada and the United States; 112 in the European Union; 112 or 999 in the United Kingdom; 111 in New Zealand; 000 in Australia).

Patients may also *self-refer* (present themselves on their own initiative without referral) or they may be brought in by friends and family. Some critically ill patients may be referred to the ED by their primary care doctor, in which case their own doctor may order an ambulance to take the patient to hospital.

When patients turn up at the ED themselves ED staff will have no prior knowledge of what condition or problem they are presenting with. In contrast when patients are referred by their primary care doctor or provider, or brought in by ambulance staff, ED staff will be aware of their condition and history before they arrive. As an example, a primary care doctor who examines a patient with acute chest pain and who suspects the patient is having a heart attack, may ring the doctors at the ED, write a quick letter of referral and arrange for an ambulance to take the patient to the ED.

4.   Some common reasons for admission to ED

Reasons for admission to ED may include:
–   medical problems – See Section 4.1
–   accidents (including orthopedic problems) – See Section 4.2
–   issues requiring surgical intervention – See Section 4.3

The most common problems for each of these categories are listed below, starting with medical problems.

4.1   Common medical problems

1.   *Anaphylaxis or severe allergic reaction* – This can be a life-threatening response to 'allergens' (substances which cause an allergic reaction).

Causes: Allergens include foods (sea food, peanuts, strawberries, chocolate, milk), bee stings.

Symptoms: The body's response is exaggerated causing all blood vessels widen, leading to a severe drop in blood pressure. A rash may appear, the person may lose consciousness, and may even die, unless action is undertaken quickly. The Emergency Services need to be called.

Questions: Questions may be asked of witnesses, as the patient may be unable to answer any questions. These include

–   What happened; where was the patient (garden, kitchen, dining room); what was the patient doing, what was the patient eating, drinking or inhaling?
–   Does the patient have any known allergies?
–   Do allergies run in the family?

Treatment: The patient will most commonly be given adrenaline, to make the blood vessels constrict (narrow), which will help the blood pressure go up.

2. *Asthma* – Very common, especially amongst children. In asthma, the bronchi (breathing tubes) become narrow and the patient has problems breathing out. Attacks can be life-threatening.

Causes: Attacks may be triggered by breathing in pollen, dust or other allergens, or by breathing in cold air, exercise, or infections.

Symptoms: The patient's bronchi respond to these triggers with a hypersensitive reaction, become narrowed and start producing mucus (slime). This makes it difficult for the patient to breathe out and they may either wheeze (make a whistling sound) or cough when breathing out. Children will often cough a lot, especially at night.

Questions:
– Is there a family history of asthma or hay-fever.
– Have you got any allergies or is there a family history of allergies?
– What brought on this attack?
– Have you had a similar attack before?
– Are you on any medication? What?
– What was your last peak flow (maximum amount of air the patient is able to breathe out (measured by a small hand-held device called a peak flow meter)?

Treatment: Medication to open up the airways called *bronchodilators*. Brand names include: Ventolin® or Salbutamol, Respolin, Bricanyl. These may be given as *inhalers* or as *nebulizers* (see Chapter 19). Patients may be given steroids (hydrocortisone) into the vein (intravenously) to help the body overcome this crisis situation.

3. *Bronchitis* – Inflammation of the bronchi (breathing tubes) (see Chapter 19, Page 198).

4. *Chest pain*

Please note: Chest pain means 'pain in the chest' and should always be interpreted as such. It should never be interpreted with 'heart pain' as chest pain may have a range of causes.

Causes: Chest pain may originate from:
– the stomach – Stomach acid may cause a burning sensation behind the chest bone. This is usually referred to as heart burn, which is often due to reflux (see below)
– the esophagus or gullet – Stomach acid can go back up the oesophagus and cause a burning sensation there. This is usually referred to as reflux. If reflux causes inflammation, the doctors will use the word *esophagitis* (inflammation of the esophagus)

- the muscles between the ribs – Caused by too much coughing or by a torn muscle (e.g. due to playing racket sports)
- the lungs – Inflammation of the pleura (the outer lining of the lungs) or by an embolism (very large blood clot) in the lungs. The pain will then be *associated with* breathing
- the heart muscle – If the heart muscle does not get enough oxygen, because the arteries to the heart muscle are narrowed or even completely blocked, the patient will experience pain in the chest, possibly radiating (spreading) into the jaw, neck or arms. This is called *angina pectoris*.

Questions asked may include the following:
- When did the pain start?
- Have you ever suffered stomach complaints or a stomach ulcer?
- Have you been playing any sports recently?
- Have you had a (chest) cold recently?
- Have you been coughing a lot?
- Have you brought up any phlegm/spit?
- Have you ever had any problems with your heart?
- Do you have to sleep propped up with pillows or sitting up in bed?
- Do you get any swelling of the ankles?
- Can you walk a kilometre (half a mile) without getting breathless or without getting pain in the chest?
- Can you walk up the stairs without getting breathless/without getting pain in the chest?
- Is there a family history of heart problems?
- Have you ever had angina? Have you ever had a heart attack?
- What is the pain like? (dull, sharp, heavy, crushing, like a belt around the chest? just a 'niggling' pain or very slight pain?)
- Does the pain spread into the neck or arms?
- Have you every had surgery on the heart?
- Is there a family history of coronary artery disease (problems with the blood-vessels going to the heart muscle itself)
- Do you take any medication for your heart? What is it called? What dosage do you take? How often?
- Do you carry any medication with you to relieve pain in your chest? What type of medication is it?

Medication: The patient may be given medication such as an antacid drink to neutral-ise stomach acid. Alternatively the patient may be given oxygen to see if this relieves the pain. If pain persists the patient may be given a special spray under the tongue. This spray may help to open up the *coronary arteries* which supply the heart muscle with oxygen.

Investigations: The doctor may order certain tests such as:

- *Chest X-Ray* – to look at the structures in the chest, especially heart and lungs
- *Blood tests* – these can show signs of infection or evidence of damage to the heart muscle
- *EKG or ECG (Electro-Cardio-Gram)* – to check the electrical activity in the heart – an ECG might show that the patient has had or is having a heart attack

5.   *Congestive Heart Failure (or CHF)* – Heart is not able to pump blood through properly. The doctor may never mention the term heart failure, but may say things such as: 'You have some fluid on the lungs' or 'We need to give you something to get rid of some extra fluid.'

Questions asked:

- Do you have to sleep sitting up or propped up with pillows at night?
- Do you get swelling of the ankles?
- Do you frequently have to urinate or pass water at night?
- Do you get short of breath on exertion?

Medication: Diuretics are frequently given – these help the body get rid of excess fluid by increasing urine output. As a result, there is less fluid for the heart to pump around the body.

Digoxin is a drug that may be given to strengthen the pump action of the heart.

6.   *CORD – Chronic Obstructive Respiratory Disease* also *COPD*
CORD patients are people with a long history of breathing disorders which cause obstruction of the airways, making breathing difficult and forced. This includes longstanding asthma, chronic bronchitis, emphysema (see Chapter 19 for more information).

7.   *Coughing up blood or hemoptysis (hemo:blood; ptyo:to spit)*

- There can be many different reasons why the patient is coughing up blood: Bronchitis; an abscess in the lung; tuberculosis (Tb) or lung cancer
- Tuberculosis is now making a come-back in some countries.

Please refer to Chapter 19 for some commonly asked questions and common tests to do with breathing problems.

8.   *CVA – or stroke*

Cerebro-vascular accident – An 'accident' involving the blood vessels in the brain (cerebro: brain; vascular: to do with the blood vessels). A stroke can be due to a blood clot obstructing the blood supply leading to part of the brain. A stroke can also be due to a bleed in the brain (brain *hemorrhage*). Without oxygen, the affected part of the brain will stop functioning or function less well.

Symptoms may include: Paralysis (inability to move); paresis (weakness); aphasia (inability to speak or to understand speech); blurred vision; hemianopia (half-sided loss of vision).

Questions:

It is often necessary to obtain a 'history' from the patient's relatives as the patient may be unable to speak, or the patient may have no recollection of what happened while they were having the stroke.

Important questions to the patient's relatives would include:
–   Did the patient smoke? How much? For how long?
–   Has the patient every had a TIA (Transient Ischemic Attack) also called a mini stroke or a warning stroke. The symptoms are similar to those of a real stroke, but do not last very long.
–   Was the patient able to move all his/her limbs before the attack?
–   How long was the patient unconscious for?

Questions to the patient would include:
–   Did you black out?
–   Can you move your arms/legs?
–   Do you have blurry vision? Can you see me if I stand on this side?
–   Are you experiencing any abnormal sensations, such as numbness, tingling, pins and needles?

Investigations might include:
–   CT scan or MRI scan of the brain.
–   Shining a light in the patient's eyes to check the reaction of the pupils.
–   Checking the patient's pulse, blood pressure and breathing rate.

9.   *Diabetic Coma* – **A** life-threatening condition – deep level of unconsciousness

A diabetic coma can be caused by either a very low blood sugar level (*hypo*-glycemia where hypo means 'below', glyc- means glucose or sugar, and (h)emia means in the blood) or by a very high blood sugar level (*hyper*-glycemia where hyper (just like *super*) means 'too much'). As the patient will be unconscious, it will not be possible to take a history from the patient. See also Chapter 25.

If relatives or friends are present they might be asked the following questions:

- Did the patient inject insulin or did he take tablets for his diabetes?
- Did the patient take his normal dose this time?
- Did the patient eat his normal breakfast/lunch/dinner/snack?
- Did the patient have a fever/infection/cold?
- Has the patient just undergone surgery/a stressful situation/ an accident or has the patient just exercised to excess? (Stress may raise the body's blood sugar levels.)

Treatment
- The patient may be given *glucose* or glucagon (if the coma is caused by a low blood sugar). Glucagon injections will help to raise the blood sugar quickly.Patients may also be given *Sodium bicarbonate* and *insulin* (if the coma is caused by a high blood glucose level). This will be given to treat *metabolic acidosis.*

Once the patient is out of the coma, he or she will almost certainly be kept in hospital for observation and to try and get the patient's diabetes under control again.

10.   *Heart Attack or Myocardial Infarction (MI)* – blood supply to part of the heart muscle is cut off completely, usually due to a blockage of the coronary artery.

Questions: please refer to the section on *Chest pain* above

Treatment:
The patient will usually be transferred to the Coronary Care Unit or CCU for observation. The patient will be placed on a heart monitor and will have frequent blood tests. Blood pressure and pulse will be recorded frequently.

Medication may include:
- Medication to relief pain and anxiety
- Medication to preventventricular fibrillation (ventricles quiver but do not contract). A diuretic to get rid of excess fluid in the bloodstream
- Anticoagulants (drugs to prevent clotting) or
- Thrombolytic drugs to dissolve clots
- Beta-blockers to reduce the effect of stress hormones on the heart (rate)
- Anti-arrhythmic drugs to encourage normal heart rhythm
- Drugs to reduce blood pressure and blood volume, including ACE *inhibitors* and An*giotensin receptor blockers*

11.   *Heart Failure* – please see *Congestive Heart Failure* above.

12.   *Hyperemesis gravidarum* – Excessive vomiting during pregnancy which may lead to dehydration or loss of electrolytes

Questions will include:
- Are you able to keep down foods and fluids?
- How much have you vomited over the last 24 hours?
- Are you still passing urine? What colour is your urine (dark, concentrated, light)? Have you got a headache?

If the doctors find that the woman is dehydrated, they may admit her for treatment and observation. They may put her on an intravenous drip with electrolytes to restore her fluid and electrolyte balance.

13.   *Meningitis* – inflammation of the meninges, the outer lining of the brain and spinal cord
Patients will complain of fever, neck stiffness and severe headache. The cause may be a virus infection or a bacterial infection (serious).

Questions may include:
- Have you taken your/his/her temperature? What was it?
- Have you had the chills? (high fever/ feeling hot then cold and shivering)
- Have you vomited at all?
- Any convulsions/seizures?
- Have you (he/she) been more irritable than usual?
- When baby cries does it sound normal? Any high-pitched cry?
- Does baby cry when you change baby's nappy?
- Have you noticed any blotches/red spots on the skin? (meningitis rash)

Investigations:
- Lumbar puncture or spinal tap (to check for presence of bacteria in the spinal fluid).
- CT scan of the brain.

Treatment:
- Antibiotics to treat the bacterial infection.
- Drugs to stop convulsions (anti-convulsants).

14.   *Miscarriage* – Bleeding during pregnancy associated with fetus and placenta coming away.

Questions:
- Any woman who comes in with vaginal bleeding will be asked if she is pregnant; What was the first day of your last period?
- Have you been feeling nauseated?
- Did your breasts feel tender? Do they still feel tender now?

Investigations:
- A blood test to check HCG (pregnancy hormone) levels in the blood. Ultrasound scan of the lower abdomen
- Vaginal examination

Treatment:
Incomplete abortion: If the fetus has died and has come away from the womb or if some products of conception (fetal or placental tissue) are still inside the womb, a dilatation and curettage (D & C) may be needed – the woman will have general anesthetic (generally) and the doctor will open up the neck of the womb and scrape the lining of the womb clean. Any remaining products of conception may result in a risk of infection or molar pregnancy, a form of cancer.

Complete abortion – If the fetus has died and the scan shows that the womb and the cervix are empty a D & C may not be considered to be necessary – a blood test will be taken to check on HCG (Human Chorionic Gonadotropin) levels and repeated later on to ensure that there is nothing left inside the womb.

15.   *Peritonitis* – Inflammation of the peritoneum – the inner lining of the abdomen
Causes: Infection by bacteria. Peritonitis may develop in people with appendicitis or in patients who are on continuous ambulant peritoneal dialysis (CAPD).

Symptoms: Fever, chills, pain in the abdomen; guarding (muscle defence by abdominal muscles).

Questions:
- Does it hurt when I press here?
- Are you feeling nauseated/have you vomited?
- Do you have diarrhea?
- When did the pain start?/Where did the pain start?
- Have you had a fever?/Have you had chills?

Treatment:
Sometimes laparoscopy or laparotomy (see Page 157) to find the cause.

16.   *Shock (anaphylactic shock; hypovolemic shock)*
Anaphylaxis – see under anaphylaxis above under medical problems.
Hypovolemic shock: The amount of circulating volume (blood and fluid) is very low. The heart cannot pump enough blood around the body and this may cause vital organs to stop working.

Causes: Severe and prolonged blood loss; diarrhea; weakness,

Symptoms: Low blood pressure; weak, thready pulse; sweating, cold clammy skin; rapid breathing; paleness; loss of consciousness

Investigations: Blood tests (Complete Blood Count); CT scan (to see where bleeding is); echocardiogram;

Treatment: keeping person warm; replace lost blood and fluids; medication to increase blood pressure; urinary catheter; Swan Ganz catheter (into the heart) to check cardiac output.

Outlook: Possible complications include damage to kidneys, heart and brain and possible death.

17.   *Vomiting up blood*

Causes: This can be due to a variety of causes: including an ulcer in the stomach (peptic ulcer) or in the first part of the small intestine (duodenal ulcer); varicose veins in the gullet (esophageal varices) which often occur in patients with cirrhosis of the liver; irritation of the lining of the gullet by reflux of stomach acids into the gullet (reflux oesophagitis); taking aspirin or NSAIDS (non-steroidal anti-inflammatory drugs) which can irritate the lining of the stomach.

Questions:
– Do you have a history of ulcers?
– Do you have a history of taking of aspirin or NSAIDS (on an empty stomach)?
– Have you been feeling nauseated (before food, during meals, after meals)?
– Have you been experiencing pain in the stomach (before/during/after meals)?
– How much alcohol do you drink/for how long/how frequently?
– Have you ever been diagnosed with Hepatitis (B or C) or cirrhosis of the liver?

Investigations and Treatment:
– urgent *endoscopy* (*gastroscopy* or *esophago-gastroscopy*) to find the cause of the bleeding or to treat the cause (in some cases)
– *laparotomy* (operation to open the abdomen)

4.2 Accidents

1.   *Assault*

Questions
– Who assaulted you (man, woman, young, old)
– What with? (blunt weapon: wood), or sharp weapon (flick-knife, kitchen knife, machete); what material was it made of: iron bar, wooden club.
– Where did they hit you?
– With what force did they strike/hit/stab you? Did you black out?
– Where is the pain?
– Is there any pain associated with breathing?

2.   *Burns*

It is very important to determine how 'deep' the burn has gone.

1st degree burn: superficial only

2nd degree burn: deeper

3rd degree burn: underlying tissues burnt (including muscle)

Questions:
–   How did you burn yourself with: water or oil ? Fire ? (wood fire/electrical fire?)
–   What type of first aid did you get? (10 minutes under cold running water? Cremes?)

Treatment:
–   IV fluids (Intravenous fluids) and a high-protein diet
–   Dressings and saline baths
–   Skin grafts (mesh)

3.   *Drowning or near-drowning*

Questions:
–   How long was the patient under water?
–   Did he/she drown in fresh water or salt water?
–   Did he/she breathe or have a heart beat when he/she came out of the water?
–   How cold was the water?

Investigations:
–   Neurological observations: response; pupillary reaction; pulse/blood pressure
–   Temperature: undercooling (hypothermia)? To what extent?

Treatment:
–   CPR (cardio-pulmonary resuscitation) followed by artificial respiration (patient placed on a ventilator)
–   Drug treatment (given intravenously)
–   Warming up with a special thermal blanket and/or pre-warmed intravenous fluids
–   Monitoring of blood gases (oxygen etc.)

4.   *Drug overdose – see poisoning*

Can be accidental or intentional (suicide attempt)

5.   *Falls*

Questions:
–   How did you fall? Did you stretch out your arms to try and break your fall?
–   Did you fall on your head/neck/back?
–   Did you black out or lose consciousness at all?

- Can you feel your toes/legs? Can you move your toes/legs?
- Where does it hurt? Does it hurt when you breathe in/out? Did you fall from a moving vehicle? How fast was it moving?

6. *Head injuries*

Questions:
Some questions will be the same as those for falls and accidents

- Can you squeeze my hand? Can you push my hand away with your foot? Can you grimace?
- Can you lift your hand up?
- What is your name? Do you know where you are? What is today's date?

Investigations:
- Neurological observations: response; pupillary response; pulse/blood pressure; level of consciousness (LOC).
- Giving the patient instructions and checking whether he is able to respond to these
- CT Scan or MRI Scan of the brain.

Treatment:
May include urgent surgery on the skull if there is bleeding inside the skull or into the brain; the aim is to reduce pressure and swelling on the brain.

7. *Poisoning* – can be accidental or intentional
Some common drugs (e.g. Paracetamol® and aspirin, tranquilizers and antidepressants) may cause serious problems. It is absolutely essential to find out exactly what was taken, as each drug acts in a different way and may cause damage in different ways and to different parts of the body.

Questions:
- What was taken (ingested)/when/how much/by what route (mouth, sniffing, inhaling, huffing (sniffing inhalants), injecting intravenously)?
- Was anything done to induce vomiting?
- Did the patient take or drink anything (e.g. milk) to counteract the poisoning?
- What/when/how much?

Investigations:
Blood test (drug levels)

Treatment: This can include:
Gastric lavage (emptying stomach out by means of tube and then flushing it clean with water).

Antidotes – Drugs to reverse the action of the first drug;.

Charcoal – Charcoal can absorb what was ingested, and stop it from being absorbed into the body.

8.   *Road Traffic Accident (RTA)*
Also known as motor vehicle accident (MVA), motor vehicle traffic collision (MVTC); car wreck, motor vehicle collision (MVC), road traffic collision (RTC), road traffic incident (RTI).

Questions may include:
– Where were you sitting (driver seat, front passenger, rear seat passenger)?
– Were you wearing a seat belt?
– Were you thrown clear off the car?
– Did you have an airbag?
– Did the car have side-intrusion bars?
– Did the car roll?
– How fast was the car going at the time of impact?
– Did you black out/lose consciousness at all?
– Can you remember what happened just before the accident?

Investigations:
Blood tests; imaging such as X-Rays/CT Scans/Ultrasound Scans/MRI scans; exploratory surgery to check for internal injury or problems medical staff are not aware off.

Treatment:
Urgent surgery may be required, especially to stem any internal bleeding.

9.   *Shock (all types)* – see page 82.

10.   *Orthopedic problems*
These usually relate to broken bones (fractures) or to dislocations (e.g. dislocated shoulder); sometimes they relate to 'avulsion fractures' where a small piece of bone has been torn off usually due to pull of the surrounding muscles or tendons

Questions:
– How did the accident happen?
– Do you have osteoporosis?
– Where does it hurt?
– Have you had surgery before? (Followed by all the common pre-operative questions as per Chapter 10).

Investigations:
X-Rays; CT Scanning; MRI Scanning;.

Treatment – see Chapter 20.

4.3 Surgical problems

Some of the most common surgical problems (problems requiring surgical treatment) would be:

1. *Appendicitis:* Inflammation of the appendix (see also Chapter 26)

Questions:
– When did the pain start?/Where did the pain start?/Where is the pain now?
– Do you feel nauseated?/Have you vomited?/Have you had diarrhea?
– Have you had the flu/a viral infection?

Investigations and treatment:
Palpitation (rebound tenderness); blood tests; ultrasound scan.
Laparoscopy and laparotomy and possibly an appendectomy (surgical removal of the inflamed appendix).

2. *Collapsed lung:* Air (pneumothorax) or fluid or blood (hematothorax) has entered the space between the pleurae and the lung has collapsed as a result. This may be the result of a broken rib or a stab wound, or an asthma attack where air cannot be breathed out.

Investigations:
Chest X-ray shows a white-out (area where there is little or no air movement or gas exchange); patient very short of breath

Questions:
– Do you have asthma?
– What were you doing when your lung collapsed?
– Were you assaulted/stabbed? What with? How long was the knife? How far did it go in?

Investigations:
X-Ray.

Treatment:
Drains to drain fluid/blood:
– Intra chest wall drain (ICWD) to keep the lung expanded
– Pleural tap: To drain fluid from the space between the pleura layers with a long hollow needle.

3. *Perforated stomach ulcer*

Questions:
– Where is the pain? When did the pain start? Does the pain radiate anywhere?
– Do you have stomach ulcers /duodenal ulcers?

Investigations: Laparotomy (to check for damage and repair at the same time)
Treatment: Surgery to repair the perforation and stop the bleeding

4.   *Sub-acute bowel obstruction* – Bowels are almost completely blocked and food cannot pass through. Normally – patient vomits up fecal fluid and bowels do not function at all. This may be due to the presence of tumors in the abdomen (bowel cancer, ovarian cancer) or to the patient having swallowed something large (e.g. a whole orange) without chewing.

Questions:
–   What did you eat before this happened?
–   Have you had previous abdominal surgery?

Treatment: Drip and suck: IV drip (to keep the patient hydrated) and nasogastric tube to drain fluid out of the gastro-intestinal tract.

Summary of main points

This chapter has looked at Emergency Departments and ERs including:

–   health professionals involved
–   three main reasons for admission into the ER, including
    –   medical conditions
    –   accidents
    –   surgical problems

Chapter 9

Informed consent

Informed Consent forms or Agreement to Treatment forms are used in all hospitals. The Informed Consent procedure is a legal requirement for all invasive and/or potentially harmful procedures. It involves an agreement between the patient and the health professional and means that the patient is consenting to a certain procedure, having been informed what is to be done, what is involved, and what the potential risks and complications are.

The procedure involves the medical professional explaining the intended operation or procedure to the patient. The outcome of the doctor's explanation should be for the patient to understand what is going to be done, why, how, who is going to do it, what the risks will be, and what the expected result will be.

The Informed Consent form is a legal document. It protects both the patient and the health professional. The patient cannot undergo a potentially risky procedure without being fully aware of the possible risks. Also, the patient cannot have limbs, body-parts or even tumors removed without having given his or her express consent. The health professional is protected in that, if the outcome of the procedure is not good, he or she can state that the patient was aware of the risks and had agreed to the procedure.

There are circumstances in which 'Informed Consent' cannot be obtained in writing and from the patient themselves, for example:

–   the patient is unconscious, but in need of urgent surgery
–   the patient is a minor 'under the age of consent'. Consent procedures will vary from country to country and state to state. Typically in such cases, the 'Consent' form is signed by the parents or legal guardians of the child.
–   the patient is under the influence of mind-altering substances (e.g. alcohol, drugs) or sleep-deprived to such an extent that they are incapable of reaching an informed decision.
–   the patient is *not compos mentis* (mentally incapable of reaching an informed decision). This may be the case if a patient suffers from Alzheimer's dementia or is otherwise intellectually challenged or under the influence of mind-altering substances. This can be quite a hazy area, and psychiatric assessment may be required to gauge whether the patient is capable of giving Informed Consent.

If the patient is not capable of giving Informed Consent himself/herself, the medical staff will try to get hold of the patient's next of kin to act in the patient's best interests and sign the Informed Consent form on the patient's behalf.

In an emergency, where immediate action needs to be taken, consent may be obtained over the phone. If time does not permit this, doctors may proceed with treatment, providing they are acting in the best interests of the patient and death or permanent harm will result if they do not intervene. Note if a doctor knows that the patient would not have consented, but proceeds with intervention nonetheless, he or she could be held liable in some countries. As an example, if an adult patient tells the doctor that he refuses a blood transfusion for religious reasons (e.g. if the patient is a Jehovah's witness), and the doctor gives the patient blood all the same, the doctor has acted against the patient's consent and can be held liable. With regard to a minor, however, doctors may overrule the parents/guardians, and may act in, what they consider to be, the child's best interests. In some countries/jurisdictions, a court order may be taken out, to place the child temporarily under guardianship of the court, so that medical treatment can be carried out. In emergency cases, doctors may proceed with urgent treatment without waiting for a court order.

1. Issues which might arise for interpreters during the Informed Consent process

Ideally, the doctor/professional should explain the following:

- *What* they aim to do (the procedure);
- *Why* they think this procedure is necessary or desired
- *How* the procedure will take place
- *Who* will undertake the procedure (i.e. an experienced person or a trainee)
- *What* the *expected outcomes* are
- *What side-effects* or *risks* could be involved. This is often expressed as a percentage of patients who have experience harmful side-effects (morbidity rate), or who have died (mortality rate)
- Whether there are *any alternatives*/other options to the proposed treatment

However, in practice the whole Informed Consent process may be fraught with issues which may catch the interpreter unawares. These may include, but be by no means limited to the following:

- Some medical staff expect the interpreter to do a sight translation of the form and even complete it on behalf of the patient, rather than interpreting for the medical staff who are taking the patient through the Informed Consent process.

- Some medical staff may want to absent themselves during this process, leaving the interpreter 'in charge'.
- Some medical staff orally convey certain risks and side-effects to the patient which are interpreted by the interpreter. They may then add other issues in writing to the Informed Consent form, without either mentioning or clarifying these. An example would be where the medical practioner mentions 'post-operative infection' as a possible side-effect, but then writes down 'death' on the form, without mentioning this. The interpreter is then caught in a difficult situation (see also mention of Duty of Care in Chapter 2).
- In most cases, surgical consent will be obtained before the anesthetist takes the patient through the Informed Consent for the anesthesia, however it may happen that the surgeon rushes through the Informed Consent process while the anesthetic agents are already starting to take effect. This means the patient is no longer able to give 'informed' consent.
- Medical practitioners may also rush through the Informed Consent process for other reasons, leaving interpreter (and patient) to feel that the process has not been properly administered.
- The interpreter may find himself interpreting for the patient and his family, with the family answering or asking questions on behalf of the patient. This may particularly be the case in situations where the question of whether the patient is capable of giving informed consent is borderline. The interpreter may need to convey different 'voices' simultaneously without being fully aware who is saying what, and may feel he is losing control of the interpreting process.
- The term next of kin may also pose a problem for interpreters, as it conjures up associations of 'close family members'. In reality, relationships between the patient and close family members may sometimes be strained. For this reason, patients are always asked who they wish to nominate as next of kin when they are admitted to the hospital. In practice, patients may in fact nominate their best friend, their niece, or even their wonderful neighbor, to be the person who is notified when things go wrong, or when they need support.

Other issues pertain to the particular type of legal English often used in Informed Consent forms. In the event that the interpreter is required to do a sight translation (reading the English text out in the patient's language) he needs to be aware of crosslinguistic and sociopragmatic issues in conveying the linguistic features of the legal English often used in these forms. Prominent features of legal English may include:

- the passive voice ('we transferred the patient' -> 'the patient was transferred')
- nominalizations (turning a verb into a noun, e.g. 'to heal' -> 'recovery/healing')
- words originating from the Latin or the Greek, rather than from Old English (deceased rather than dead)

Both the passive voice and nominalizations are grammatical structures which can leave the listener confused as to 'who did what'. An example of the use of the passive voice in a medical context would be: 'Mrs Z *was noted* to have diffuse swelling of the right arm'. This sentence would be easier to understand if it read: 'I/The Nurse/Doctor X saw that Mrs Z had widely spread swelling of the right arm'. An example of the use of nominalization would be: 'Intubation proved to be very difficult' when we could say: '*I* found it very difficult to intubate *him*', which tells us *who* intubated *whom*.

In other words, the interpreter may have to decide what the text really means, but must at the same time leave ambiguities ambiguous. If the text is intended to have a double meaning, the interpreter must convey the double meaning. When dealing with either the passive voice or nominalizations, the interpreter could use a reflexive verb in some languages (e.g. '*Se notó que tenía…*' in Spanish) or a null subject (or '*Man hat beobachtet dass…*' in German). Please see Tebble (2003), Meyer (2003) and others for a detailed analysis of medical discourse. Suggested further readings include Faden and Beauchamp (1986), Hunt and Voogd (2007), Simon, Zyzanski and Durant (2006).

Summary of main points

The informed consent process requires accurate and impartial interpretation of all relevant information, but may in practice be fraught with issues, leaving the interpreter in a difficult dilemma.

Chapter 10

Pre-operative and post-operative procedures

The words pre-operative and post-operative refer to what happens before (pre) and after (post) procedures such as operations (surgery). The interpreter may also hear these abbreviated as pre-op and post-op.

Pre-operative procedures and questions

There are a number of procedures which are commonly carried out prior to surgery. Similarly, there are a number of questions which are commonly asked prior to the patient having surgery. Many of these procedures and questions are necessary to prevent things from going wrong during or after surgery (e.g. fasting prior to surgery reduces the risk of stomach contents being inhaled into the lungs by the unconscious patient). Most of the questions below may be asked by nursing personnel or anesthetic assistants, while others will be asked by the anesthetist (see next page).

Some commonly asked pre-operative questions:

- Have you had any previous surgery? (Meant to check whether everything went okay and how you responded to the anesthetic.)
- Where and when and what for? (Meant to trace the information we need, and we know something about your general health status)
- Are you allergic or 'hypersensitive' to any medication/sticking plaster? (Allergies can cause life-threatening reactions which lead to the patient going into a severe allergic reaction known as *anaphylactic shock*.) Sometimes common substances which may cause severe allergic reactions are included in the question:
- Are you allergic to:

    - aspirin
    - antibiotics
    - bee stings
    - blood and blood products
    - plasma expanders (used to treat low blood pressure)
    - iodine (commonly used in contrast dye, for instance during angiography procedures)
    - penicillin
    - sticking plaster (any colour)
    - sulfa drugs (antibacterial *sulfonamides*)

NB: A common answer to this question is: 'Not that I am aware of' or 'Not as far as I know', which is 'translated' into the medical notes as *nil known.*

- When did you last have anything to eat or drink (if the patient has something in his/her stomach, the contents may be accidentally 'aspirated'/inhaled into the lungs while the patient is unconscious.
- When did you last void or pass urine (pee/go weewees/pass water) – a full bladder may empty itself while the patient is relaxed/unconscious; or it may be accidentally 'perforated' during surgery.
- Are you Hepatitis B positive/HIV positive?
- Do you drink (alcohol)? How much/how often? (People who consume a lot of alcohol may require more anesthetic to 'go under'; they may also require more pain relief after surgery.)
- Do you have any crowns/caps/loose teeth/bridges or plates in your mouth? (This is an important question as the anesthetist wants to be sure he does not run the risk of knocking out any loose teeth when he or she inserts the breathing tube or, worse still, push the loose teeth down into the airways with the breathing tube!)
- Do you wear dentures? (This question is asked for the same reason as the previous question – the patient will have to leave both pride and dentures behind in a named container on top of his/her locker.)
- Do you wear make-up (lipstick/blusher) and/or nail-polish (the anesthetist can gauge the patient's well-being partly from looking at the colour of lips and finger nails – in some private hospitals patients are allowed to go to the operating theatre wearing make-up!)
- Have you removed all your hairpins/rings, earrings, etc? (These metal objects can lead to electric shock and burning when the doctor is using the cauterization equipment (see glossary) during the operation or they may quite simply slip off people's fingers and get lost); Would you like us to lock them up in the valuables cupboard?

The anesthetist will visit the patient before the patient goes into the operating theatre. The main reason for this visit is to check whether there are likely to be any problems with the anesthetic. The anesthetist does this by looking the patient over (eye-balling) and by asking the patient if he had any problems with previous anesthesia. The anesthetist will look at any aspects of the patient's build that may need to be taken into account when administering anesthesia. If the patient has a very short thick neck, for example, the anesthetist may have to use a shorter breathing tube.

In addition to looking at the patient, the anesthetist may ask questions such as:

- Have you had previous surgery?
- Did they perform the surgery under general anesthesia or under regional anesthesia?
- What type of regional anesthesia was used: epidural anesthesia, spinal anesthesia, local anesthetic injected under the skin, an arm block, etc?

- Did you experience any side-effects or after-effects from the anesthetic?
- What type of side-effects did you experience? (e.g. headache, pain in the back, vomiting, drowsiness)
- Do you have any preferences (type of anesthetic)?
- Do you have a latex allergy?

In addition, the anesthetist will probably like to decide what type of anesthetic would be best for this patient in view of the patient's medical history and current condition and to discuss options, benefits and possible side-effects or risks with the patient.

Intra-operative: during surgery and anesthetic

Main types of anesthesia
- General Anesthesia
- Regional Anesthesia: epidural, spinal, caudal block, arm block, superficial local anesthesia

NB: No matter what type of anesthetic is used, the patient will almost always have a small needle inserted into a vein. This enables the anesthetist to administer medication, blood or fluids quickly, should this be necessary. The interpreter may be involved in interpreting whilst the patient is being given anesthetic, and after the patient has returned from the Operating Room.

General Anesthesia or GA
Basically, in General Anesthesia, the patient is given a combination of drugs intravenously. These drugs have different effects on the body. Most commonly they include:

- something to put the patient to sleep (a hypnotic)
- a muscle relaxant – this will relax all muscles in the body, including the breathing muscles, so the anesthetist will have to look after the patient's breathing. He can do this by putting in a breathing tube and connecting the patient to a ventilator or breathing machine. Anesthetists may also use a laryngeal mask (inflatable silicone mask and rubber connecting tube which cover the opening of the windpipe)
- something to suppress the patient's reflexes
- a pain killer (long-acting/short-acting; strong or less strong)

For very short procedures, the anesthetist may induce sleep by putting a mask over the patient's face. The patient will breathe in the anesthetic gas and fall asleep.

Epidural Anesthesia and Spinal Anesthesia
The anesthetist will ask the patient to either sit on the edge of the bed and bend forwards, making a curved back. For some patients, this is really difficult, and in those cases, the anesthetist may ask the patient to lie on his side, with a curved back.

In the case of epidural anesthesia, the anesthetist will then insert a hollow needle and check whether he has found the correct space. Once he has found the right space, the anesthetist will inject the anesthetic into the epidural space.

After this, he will insert (through the needle) a very narrow tube and attach this catheter to the patient's back with tape. The catheter can be used to give the patient a top-up of additional anesthetic if required. All spinal nerves which exit the spinal canal, will pass through the epidural space first. By putting the anesthetic into the epidural space, the spinal nerves are anesthetized at the point of exit.

For spinal anesthesia, the anesthetic is injected into the spinal canal itself and mixes with the spinal fluid. By putting the anesthetic into the spinal space, the spinal nerves are anesthetized below a certain level.

The purpose of this type of anesthesia is to block messages from the brain to the body and vice versa at a certain point. If the patient is to have knee surgery, the anesthetist can ensure that the patient does not feel any pain from the waist down (the pain signals do not reach the brain, and the patient does not feel any pain). If the brain sends a message 'Move that leg', that message is blocked as well.

The nurses will test the effectiveness of the anesthetic using different methods. Some nurses apply an ice cube to the skin and ask the patient if he can feel the cold. Some nurses use cotton wool soaked in ether (which will also feel cold) and ask the patient if he can feel that.

Nerve Blocks
For surgery on the fingers or hand, many anesthetists prefer injecting anesthetic into the bundle of nerves going into the patient's arm. This type of anesthesia is called an 'arm block'.

The anesthetic is injected into the underarm, into the 'plexus' or bundle of nerves going into the patient's arm. Once the block takes effect, the patient may feel as if his arm has been replaced by a heavy block of wood. The arm will feel heavy, and the patient will lose all sensation or feeling in that arm.

Local Anesthesia
The anesthetist or doctor will inject the local anesthetic agent into the superficial tissues, under the skin, through a very fine needle. If adrenaline has been added to the local anesthetic, the blood vessels will contract and skin may start to look very pale. The adrenaline is added to ensure that the anesthetic agent stays in place, therefore lasting a bit longer. It also helps to reduce bleeding.

Post-operative Care Unit or Recovery Room
After surgery, most patients spend some time in the Post-Operative Care Unit (PACU) or Recovery Room, before going back to the Ward.

Those who may have developed complications or who are showing signs of instability, go to the Intensive Care Unit. These are usually patients who need special attention for a longer period of time, before being able to return to a normal nursing ward. It is standard procedure for patients to spend some time in the Intensive Care Unit after certain types of procedures (e.g. after coronary artery by-pass surgery).

When the patient is in the PACU, he will still be sleepy and it is not very likely that interpreters will be called in to interpret here.

For the sake of completeness, though, I will mention some of the most common pieces of equipment that will be used in the PACU and some of the most commonly performed observations.

IV drip – most patients will still have an intravenous needle (or luer) in their veins. Fluid can be given through plastic tubing, straight into the patient's vein. There are several reasons why patients are left with intravenous lines of IV's connected after surgery:

– they can be used to give extra fluid quickly, if need be.
– they can be used to give the patient medication accurately and quickly, for immediate effect, if need be.
– they can be used to give the patient a blood transfusion, if the patient needs this.

Some related terms:

Long lines – the term long line refers to the fact that the intravenous catheter (inside the patient's vein) is pushed almost as far as the patient's heart. Long lines can be used to monitor blood pressure at a point just before the blood flows back into the patient's heart.

Arterial lines – these lines are inserted into the patient's artery and can be used to take arterial blood off the patient or to monitor the patient's blood pressure; arterial lines can also be used to take blood samples off the patient.

Bleeding lines – these are usually inserted into a large vein and closed off with a little cap. Central Venous Lines – are usually put into the patient's large hollow vein, just below the collar bone (subclavian vein). However, sometimes Central Venous lines are lines inserted into the jugular vein (in the neck), or long lines inserted into the vein in the crook of the arm. Central Venous Lines can be used to monitor Central Venous Pressure. Central venous lines are also used to give patients IntraVenous Nutrition (IVN) or Total Parenteral Nutrition (TPN – which means by-passing the bowels), containing fats, carbohydrates, sugars, vitamins, minerals and trace elements.

Position of IV (Intra-Venous) lines

IV lines are usually put into the veins on the back of the patient's forearms or hands. Occasionally, they are put into the crook of the patient's arm. They can also be inserted into the patient's neck vein (jugular vein) or in a larger, more central vein (e.g. a subclavian catheter inserted in a large vein close to the heart, *below the collar bone*).

Pain pump – also known as *PCA pump* for *Patient Controlled Analgesia*. The PCA involves an infusion pump which delivers pain relief from a syringe filled with a pain-killing solution. The syringe is placed in a chamber. The syringe is connected to tubing which connects on to the patient's IV line (or spinal catheter, see below). A push button is connected to the chamber and the patient can give himself a dose of pain killer before painful procedures, such as turning.

The amount of pain killer the patient is allowed to have (either continuously or intermittently) is prescribed by the anesthetist and programmed into the PCA pump by nursing staff. The prescribed dose cannot be exceeded, as the pump will refuse to give the patient more than the patient is allowed to have.

Pain pumps may also be connected to the nerve block catheter, e.g. an intrathecal pain pump will be connected to a spinal catheter and anesthetic drugs will be delivered straight into the spinal fluid.

Various types of monitoring equipment used in PACU
Monitoring equipment used in the PACU may include:

- *ECG dots* – three or four dots are usually attached to the patient's chest, sometimes to the shoulder or shoulder blades if there is no room on the chest. These dots are connected to leads which connect to an ECG monitor which shows the patient's heart beat and pattern of electrical activity in the patient' s heart.
- *Sphygomanometer and stethoscope* or
- *Automatic blood pressure monitoring* or
- *Invasive blood pressure monitoring equipment* – arterial line connected to a 'transducer'

The sphygmomanometer and stethoscope may still be used for monitoring the patient's blood pressure by hand, using an inflatable cuff and a mercury manometer.

If the patient needs to have a blood pressure taken very frequently, automatic blood pressure monitors such as the Dynamap® may be used. A cuff is placed around the patient's arm. The cuff is connected to monitoring equipment. At set intervals, the cuff fills with air and the patient's blood pressure reading will show up on the screen of the monitor.

Thermometer – used to check whether the patient's temperature is within normal range. The thermometer can be a clinical thermometer which is put under the patient's tongue, or underarm, or, occasionally, in the patient's back passage (rectum). More and more hospital use the *tympano-thermometer*, which is held briefly inside the patient's ear, until it bleeps. This last thermometer gives a very accurate reading of the patient's central body temperature when used correctly.

Oxymetry – pulse oxymeters are used to monitor to what extent red blood cells are saturated with oxygen. Usually they consist of a little machine, with a cord and a finger clip with a red LED light in it. The finger clip is placed over the patient's nail and used to measure the oxygen saturation in the small arteries in the tip of the finger.

Drains – drains are often left in to drain the operation site of excess fluid which might hamper recovery and healing.

Types of drains:

Vacuum drains – most drains are of the vacuum type: they actively drain wound fluid from within the body.

Harmonica drains – tiny drains shaped like a harmonica

T-drains or T-tubes – used to drain bile (usually dark green-brown in colour) from the body. They look like a T-junction, hence the name. These passive drains are usually connected to a simple catheter type bag.

Chest drains – chest drains are used in patients who have had a collapsed lung or blood in the lung. They taped securely and connected to one or two big glass jars which are half-filled with water. Chest drains are often connected to suction and thus bubbling.

Urinary catheter – also called indwelling catheter or Foley catheter. Indwelling catheters drain urine from the patient's bladder.

Irrigation systems – (continuous) bladder irrigation systems may be used in patients who have had surgery on the prostate. These patients will have a three-way 'balloon' catheter in. The balloon catheter serves a dual purpose: The balloon is blown up and puts pressure on the space inside the prostate, to stop the bleeding. The catheter will drain urine from the patient's bladder. The catheter is irrigated with a saline (salt water) solution from time to time, to stop the catheter from getting blocked.

Once the patient is breathing consistently by himself, and temperature, blood pressure and heart rate are normal, and there is no uncontrolled bleeding or oozing from the wound, the patient is escorted back to the ward.

Possible complications after surgery

- Vomiting and nausea
- Patient breathing very slowly or very superficially
- Patient losing a lot of blood, either via the drains or straight into the gauze dressing which has been placed over the wound; bleeding can be a slow ooze or trickle. If the patient loses a lot of blood, he may need a blood transfusion, or he may need to go back to the Operating Theatre.
- Blood clot forming in the lower leg (Deep Vein Thrombosis)
- Rise in body temperature
- Patient is unable to pass urine
- Patient is unable to have a bowel movement within a few days of surgery – bowels usually 'go on strike' for a few days after surgery, especially after surgery in the abdominal area.

Commonly asked questions after surgery

- Most of the questions asked after surgery are aimed at ensuring that there are no complications from surgery and that all systems (e.g. the renal system and gastro-intestinal system) are working normally again. Questions may include:
- Have you passed water? How much/How often?
- Have you passed wind yet?
- Have you moved your bowels yet?
- Are you in any pain? Where does it hurt?
- Would you like some pain relief? What type of pain relief would you prefer (injection into the muscle/tablet/suppository/intravenous (IV) pain relief)?
- Are you feeling nauseated? Have you vomited?
- Are you feeling drowsy?
- Can you move your toes? Any tingling/pins and needles?
- (After epidural): Have you got full movement and sensation in the legs?

Summary of main points

This chapter has touched on pre- and post-operative care settings; it has also touched on some of the knowledge competent health interpreters need to possess to interpret in these settings. It has also offered a brief overview of:

types of questions asked before surgical procedutres
types of anesthesia
equipment encountered in pre- and post-operative care settings

---

Chapter 11

Intensive Care

Intensive Care Units or ICUs are units which specialize in the care of seriously ill or potentially seriously ill people, who require round the clock nursing and medical attention. Patients are monitored closely and treatment is generally aggressive. Life support systems are often used. Often patients are deliberately paralysed and sedated by drugs and thus unaware of their surroundings.

Intensive Care units may vary in their specialty and in the age group they cater for. There are special Intensive Care Units for newborn babies (usually called Special Care Baby Units, abbreviated as SCBU or Neonatal Intensive Care Units, abbreviated as NICU) and special Intensive Care Units for children (usually called Pediatric Intensive Care Units, abbreviated as PICU). Some Intensive Care Units focus on a specific group of patients. There are Neurological Intensive Care Units for patients with neurological problems or head-injuries. Coronary Care Units focus on patients who need round the clock monitoring for their heart condition.

Some areas for intensive monitoring and treatment are indicated by different names again, including names such as: Intensive Care Room, High Dependency Unit or Department of Critical Care.

The three main reasons for admission to an Intensive Care Unit are:

– Monitoring
– Rest
– Treatment

A wide range of patients may be admitted to an Intensive Care Unit, including the following:

Major trauma: Patients who have multiple life-threatening injuries following accidents or falls.

Respiratory System: Severe asthma attacks; pneumonia; pulmonary embolism; near-drowning; severe lung contusion; respiratory arrest; also: patients who are making a slow recovery from the anesthetic

Heart and cardiovascular complications (such as those following cardiac arrest or heart attacks): heart shock; arrhythmias (irregular heart rhythm); congestive heart failure (CHF); different types of shock: septic shock; anaphylactic shock; cardiogenic shock (heart shock); aneurysms; diffuse intravascular coagulation; hemorrhages

Neurological: Brain hemorrhages (bleeding into the brain): head-injury (as a result of assault/traffic accident/fall)

Renal: Renal failure (kidney shutdown)

Obstetric Problems: Pre-eclampsia (please refer to Chapter 28); hemorrhages (bleeds) before or after childbirth

Burns: Patients with deep and/or extensive burns who suffer from swelling of the airways, shock, loss of protein and electrolyte imbalance and who need special dressings and pain relief

Major surgery: Patients recovering after major surgery, such as extensive abdominal surgery or radical head and neck surgery, or any other surgery where the patient's condition is compromised (serious)

Equipment

The amount of equipment and the extensive use of technology sets Intensive Care Units apart from other patient care areas. Equipment is used for diagnosis, monitoring and treatment of patients.

Some of the most commonly used equipment found in ICU includes:

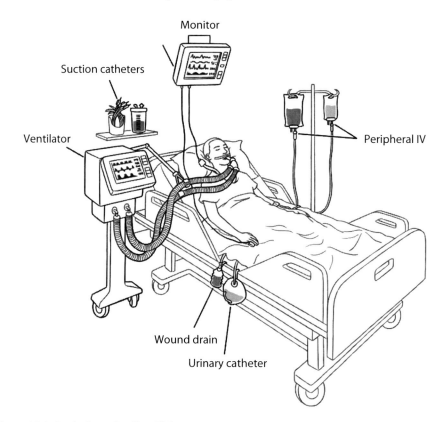

Figure 11.1. In the Intensive Care Unit

1. *Ventilator*

The ventilator or respirator is sometimes referred to as a breathing machine' and is used to maintain breathing for the patient.

Intubation is the name of the process whereby a tube is inserted into the patient, either

–   through one nostril, down the throat, through the vocal cords into the windpipe (naso-tracheal tube), or
–   through the mouth, down the throat, through the vocal cords into the windpipe (oro-tracheal tube) or
–   through a special incision called a tracheostomy straight into the windpipe (endo-tracheal tube).

Nasotracheal tubes may be used in children. Endotracheal tubes are used in patients who need to be intubated for longer periods of time. The endotracheal tube is often referred to as the '*trachy*'. The trachy is a relatively short and curved tube, which can usually be removed for cleaning purposes or replaced with a clean trachy.

Intubated patients are often unable to cough up their own phlegm, so suctioning tubes are used to suction off these secretions.

As mentioned previously, patients in the Intensive Care Unit are often paralyzed and sedated – they are unconscious, due to an induced coma (a level of deep unconsciousness, brought about by drugs), and need help with their breathing for that reason. Patients who have fractured their spine at neck level may be unable to breathe because the nerve supply to the breathing muscles has been interrupted. In other instances, the patient may simply be unable or too weak to breathe in by himself.

Usually, staff will try to wean the patient off the ventilator gradually, whenever possible.

The ventilator can be set in such a way that the patient is helped with any spontaneous attempts at breathing. If the patient makes a small attempt at breathing in, this triggers the ventilator, which will then deliver a 'full breath' to the patient. The patient can then be extubated (i.e. the breathing tube can be removed).

2. *Monitoring equipment*

Most Intensive Care patients will be attached to a variety of monitors and the monitor screens may show a lot of different information depending on the different equipment which has been attached to the monitor. Monitors may include:

–   monitors showing information about cardiac and pulmonary (lung) pressures (using a Swan Ganz Catheter in the heart)
–   an electrocardiograph (ECG) or EKG monitor which shows heart rate and rhythm
–   a pulse oxymeter which shows the amount of oxygen in the patient's blood (oxygen saturation)
–   a temperature probe, which monitors the patient's body temperature

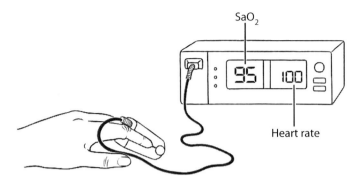

Pulse oximeter - measuring the oxygen saturation (SaO$_2$) % of the blood

Figure 11.2. Pulse oxymeter

3. *IV pumps*

Intravenous lines or IV lines are very often used to administer medication to the patient – in a lot of cases the rate at which medication is administered is very important and 'pumps' are used to ensure that the patient gets exactly the right amount of medication in exactly the right amount of time.

IV pumps are pumps which accurately regulate the amount of fluid administered to the patient. The IV fluid often contains medication, either in an IV fluid bag or in a syringe.

Where patients are conscious, *PCA (patient controlled anesthesia) pumps* or *pain pumps* may be used to provide the patient with a constant amount of basic pain relief. These pumps enable the patient to administer some pain relief when he wants it or just prior to painful procedures such as being washed or turned.

4. *Lines and tubes*

The term 'lines' generally refers to long narrow plastic tubes inserted into blood vessels for various purposes. Tubes may be inserted into the body for drainage of fluid or sometimes for the administration of fluid.

The various lines and tubes used in Intensive Care Units (and other wards) may include:

–   *Intravenous lines or IV lines:* used for administering fluid, medication and nutrition, and also for monitoring pressures inside the patient's heart, lungs and major blood vessels. Common IV lines include:
–   *peripheral lines* – inserted into peripheral veins usually on the hands, or forearms, occasionally in veins on the foot; peripheral lines ir stomachs and bowels. The IV lines may be used to give the patient fluid, glucose and electrolytes (such as Sodium, Potassium). Medication may be added to the IV fluid. Blood may also be given through a peripheral line.

- *Central Lines* – inserted into the jugular (neck) vein or into the subclavian vein (under the collar bone). Central lines may be used to give the patient complete nutrition, known as Total Parenteral Nutrition (TPN) or Intravenous Nutrition (IVN).
- *Arterial Lines* – inserted into arteries; arterial lines are often connected to a monitor for monitoring various types of blood pressures; they are also used for taking arterial blood samples.
- *Drains* – may be used to drain fluid away from the body for specific reasons. See Chapter 10 for a list of drains.
- *Nasogastric tubes* may be inserted through the nose, down the gullet into the stomach to drain away stomach juices (and other fluid produced in the gastro-intestinal tract).
- *Chest Drains* – may be used to drain air, fluid or blood from the lungs, to enable the patient to breathe better.
- *Urinary Catheters* – also called indwelling catheters (IDCs). IDCs are used to drain urine out of the bladder into a container. In the Intensive Care Unit, the urine usually drains into a urine meter, which enables staff to measure exactly how much urine the patient produces.

1. Staff

The staff in the Intensive Care Unit are especially trained to look after patients who need intensive care. Staff are ever-present and there is usually one nurse assigned per patient. This nurse will be the contact person for interpreter and family.

The medical staff will usually consists of Intensive Care Specialists (sometimes known as Intensivists (specialists in providing intensive care) and Intensive Care resident medical officers or registrars.

In some smaller centers, anesthetists, medical and surgical specialists provide medical back-up for nursing staff.

2. Some notes for interpreters and translators

Interpreting in the Intensive Care Unit will usually take place during interviews between the patient's relatives and medical staff. Sometimes Informed Consent may need to be obtained from relatives for procedures or for permission to switch off the support systems. On some occasions the interpreter may have to interpret for a semi-conscious patient (who may just be waking up from sedation), to convey messages to and from medical and allied staff.

Summary of main points

This chapter has touched on intensive care settings; it has also provided an overview of the knowledge competent health interpreters need to possess to interpret in these settings. It has also offered a brief overview of:

- types of cases requiring treatment in the ICU
- equipment encountered in ICU settings

Chapter 12

Obstetrics

Adapted from a contribution by Maureen Kearney, RN, RM

This chapter aims to present a brief overview of obstetric care. It aims to give healthcare interpreters an idea of what tests are done and what questions are asked. This chapter will mention some of the complications of pregnancy, which are discussed in more detail in Chapter 28. Problems of sick newborns will be discussed in Chapter 13.

Depending on the country women may be able to choose from a variety of healthcare providers to care for them during pregnancy. This includes (Independent) Midwifes; Primary care doctors; Hospital staff (doctors and midwives) or Private Obstetrician (specialist dealing with pregnancy and childbirth) or Ob Gyn (specialist in Obstetrics and gynecology). In former Commonwealth countries, all options *except* the private specialist are publicly funded.

Similarly, again depending on country, women may be able to choose from a variety of locations; in which to deliver their baby, including home; a Level One Hospital (obstetric hospital or public maternity unit in which there is only minimal support and backup); Tertiary Teaching Hospital (backup services such as an Operating Theatre and Special Care Baby Unit etc. are available) or private birthing clinic (paid for by the woman).

The woman discusses these options with her practitioner, who will also take into account her past obstetric history, her diet, any current health or pregnancy-related problems. In former Commonwealth countries the first three options may be publicly funded.

Prenatal care is very important. The first visit is done to obtain all the relevant information early on in the pregnancy and further check-ups are done to ensure that mother and baby continue to be healthy and that baby continues to grow well in respect to its gestation or age. If there are any problems, it is vital that these can be detected and treated as early as possible, to ensure the best possible outcome for mother and baby.

The practitioner may discuss antenatal education classes and encourage the woman to attend these, so that the woman feels she has knowledge of and feels confident about the coming birth. Classes may be held at her chosen delivery hospital or through independent midwife groups, private classes or the Home Birth Association.

1.   Prenatal care

Once her pregnancy has been confirmed, the woman will generally visit one of the above-mentioned practitioners for her first visit. This first visit will be a very thorough visit (as described below). After this visits generally increase from once a month (first two trimesters from week 1–28), to once a fortnight (week 28 to 36), to once a week (after week 36) as the expected date of delivery approaches. Obviously, this schedule may vary, depending on how the pregnancy progresses.

During the first antenatal visit the woman may be:

–   Booked in for delivery in hospital (even though she may express the wish to deliver elsewhere). It is important that the woman is booked into a hospital, just in case it becomes necessary to transfer the woman there in the course of delivery.
–   History will be recorded. This is a very important part of the first visit and will include:

Obstetric History
–   The first day of the last menstrual period (LMP)
–   Past child bearing experiences
–   Previous terminations of pregnancy
–   History of repeated spontaneous abortions
–   Complications in previous childbirth

Social History
–   Planned/unplanned pregnancy?
–   Wanted/unwanted pregnancy?
–   Support from partner/family
–   Response of mother and whole family to the pregnancy
–   Financial Support
–   Environmental factors (housing, heating, diet, and so on)
–   Age – is it a teenage pregnancy?
–   General Health (Practitioner will give advice on this if necessary)
–   Exercise
–   Cigarette smoking, use of alcohol and drugs (practitioner will discuss these with the woman if necessary)

Menstrual History
–   The practitioner will try to determine the date on which the woman started her last menstrual period (LMP). The practitioner will then add 9 months plus 7 days to the first day of the LMP to arrive at the approximate Expected Date of Delivery (EDD).
–   The practitioner will discuss the woman's normal cycle and amount of bleeding and will find out if any pain is associated with this menstrual cycle.
–   The practitioner will discuss the woman's contraception history with her.

Medical History

- The woman's past health is very important, as medical conditions may affect the pregnancy. These may range from severe heart conditions to common urinary tract infections. Some of the more common medical conditions are asthma; epilepsy; diabetes; high blood pressure or hypertension; mental health problems; heart disorders (including rheumatic fever) and any other condition that the woman may be taking medication for.

Family History

- Certain conditions are genetic in origin while others are familial (occuring in certain families) or racial (confined to certain races) or social (influenced by social conditions). It is important to know the woman's family history and that of her partner, if they know of them, so the caregivers can be more aware of any risks to the baby. Obviously, if either the father or the mother has been adopted, this information may not be available.

- *Physical Examination.* The practitioner will carry out a thorough physical examination of the woman, which may include height and weight; blood pressure; height of the fundus (the top of the womb)
Investigations may include:

  - Urine test for glucose/sugar (this may be a sign of gestational diabetes) and protein (this may be a sign of pre-eclampsia)
  - Blood tests for hemoglobin (to check for anemia and thalassemia); Complete Blood count (CBC) or Full Blood count (FBC); blood group and Rhesus Factor; antibodies in the blood (Rubella, Hepatitis B); VDRL (to check for venereal disease – syphilis)
  - Vaginal speculum (vaginal smear) (cells are checked for cervical cancer) and vaginal swabs (check for infection, e.g. Chlamydia)
  - Baby's heart beat (depending on how long the woman has been pregnant)

2. Follow-up visits

Once all the above information has been recorded during the booking visit, further antenatal check-ups are usually less involved. The following would be checked during a typical check-up:

- mother's general well-being
- blood pressure
- weight
- urine test for sugar and protein

- abdominal palpation (feeling the mother's abdomen). Feeling and measuring the baby's growth is an important factor in determining whether baby's growth equals its *gestation* or age.
- checking fetal movements. It is very important that the mother is aware of the babies movements and that she feels at least 10 movements a day (this becomes more significant after approximately 25 weeks)
- checking if mother has any swelling in face, hands and feet (signs of pre-eclampsia)
- checking baby's heart beat

Other tests may be done during the antenatal period if the practitioner, or the woman, think these are necessary or desired. These may include:

- alphafetoprotein (AFP) – Test done at approximately 13 weeks to check whether there may be a risk of congenital abnormalities (birth defects), such as spina bifida or chromosomal problems such as Down Sydrome.
- amniocentesis – Usually done between 16 and 18 weeks. Some amniotic fluid is taken from around the baby. This is withdrawn with a needle which is inserted through the abdominal wall under ultrasound guidance. The amniotic fluid is then tested for abnormalities. This is a very accurate test which can also tell the sex of the baby.
- cardiotocograph or CTG- Can record the baby's heart beat via an abdominal disc which has been strapped to the mother's stomach. The heart beat will show up on a graph. The same graph can also record any contractions (or tightening) the mother may have. It can show the strength of these contractions and how often they come.
- Chorionic villus sampling (CVS) – Usually done between 9 and 11 weeks where a sample of early placental tissue is taken to check for abnormalities.
- ultrasound scan – Imaging with the aid of high-frequency sound waves, usually done by a radiographer. The ultrasound can show the baby on the screen and can detect growth and abnormalities (if any). A 3D-scan will show the developing fetus (baby) in 3-D.

3. Term of pregnancy

As a large proportion of infants admitted to SCBU and NICU are premature, it is necessary to understand what is meant by term pregnancy so as to understand the implications of preterm delivery or premature birth.

A normal term of pregnancy is 40 weeks from the first day of the last menstrual period (LMP). The expected date of confinement (EDC) or expected date of delivery (EDD) is calculated by adding 9 months and 7 days to the date of the LMP. The number of weeks of gestation is calculated accordingly. A pregnancy is regarded as term when it reaches 36 to 38 weeks. Once the pregnancy passes 40 weeks it is regarded as postterm. Any gestation before 36 weeks is treated as preterm, therefore delivery before 36 weeks' gestation would be regarded as premature birth.

However classification based on the date of the LMP may, sometimes, be inaccurate. A lot of women have irregular menstrual periods which can make LMP quite unreliable, while other women *may not remember, or may conceal* for a variety of reasons, their actual date of LMP. As a result ascertaining gestation can be very difficult, and gestation could be different from the actual size and development of the fetus. Thanks to ultrasonography (ultrasound scanning or USS) the maturity of a pregnancy can now be assessed quite accurately. USS uses high-frequency sound waves to reflect the image of the fetus in the mother's abdomen, enabling healthcare professionals to measure the actual size of the fetus. Comparing these measurements to a standard measurement gives a fair indication of how mature the fetus is.

The biparietal diameter (BPD) of the fetal head offers a reliable parameter in *ultrasonography* to assess how far along the pregnancy is, because the head of the fetus grows at a fixed rate. The head-abdomen ratio (H:A ratio) is another measurement done to ascertain duration of pregnancy. Since head and abdomen grow at different rates, the H:A ratio is usually larger in early pregnancy and lower in late pregnancy when the abdomen grows faster than the head.

Most babies are delivered near term, i.e. after a pregnancy of around 40 weeks. However, some babies are delivered preterm or post-term. Most preterm deliveries, and some term or post-term deliveries, may cause problems for babies. The more preterm the infant the more problems can be expected. Please see Chapter 12 for more detail.

4. Labor and childbirth

Childbirth is a major life experience. Labor is described as the process by which the baby, placenta and membranes are expelled through the birth canal. Normal labor occurs spontaneously at 'term' (38–42 weeks of pregnancy), with the baby presenting head first. It is considered normal for the woman to deliver between 37 and 42 weeks.

Note the interpreter may need to stay close to the mother and interpret the health practitioner's comments and instructions. If the interpreter feels faint, he or she may have to sit down.

There are three stages of labor:

-   *Stage one:* The cervix (or neck of the womb) dilates, beginning with regular rhythmic contractions of the uterus. Dilatation of the cervix is complete when the cervix is fully dilated (opened) to 10 cm.
-   *Stage two:* The baby is born. This stage begins when the cervix is fully dilated and finishes when baby is born.
-   *Stage three:* This stage involves the placenta (afterbirth) and membranes coming away from the wall of the uterus and being pushed out. This stage also involves the control of bleeding. It begins after the birth of the baby and ends when the placenta and membranes have been expelled.

5. Common terminology

-   *Contractions or tightening:* The pain of the contractions comes and goes, and is mostly felt in the lower abdominal and upper stomach areas, due to the muscles in the wall of the womb squeezing and relaxing.
-   *Drip:* An intravenous line inserted into a vein, usually in the back of a hand, so fluids can be given straight into the blood.
-   *Entonox:* A form of pain relief which is inhaled by mouth piece: it consists of nitrous oxide mixed with oxygen.
-   *Epidural:* Injection of local anesthetic into the epidural space near the base of the spine. See Chapter 10.
-   *Fetal scalp electrode (FSE):* This is a clip which is attached to the baby's head via the vagina. The lead is plugged into a machine which will record the baby's heart beat very accurately.
-   *Meconium:* Baby's first, greenish-black bowel movement. When the baby has passed a bowel movement while still in the uterus, the amniotic fluid around the baby will become a greenish color. When amniotic fluid appears this color it is a sign that baby has been distressed at some stage. Meconium in the amniotic fluid also means an increased risk of infection. If meconium has been observed, a fetal scalp electrode will be used.
-   *Membranes ruptured* (waters leaking or waters have broken or the bag of waters has broken): The amniotic fluid (waters) is contained within two layers of membranes around the baby, which protect the baby from any infection. These membranes should not rupture (break) until labor has begun. Women are often unsure as to whether the membranes have ruptured. They describe feeling wet as though they have passed urine. Once the waters have broken, baby will need to be delivered within a certain time-frame, depending on the Lead Maternity Carer (LMC).

- *Narcotics:* Are sometimes still given as pain relief.
- *Perineum:* The area between the lower vagina and the rectum. The perineum is stretched, particularly when the baby's head is born. It may tear or be cut in a procedure called an episiotomy to allow for baby's head to pass through. After a tear or episiotomy the perineum is repaired with dissolving sutures (stitches).
- *Position:* Refers to the way the baby's head is lying and is assessed by feeling (by vaginal examination) the sutures and fontanelles on baby's head.
- *Show:* A sticky discharge of mucus (slime) and blood, that appears usually early in labour. This is a plug of mucus that was situated in the neck of the cervix during pregnancy, protecting the baby from infection. Once the cervix begins to soften up and dilate, this mucus comes away.
- *Vaginal examination:* This is done by the practitioner to assess whether the cervix is changing and is the most accurate way of assessing progress in labour.

6.   Postnatal care

The postnatal period is also called the *puerperium*. This is the period between birth and 6 weeks after birth. The mother may or may not stay in hospital for the first few days. This is a time of great physical, emotional and psychological change. It is important to establish a bond between mother and baby and to establish breast-feeding. Although breast-feeding is a natural process, lots of help and support is often needed.

Postnatal checks and care of the mother generally includes:

- *Physical check on mother* – This is done daily for the first few days and every other time she is visited.
- *General well-being* – Does mother feel well?
- *Breasts* – Breasts are checked for red, painful areas, lumps or any other problems
- *Nipples* – Nipples are checked to ensure that there are no blisters, cracks, bleeding areas, etc. Are the nipples coping with the breast-feeding and the constant sucking from baby?
- *Fundus* – The fundus is the top of the uterus. After the baby is born, the fundus should be at umbilicus (belly-button) level. From thereon, the fundus drops a bit each day (approximately 1 centimeter), until it finally returns to the pelvis, under the pubic bone. This process is called involution and feeling the level of the fundus forms part of the postnatal check.
- *Vaginal discharge or lochia* – The vaginal discharge begins as fresh bleeding. Over a period of time (different for each woman), the *lochia* changes into a whitish discharge. Some women may bleed on and off for up to six weeks.

   – *Legs* – Women are encouraged to be up and about early after the birth of their babies to stimulate a good blood flow through the legs and thereby avoid the formation of blood clots (thrombosis).
   – *Urine* – After birth, women will pass urine in larger quantities and more frequently than usual, in order to get rid of the excess fluid they have been carrying during pregnancy. Urinary tract infections can be common after birth so the practitioner will check that there is no pain, stinging or unusual smell associated with the urine.
   – *Sleep* – The mother will be encouraged to sleep when her baby sleeps, as over-tiredness is very common in the postnatal period.
   – *Nutrition* – The woman needs to eat regular, nutritious meals and snacks, especially if she is breast-feeding.
   – *Hydration* – The woman needs to be encouraged to drink lots of fluid, especially if she is breast-feeding, as the baby will take a lot of fluid away from her.
   – *Bowel function* – Often mothers do not have a bowel movement for a few days and may find themselves constipated. The practitioner may advise her to take gentle laxatives or high fibre food and to drink a lot of fluids.
   – *Postnatal exercises* – These should be started in a gentle way, soon after the birth. The so-called pelvic floor exercises, which aim to strengthen the pelvic floor muscles, are especially important. Abdominal exercises and other exercises can be introduced later.
   – *Postnatal blues* – Major emotional and hormonal changes can occur postnatally. It often takes 6 to 12 weeks to return to a normal emotional state. 'Blues' or 'feeling down' can occur at anytime between 3 to 10 days after birth. 'Blues' are most common on the fifth day after birth. This is a normal reaction to childbirth, which affects approximately 60% of women. Signs are tearfulness and a feeling of panic. The first days after birth are a time of great hormonal changes, with progesterone levels dropping to almost zero, and tearfulness usually settles down after 24 hours.

7. Postnatal checks

At one and five minutes after birth, the practitioner will check the Appearance, Pulse, Grimace, Activity, Respiration (APGAR) score. Appearance involves the baby's complexion or skin colour (pink, pale, blue); Pulse relates to baby's heart rate; Grimace relates to baby's reflex to stimulation (none, grimace, crying); Activity relates to muscle tone (none, some, flexion), and Respiration relates to breathing (none, weak, strong). A score of 0, 1 or 2 is given for each aspect. Best outcome would be a total score of 9 or 10 overall, while an overall score of < 3 means the baby needs immediate medical attention.

A thorough baby check is done after birth, including listening to the baby's heart sounds, lungs, testing the baby's reflexes, hips and so on. This thorough check is repeated at six weeks. Any baby that is feeding well and sleeping well should thrive. The baby will be checked by Child Health Nurse (Plunket Nurse in New Zealand) once the Practitioner hands over the care of the baby, usually at between 2 to 6 weeks after birth.

The following are typical baby tests:

– *Feeding* – It is important to know whether baby is going to be fed on formula or breast-milk. The practitioner will check how much baby drinks and how often, and if there are any problems.
– *Skin* – The practitioner will check for spots, rashes, marks, skin infections, and so on.
– *Head* – The practitioner will check fontanelles, ears, eyes, nose, mouth and so on, for any signs of infection, redness and so on.
– *Cord* – The practitioner will check whether this is drying or moist. The practitioner will also check for redness, an offensive smell, or whether the cord has fallen off (usually around the fifth day).
– *Bottom* – The practitioner will check for redness, nappy rash, spots or thrush.
– *Urine and bowel function* – The practitioner will check whether baby is passing urine and bowel movements normally.
– *Sleeping pattern* – The practitioner will check baby's sleeping pattern and give advice if necessary.
– *Crying or agitation* – The practitioner will check for crying, agitation or any unusual behavior.
– *Growth* – The practitioner will check baby's height and weight.

Summary of main points

This chapter has offered a brief overview of:

– the three stages of pregnancy
– health professionals involved in the period leading up to, during and after childbirth
– common procedures and investigations

Chapter 13

Child health

Interpreting in the area of child health may be very rewarding but can also be extremely taxing. The parents' strong emotional involvement may place additional strains on the interpreter. Sometimes interpreters will need to interpret for children. They will need to make sure they convey information in appropriate language. It is important to remain calm and collected during the interpreting assignment, but equally important to seek debriefing from a counselor or supervisor after difficult interpreting situations.

1. Neonatal Care

Adapted from a contribution by Dana Lui

Newborn infants are classified as neonates from the day of birth to one month of age. Newborn services provide healthcare service for this group of babies. Other health professionals may provide follow-up services. This section will focus on delivery of care within the Special Care Baby Unit (SCBU) and Neonatal Intensive Care Unit (NICU), as these provide immediate care for sick neonates as soon as they are born.

1.1 Neonate Care

In most countries neonatal care can be divided into three levels:

Level 1 is the basic care provided to all newborn babies. This generally refers to mother crafting like feeding, bathing, changing diapers/nappies, looking after the umbilical cord, etc.

Level 2 care is provided to sick newborn infants who require close observation and special management. Level 2 neonatal care may be referred to as Neonatal Care (Specialty) (USA), Special Care Newborn Nursery (Canada), Neonatal High Dependency Unit (UK), Special Care Baby Unit (SCBU) (Australia, NZ).

Level 3 care is intensive care delivered to newborn infants who are extremely premature (under 31 weeks' gestation) or with a low birth weight (less than 2 pounds 12 ounces or 1250 grams), or very sick infants requiring ventilation support, blood exchange transfusions, or those newborn babies who cannot be appropriately cared for at level 2. Level 3 units are mostly located in academic teaching hospitals (tertiary hospitals) which have maternity units and which serve as teaching units or research centers. Level 3 care units are referred to as Neonatal Intensive Care Units (NICU) in most countries and have easy access to most of the back-up services, such as laboratory and radiology services.

Circumstances for admission to Level 2 Neonatal Care may include:

– Babies of low birth weight. Low birth weight babies weigh less than 5 pounds 8 ounces or 2.5 kilograms at birth, regardless of gestational age. Low birth weight babies may be preterm, born before 37 weeks gestation or babies small for gestational age (birth weight below tenth percentile for gestational age). Some babies are both preterm and small for gestational age. This includes babies who are born at less than 31 weeks' gestation who do not need ventilation support.
– Babies with respiratory distress (breathing problems) as a result of prematurity e.g. birth asphyxia, meconium aspiration or infection. These babies may be admitted to either SCBU or NICU depending on the severity of the problem.
– Babies with suspected or clinical signs of infections such as pneumonia, meningitis, urinary tract infection or umbilical infection.

Other conditions that would make it necessary for a baby to be admitted into a newborn unit could include:

– hypothermia (low temperature)
– hypoglycemia (low blood sugar level)
– jaundice
– congenital abnormalities
– gastro-intestinal problems, such as feeding problems severe enough to cause clinical concern, bile-stained vomit, or other signs suggesting bowel obstruction
– convulsions
– cardiovascular problems

Occasionally, babies are admitted for social issues or for terminal care when deemed appropriate after consultation between health professionals of different disciplines.

1.2 Asphyxia

The most serious problem a term infant can face at delivery is birth asphyxia. Asphyxia means respiratory failure. In a newborn this could be the result of anoxia (a complete lack of oxygen) or hypoxia (not enough oxygen, i.e. less than normal oxygen concentration). The causes of anoxia and hypoxia could be the result of events before birth (antepartum), during birth (intrapartum) or after birth (postpartum).

Hypoxia prepartum may be caused by maternal hypoxia; poor functioning of the placenta; intrinsic problems of the fetus, such as severe anemia resulting from hemolysis (break down of red blood cells); hemorrhage (bleeding) or clotting defects. These may all lead to chronic hypoxia of the fetus. If the fetus (baby) is already compromised prior to labor, going through labor may cause even more distress.

Hypoxia intrapartum may be due to cord compression (circulation of blood through the umbilical cord is compressed); fetal dystocia (where the fetus presents in a position which makes delivery difficult); acute bleeding or meconium aspiration, which can predispose the baby to asphyxia. Meconium aspiration is a condition characterized by passage of fetal stools before the baby is born. The fetus inhales these stools into its airways, thereby making the process of breathing impossible or difficult at birth.

Hypoxia postpartum may be due to hyaline membrane disease (infant respiratory distress syndrome), or surfactant deficiency, which results in the babys air sacs (or alveoli) being unable to expand, thus making breathing a very difficult process. This disease is more prominent in preterm infants (especially less than 32 weeks' gestation, although some term infants may have this problem as well).

The effect of asphyxia on the body of the newborn infant can be very serious. Before birth, the baby received oxygen through the umbilical cord, in other words, supplied by the mother. However, after birth baby is supposed to breathe for itself. However, if the baby is not getting enough oxygen, because of asphyxia, the baby's body may revert back to fetal circulation (circulation as it was before birth). The reason for this is simply that, as the baby cannot get oxygen through its lungs, the baby's blood once again by-pass the lungs via various channels that would normally close after delivery (see also Patent Ductus Arteriosus, page 133). This condition is called persistent fetal circulation or persistent pulmonary hypertension.

Persistent fetal circulation is very dangerous for the baby. Fetal circulation was helpful for the baby while it was getting its blood supply directly from the mother, but if it persists when the baby's blood supply is disconnected from the mother's blood circulation (i.e. when the umbilical cord is clamped), the baby can be in real danger.

Hypoxia after birth means that all of the baby's body will be deprived of oxygen with the brain cells affected worst of all. The infant may develop seizures as a result of hypoxia and end up in a condition called hypoxic-ischemic encephalopathy, where the brain is suffering the effects of insufficient oxygen supply. In order to deliver oxygen to the tissues of the body, the infant will need intubation (insertion of a breathing tube) and ventilation (receiving air and oxygen through a breathing machine).

1.3 Premature delivery

Sometimes babies need to be delivered prematurely, sometimes because labor starts too early. If the baby is very premature, the obstetrician will try to suppress the spontaneous onset of preterm labour by giving the mother medication. At the same time the mother will receive corticosteroid drugs which help the fetal lungs mature.

If the baby's lungs are a bit more mature, the baby may have a greater chance of survival even when it is born too early. If the woman's membranes (or 'waters') do rupture prematurely, antibiotics are also given to protect both mother and fetus from infection. If there are signs of infection (e.g. if the mother develops a high temperature) the process of delaying delivery may need to be stopped and delivery may be allowed to proceed because infection may be dangerous to both mother and child.

Most of the time it is not clear why labor starts prematurely. In some instances, if the woman starts to bleed or shows signs of an intra-uterine infection, it may be necessary to deliver the baby quickly in order to save both mother's and the baby's life. Another serious condition, known as pre-eclampsia (previously known as gestational proteinuria and hypertension), may also make it necessary to initiate premature delivery (especially if this condition is worsening). It is the mother's condition which determines how urgently the baby is delivered. Sometimes there is no time to give the mother the corticosteroid drugs. As a result, the lungs of the preterm baby may be so immature that the baby cannot survive.

Sometimes the baby is delivered prematurely, because there are signs that the baby is at risk. Signs could include poor growth and reduced movement. Often a difficult decision has to be made on the balance of either delivering the baby too early or leaving a compromised (at risk) baby inside the uterus.

1.4   Problems of prematurity

Premature birth will result in a premature baby who is not, as yet, ready for independent life. Such problems are foreseeable given all organs and systems of the infant are immature. These problems can include:

1. *Respiratory Problems*
At 24 weeks' gestation the fetal lungs have developed to a stage where they could be functional. Gas exchange is possible as the air sacs start to form. Prior to this period the fetus is not viable (cannot live). However while all the necessary tissues are there at 24 weeks the ventilation system is still very primitive. By giving the mother corticosteroids before the baby is born, baby's lungs are helped to mature more quickly. Infants born before 32 weeks' gestation (duration of pregnancy) are likely to develop hyaline membrane disease (HMD) because of the lack in production of surfactant (a substance lining the air sacs). This leads to respiratory difficulties. After delivery an endotracheal tube can be passed down the trachea (windpipe) of the baby and positive pressure can be administered to deliver oxygen-enriched air to expand the air sacs, thus making gas exchange possible and keeping the premature baby alive. This process is called ventilation. Artificial surfactant can be given directly into the baby's lungs to counteract HMD. Giving antenatal corticosteroids, maintaining the preterm baby on a ventilator (breathing machine) and early administration of surfactant enable a lot of

extremely premature babies to survive. The more premature the infant, the longer they need to stay on ventilation.

Ventilation helps preterm babies to survive, but it is has limitations and complications. One has to remember that in order for gas exchange to take place in the lungs, the respiratory system has to have developed to a stage where the basic organs and tissues are in place.

If an infant is less than 24 weeks' gestation, the infant would not survive (despite the best machines available). One can also imagine that when positive pressure is constantly being pumped into these babies' lungs, a hole can be inadvertently blown, causing a pneumothorax to develop. Pneumothorax means the presence of free air in the thoracic (chest) cavity between the layers of lung coverings (pleural layers). As free air occupies space, it stops the lungs or the air sacs, from expanding, making gas exchange ineffective. Pulmonary hemorrhage (bleeding in the lungs) can also occur due to the fragile nature of preterm infant's lung tissue (can lead to the rupture of blood vessels under pressure), the side-effect of the surfactant, or because of clotting defects resulting from prematurity.

Small preterm babies may need to stay on ventilation for a long time. The pressure exerted by the ventilator on the immature lungs can cause damage to the lung tissues, leading to a condition called chronic lung disease, where lung tissues become fibrotic and lose their elasticity. Worst of all, if a preterm baby is given increased oxygen over a prolonged period of time, can be very toxic and cause blindness.

2.   Hypothermia

In hypothermia body temperature is low. Normal body temperature is between 96.8 to 98.6 degrees Fahrenheit or 36 to 37 degrees Celsius. Normal term babies need to be kept warm by keeping them in warm environment with appropriate clothing and bedding, as, due to their big body-surface-to-room-surface ratio, they lose heat much faster than an adult.

A preterm infant has little or no subcutaneous tissue for insulation to preserve body heat. At birth, these infants come out wet (because they have been surrounded by amniotic fluid) and out of the warm environment of the uterus. In these babies the organ for heat production, the muscle, is underdeveloped, therefore heat production is basically ineffective or non-existent. In addition most of these infants need resuscitation at birth. It is essential therefore that they are dried immediately as heat loss through evaporation, conduction and convection can be very dramatic within a short time. To prevent heat loss and maintain a normal temperature, premature babies will be placed and nursed on a heat table or in an incubator. A heat table is an open crib with an overhead radiant heater with control for adjustment of the temperature according to the baby's temperature. The incubator is a transparent box that a baby can be nursed in almost naked so that observation is possible and warmth can be provided.

A cold baby needs more energy and oxygen supply to maintain its warmth, therefore when sick a low temperature will only further compromise the baby as its systems (of the body) shut down.

3. *Hypoglycemia*

In hypoglycemia blood sugar levels are low. A preterm baby has very little fat and muscle therefore its energy storage is low and any sugar in the blood can be used up very quickly. If a baby is cold it will also need more energy in order to keep itself warm. As all tissues and cells need energy to function properly a low blood glucose (sugar) level means problems. Again, the brain cells will be the worst affected. A baby will start to fit (have seizures) if the blood sugar level drops down too low. A term infant, who is healthy and who sucks well, will be offered the breast or a bottle of formula as soon as possible after birth. A preterm or sick infant will typically be started on an intravenous infusion of glucose water.

4. *Blood problems*

All newborn organs and systems are immature, including blood making mechanisms and organs. Most sick preterm infants will be anemic (have low levels of red blood cells) as they may have bled before birth and may have a comparatively low blood volume. Therefore, newborns may require more frequent blood tests to assess their clinical condition, and blood transfusions may be necessary to compensate for their anemia. Newborn babies may also have low levels of white blood cells (leukocytes) and platelets (thrombocytes). As white cells are responsible for fighting infection a decreased white cell count, or a decreased white cell response, makes the baby more vulnerable to infection and or may make the effects of infection more profound. A reduced platelet count increases the chance of bleeding, both internally and externally, which can lead to life-threatening events or very poor outcomes. Newborns are particularly vulnerable to pulmonary hemorrhage (bleeding into the lungs) and intraventricular hemorrhage (bleeding into the brain).

5. *Infection*

Sepsis is another term used for wide-spread infection. When a baby is preterm, the immune system is also immature. Response to infection may be delayed or inadequate, therefore making any infection, that would be harmless to an adult or term infant, very severe. In addition because premature infants are so small infection can spread throughout the whole body in a very short time. Most preterm neonates will receive antibiotic cover (protection) straight after birth to prevent any infections from entering the body.

Simple measures like hand-washing are very important in preventing infection and cross-infection. Aseptic techniques are necessary for all traumatic procedures, such as blood taking, so as to minimize the chance of introducing infection. Nursing an infant in an incubator (special bed for very sick newborns) also provides a protective environment.

6. *Cardiac problems*

There is one cardiac problem specific to very preterm neonates, Patent ductus arteriosus (PDA). PDA is the persistent opening of the duct between the aorta and pulmonary arteries which normally closes after birth. This duct is open in fetal life so that oxygenated blood that comes in from the mother (through the umbilical cord) can by-pass the lungs. After delivery, the neonate should be able to breathe and supply its own oxygen, therefore this duct normally closes. In some cases however the duct remains open. This causes problems for both the lungs and the heart and makes a sick neonate even sicker. In order to close the PDA a special drug may be given. If this drug does not work, or if it gives rise to too many side-effects, an operation can be done to ligate (tie) the duct. In most cases, the neonate then improves instantly.

7. *Intraventricular hemorrhage (IVH)*

IVH is bleeding in the head of the preterm neonate. Because the brain of preterm babies is immature, the blood vessels in the brain are very fragile. IVH occurs most often in the first week of life, typically during the first three days after birth. There are four stages of IVH. Grade I bleeding is bleeding limited to the germinal matrix (primitive tissue), while Grade II bleeding is bleeding into the ventricles (cerebro-spinal fluid chambers of the brain). Both Grade I and Grade II bleeding will cause minimal brain damage once they have resolved. In Grade III bleeding there is bleeding into the ventricles, causing distention of the ventricles. Grade IV bleeding is bleeding into the brain tissue surrounding the ventricles as well. Both Grade III and Grade IV hemorrhages can lead to quite severe brain damage and to long-term disabilities.

8. *Necrotising enterocolitis (NEC)*

NEC is an inflammation of the gut specific to preterm babies. The wall of the gut breaks down as infection sets in. This can lead to perforation if unrecognized and untreated within a short time. If the infection is recognized early enough, and if the baby is given antibiotic cover and left without feeding for two weeks, the condition can generally be cured. If perforation occurs an operation will be necessary to remove the necrotized (dead) portion of the gut. Occasionally, a premature baby may die from this condition.

9. *Jaundice*

Many newborn babies will have jaundice (yellowish discoloration of skin and mucous membranes). This is a direct result of the breakdown of red blood cells. Most term infants are able to handle and get rid of this jaundice through their liver, and for this reason the condition is described as physiological (normal). However, in a preterm infant liver function is immature as is the processing of bilirubin (the bile pigment which causes the jaundice). Placing these infants under phototherapy (UV light treatment) helps to break down the bilirubin so that it can be passed out (via urine and stools) thus reducing the jaundice. If the bilirubin level is too high it can cause brain damage. In order to avoid this, a blood exchange transfusion may be necessary.

10.   *Feeding intolerance*

When a preterm baby is born its gut may not be ready for feeding as digestive enzymes may be absent or deficient, absorptive ability may be very limited or the gut may not be moving as yet. If the infant was hypoxic at birth the gut may take an even longer time to recover because the body attends to the major organs (e.g. brain, heart and kidneys) first.

The mother's breast milk is the first choice for preterm babies as it is more easily absorbed and contains antibodies important for fighting infections. Mothers are encouraged to express their milk regularly so as to establish lactation (breast milk production). In the initial days, when breast feeding is not possible, breast milk can be frozen so that it can be used later (can store for up to three months) when the infant starts to feed. If the baby is unlucky enough to develop necrotizing enterocolitis, introduction of feeding needs to be more cautious and slow.

1.5   Admission process

When a preterm or sick infant is admitted to NICU, ventilator support will usually be necessary. Umbilical lines (intravenous lines in the umbilical vein) may be inserted to deliver fluid to the baby. Umbilical lines also provide access for blood sampling and blood pressure monitoring. Antibiotics will be started after blood tests have been taken. Once stabilized the baby will be weaned from the ventilator (breathing machine) and encouraged to breathe, with some support, on their own. Continuous Positive Airways Pressure (CPAP) is an alternative means in which to help the infant breathe spontaneously. A tube is passed down the nose of the baby to just above the throat and a small amount of pressure is delivered to keep the airways open. Oxygen may also be given through this tube. When the baby grows or improves, CPAP may be stopped and the breathing tube removed (extubation) and head box oxygen (oxygen provided in a 'box' around baby's head space), or nasal prong oxygen (oxygen through prongs in the nostrils), will be given instead. This also allows easy handling of the baby by its mother.

Similarly, when an infant is admitted to SCBU, it may need extra oxygen to help with its breathing. Babies can receive oxygen via a head box. If they are too ill to breathe on their own they may receive a special type of respiratory support called CPAP. If the baby is very sick, medical staff may insert umbilical lines and start baby on antibiotics. If the baby's condition gets worse, baby may need to be transferred to NICU for ventilation or management.

Feeding is started when the baby's respiratory status improves. Baby will receive small but regular feeds via a nasogastric (stomach tube inserted through the nose), or orogastric tube (stomach tube inserted through the mouth), so that the baby does not need to suck. If baby tolerates these feeds, both volume and frequency will increase. When this happens, intravenous infusion of nutritious fluids can be decreased and finally stopped.

When either the baby's condition improves, or when it reaches a certain weight, or passes a certain gestational age, the infant will be transferred from NICU to SCBU for ongoing care until it can be discharged (allowed to leave the hospital).

In SCBU the baby needs to show that it is able to suck feeds effectively and gain weight (particular if the baby was born very premature) before going back to the postnatal ward or going home. Generally preterm infants have to reach a weight of 2.5 kilograms (or 5 pounds 8 ounces) or have to be close to *term* before discharge planning is organized. Prior to discharge, the baby will often go to the postnatal ward with its mother for *mother-crafting*. This involves the mother learning to be totally responsible for the care of her baby, with the backup support of the unit. Some babies may go home on oxygen and with an apnea mattress which helps alert parents to baby's apnea (not breathing). Some babies may go between NICU and SCBU a few times, especially if they are extremely premature; of low birth; deteriorate during their course of stay, or undergo surgery.

1.6   Some common investigations

Blood tests

Åstrup	See Blood gases
glucose	serum sugar level
electrolytes	important minerals which are part of the biochemistry of the blood, this includes Sodium (Na), Potassium (K), Calcium (Ca)
blood culture	to check for infection
blood gases	to check the biochemistry of the blood so as to gain information about the respiratory status
chromosome study	to rule out congenital abnormalities
Complete Blood Count (CBC)	checking the number of red blood cells, white blood cells, platelets, packed cell volume, and toxic ratio/left shift
Full Blood Count (FBC)	See Complete Blood Count
genetic study	See chromosome study
Groups and Coombs test	to check for hemolytic disease (breakdown of blood)
Phenylketonuria (PKU)	screening for a metabolic disorder which can lead to brain damage if it goes undetected.
SBR	Serum Bilirubin Level
thyroid function tests	to check levels of thyroid hormones
Urea, Creatinine	Tests to check kidney function

Radiological tests

abdominal x-ray	to assess abnormalities in the abdomen
Chest X-Ray	to assess condition of heart and lungs
radiological tests	examinations by X-Ray

Ultrasonography

cranial ultrasound	ultrasound of the head
echo cardiogram	ultrasound of the heart
renal ultrasound	ultrasound of the kidneys
ultrasonography	ultrasound tests (examinations by sound waves)

Urine tests

culture and microscopy	to detect infection; find out what organisms are causing infection

Other tests

endotracheal aspirate culture	to detect infection in the airways
gastric aspirate	to detect infection in the stomach
lumbar puncture	obtaining cerebro-spinal fluid to check for meningitis
spinal tap	Same as lumbar puncture
TORCH study	to detect congenital infection
viral study	to detect viral infection

2. Pediatrics

Pediatrics (child medicine) is a specialized area of healthcare. In children, the body's defense system is still developing and this means that they are very susceptible to a large range of infectious diseases. In addition, children are often not aware of the dangers of particular situations and may be involved in a wide range of accidents, ranging from accidental poisoning (e.g. taking their parents' medication or drinking household cleaning liquids) to falls or (near-) drowning accidents in swimming pools or small creeks.

Sadly, sometimes children become the victims of abuse (physical or sexual) or neglect (not receiving appropriate care) or they become victims in car accidents, especially when they have not been strapped into child safety seats, booster seats or seat belts.

In this chapter I will look into some of the most common childhood illnesses. Please refer to the Chapter 8 on Emergency Departments for further information on accidents.

2.1   Child health professionals

Most countries have special health providers looking after the health of young children. A doctor specializing in child health is called a pediatrician and the children's ward is referred to as the pediatrics ward.

Child Health staff check for normal growth and development, making sure that the child reaches its developmental milestones at the right stages in its development. They also provide parent support and education. Parents are often given a book in which they can record milestones in the child's development, such as the first smile, the first steps (unaided), the first words, etc. Dates for (repeat) immunizations are also recorded in this book. If the health provider has reasons for concern, he/she may refer the parents to a child specialist or to a special child development clinic. Health providers may also refer so-called *at-risk* children to other services who may then follow these children up until their sixteenth birthday.

2.2   Immunization

Immunization means 'giving immunity to'. We have immunity (defence) against certain diseases, when we have enough antibodies (comparable to specially trained defense troups) in our body to fight off an attack of these illnesses.

Sometimes doctors talk about *passive immunity* and *active immunity*

Passive immunization occurs when the child/patient becomes immune to something without having to fight the infection him/herself. Breast-feeding mothers give their children passive immunizations against certain disorders by passing on their own antibodies via their breast milk.

Children usually have passive immunity during the first 5 or 6 months of life, because their mothers antibodies still circulate in their bodies. Patients may also be given passive immunity against certain diseases, by being injected with the antibodies.

We get active immunity against certain diseases by actively fighting off a (small) attack ourselves. Health Professionals can help us get 'active immunity' by injecting us with a small amount of 'vaccine' leading to a small attack on our immune system. The process of injecting the vaccine to help us develop antibodies against a certain disease is called *vaccination* or *immunization*.

Special childhood immunization programmes exist in most developed countries. It is important that children are taken to the doctor whenever their next immunization is due. The doctor will check the child to make sure the child is in good health and able to develop the antibodies. If the child is not well the doctor will delay the immunization until the child is well again.

2.3 Common childhood health problems

1. *Attention Deficit Hyperactivity Disorder* (ADHD) – A combination of hyperactive behaviour and the inability to concentrate on anything for more than a few seconds or minutes (flitting from one thing to the next).

Causes: Thought to be caused by an underdeveloped frontal cortex in the brain.

Symptoms: An inability to sit still and listen.

Investigations: Observation of child and taking history (parents describe behaviours)

Treatment: Drug treatment may be prescribed.

2. *Autism (Autism Spectrum Disorder* or *ASD*)* – Children with ASD may be anywhere on a continuum from very severe autistic tendencies to high-functioning with much less severe autistic tendencies (Asperger Syndrome). Some children with ASD may have poor (or no) verbal skills and may have trouble relating to or understanding other people. They may avoid eye contact and go through repetitive movements such as rocking backwards and forwards or hand flapping.

Alternatively, children with this syndrome may have advanced (verbal) skills, but have poor social skills and be unable to understand nonverbal language. This may mean they have trouble making friends or understanding other people. The DSM-V (2013) offers a wealth of information on ASD.

Causes: Unknown

Symptoms: Repetitive movement; flapping; rocking; behaviours as described above.
Investigations: Observation of child and taking history (parents describe behaviours)

Treatment: Behavioural therapies; speech therapy; occupational therapy; some doctors prescribe diets free of gluten, casein or soy.

*ASD may also be an abbreviation for Atrium Septum Defect, a hole in the wall between the atria of the heart.

3. *Asthma* – Refer Chapter 19 for more information.

Symptoms: Children with asthma will often have a dry cough, rather than a wheeze.

Treatment: If the child is unable to speak, they should be taken to hospital by life support ambulance immediately. In hospital, the child may be given intravenous or inhaled steroids and special asthma bronchodilator medication through a nebulizer to open up the airways.

4.   *Bronchiolitis* – Virus infection of the smallest air passages in very young children.

Causes: The infection usually follows a runny nose or sore throat and cough; usually caused by a virus.

Symptoms: Wheezing; coughing; shortness of breath, which may lead to difficulty in feeding.

Investigations: Chest X-ray; listening to lungs.

Treatment: Oxygen, feeding through a nasogastric tube; oxygen

5.   *Bronchopneumonia* – Infection of the bronchi and alveoli (little air sacs).

Causes: Infection of the upper airways spreads into the bronchi (breathing tubes) and alveoli; may be caused by either bacteria or a virus.

Symptoms: Cough, fever, shortness of breath; *whiteouts* (areas of no air movement) on the X-Ray; loss of appetite.

Investigations: Chest X-ray; listening to lungs.

Treatment: Oxygen; bedrest; antibiotics.

6.   *Cerebral Palsy* – Damage to parts of the brain which control muscle movement, balance and posture.

Causes: Doctors think this damage usually takes place while the baby is still in the uterus, during birth, or shortly after birth; for instance in some very premature children.

Symptoms: Babies may be floppy and stiff, show a lack of head control; children may adopt particular postures and have spasticity of the muscles. Some, but definitely not all, children with cerebral palsy also have epilepsy (see Chapter 17, page 172), problems with hearing, eyesight, or an intellectual disability.

Investigations: Testing reflexes and movement by pediatrician (doctor specializing in child health).

Treatment: physiotherapy to encourage movement, posture, head control and balance; *speech therapy* to encourage movement of the mouth.

7.   *Chest infection* – Infection of the bronchi (breathing tubes) and lungs (refer *bronchiolitis* and *bronchopneumonia sections above*).

8.   *Chickenpox* – A very contagious viral infection (Varicella Zoster virus).

Causes: Viral infection.

Symptoms: Skin rash with crops of blisters (filled with fluid), accompanied by slight fever and a feeling of unwellness. Chickenpox is contagious until all the blisters have crusted over (formed scabs).

Investigations: Physical examination.

Treatment: Calamine lotion for itchiness; ensuring that blisters do not get infected. Immunization is available.

9.   *Child abuse* – Includes any instances of physical abuse; neglect; malnutrition; emotional abuse/neglect; mental cruelty; poisoning or sexual abuse.

Treatment: Children need to be protected. Children depend on adults to ensure their health and well-being. In most countries special child abuse teams have been set up to deal with instances of child abuse. Such teams typically involve a Social Worker, a Child Health Nurse, and a Police Youth Aid Officer, depending on country and/or state.

10.   *Convulsions* – Refer section on *Seizures* below

11.   *Cot Death* – Also known as *Sudden Infant Death Syndrome*, occurs when the young baby suddenly stops breathing, for no apparent reason.

Cause: In spite of ongoing research, it is still not know what causes cot death. Factors that may possibly contribute to cot death include smoking (around children or during pregnancy); bottle-feeding; cold (air) temperature; low birth-weight; placing baby's head on an adult pillow (obstructing baby's airway); adults rolling on top of baby whilst bed sharing, and possibly many other as yet unidentified factors.

Symptoms: Baby suddenly stops breathing, for no apparent reason. This is followed by cardiac arrest and the child dies.

Treatment: Prevention is the key, including no smoking and using an apnea mattress under baby (alarm will sound when the baby stops breathing).

12.   *Croup* – A viral infection of the voice-box and windpipe.

Causes: Viral infection.

Symptoms: Stridor (a rasping noise) when the child breathes in; shortness of breath and respiratory distress; indrawing of the chest.

Investigations: Physical examination

Treatment: In serious cases admission to hospital; steroids, nebulized adrenaline (epinephrine).

13. *Cystic Fibrosis or (mucoviscoidosis)* – An inherited gene which leads to production of thick mucus in the airways.

Causes: Inherited gene.

Symptoms: Production of very thick mucus which results in frequent lung infections. The thick mucus also stops digestive enzymes produced by the pancreas from going to the bowels, so there is a problem in absorbing food (malabsorption). The child's sweat will contain a lot of salt and will have loose stools and may not put on any weight or only gain weight slowly.

Investigations: Testing in early pregnancy.

Treatment: Ongoing physiotherapy (at home) to treat and prevent chest infections; antibiotics; pancreas enzymes with every meal to help absorb food; genetic counseling for couples who are known to carry the gene and who want to have children.

14. *Diabetes* – Even very young children may develop Type I diabetes mellitus, where the child's *pancreas* does not produce (enough) insulin. Without insulin, sugar cannot get into the cells, but remains in the blood. There is another type of diabetes, called Type II diabetes, which used to be seen in adults only, but is now diagnosed in children as young as 9 or 10 (refer Chapter 25, page 251 for more information).

Cause: Type 1 diabetes is an auto-immune condition, where the body attacks its own insulin producing cells in the pancreas. Type II diabetes usually follows the pathway of insulin resistance (see Chapter 25).

Symptoms: The cells do not get (enough) sugar to burn for energy, so the child feels weak and tired. The child will have a high blood glucose level (as the sugar cannot get out of the blood and into the cells). The kidneys start leaking sugar into the urine, which in turn draws more fluid from the body into the urine; the child will be very thirsty and urinate very frequently.

Investigations: Fasting blood glucose; glucose tolerance test.

Treatment: Special diet; insulin injections or insulin pump; regular blood sugar testing; changing lifestyle; diabetes education. Diabetes in children poses a special challenge as children are still growing and are generally active (playing sports, running around) which means diet and insulin dosages have to be adjusted all the time to accommodate growth and activity levels.

15. *Ear infection* or *otitis media* – Infection of the middle ear

Causes: Infections travel from nose/throat area to the middle ear via the Eustachian tubes.

Symptoms: Fever; pain in the ear; difficulty hearing (everything sounds 'muffled'); enlarged lymph nodes in the neck; sometimes also a sore throat or runny nose. Can lead to complications such as glue ear, where fluid remains in the middle ear, making hearing difficult or a perforated eardrum/burst eardrum where fluid in the middle ear leads to pressure of the eardrum, and the fluid can burst through the eardrum.

Investigations: Checking ear with the otoscope (see Chapter 23).

Treatment: Antibiotics for bacterial infections; viral infections clear by themselves. *Grommets* (tiny ventilation tubes) may be inserted in the eardrum if children have repeated ear infections. An *adenoidectomy* (surgical removal of the adenoid – lymph tissue in the roof of the throat) may be performed if the doctor feels that repeated ear infections are due to a very large adenoid.

16.   *Eczema* – Also known as atopic dermatitis, is an inflammation of the skin

Causes: Often caused by hypersensitive reactions and common in people with a family history of asthma or hayfever.

Symptoms: Inflammation and or redness of skin.

Investigations: Physical examination; history.

Treatment: Topical creams (including corticosteroid ointments).

17.   *Encephalitis* – Inflammation of the brain tissue.

Causes: Infection; can occur as a complication of measles or mumps.

Symptoms: Headache; fever; drowsiness; unconsciousness; tremors, seizures and convulsions.

Investigations: CT Scan; screen for viruses; blood tests; electroencephalogram or EEG; lumbar puncture (spinal tap) to test the cerebrospinal fluid.

Treatment: Good nursing care; fluids.

18.   *Epilepsy* – Uncontrolled activity of (part of) the brain. There are many different forms of epilepsy, what they have in common is that the child has no control over what happens.

Causes: See Chapter 17.

Symptoms: May be mistaken for febrile convulsions (see below).

Investigations: EEG (electro-encephalogram); skull X-Ray; CT Scan; temperature.

Treatment: Depending on type of epilepsy; sometimes anticonvulsant drugs; very occasionally brain surgery.

19.   *Febrile convulsions* – Results in a loss of consciousness when a child's temperature goes up.

Causes: Sudden rise in temperature

Symptoms: Staring without seeing; drooling; stiffness; jerking and shaking of body and arms/legs (fits/convulsions)

Investigations: History taking; physical examination.

Treatment: Cooling the child by removing clothing; sponging with a wet flannel; giving paracetamol.

20.   *Fetal Alcohol Syndrome* (FAS) – Occurs as a result of the mother drinking alcohol during pregnancy leading to a range of effects on the baby (heart, skeleton, neurological, mental).

Causes: Alcohol consumption during pregnancy.

Symptoms: Various problems involving heart, skeleton, neurological, mental function, including underdeveloped midface, such as small eyes, short nose, thin lips; possibly neurological defects, problems with attention, learning and behavior.

Investigations: History; echocardiogram; physical examination; observation of behaviour.

Treatment: Special education; social support; nurturing environment. Early diagnosis is important.

21.   *German Measles* – refer section on Rubella below.

22.   *Heart Murmurs* – Abnormal heart sounds.
Murmurs may be innocent (e.g. flow murmurs) or may indicate that there is something wrong inside the heart.

Causes: A flow murmur is an innocent murmur caused by the blood flowing rapidly through the heart, especially if the child has a fever. Other causes include narrowed valves (blood makes extra sound as it goes through the narrowing); hole in the heart (hole in the wall separating the left from the right atrium or the left from the right ventricle; a narrowing of the aorta called coarctation of the aorta; Patent Ductus Arteriosus (PDA). The ductus arteriosus is a by-pass which exists before the child is born, to make sure that oxygen-enriched blood from the mother by-passes the lungs and goes straight to the aorta. Soon after birth this by-pass closes up. If this by-pass does not close up, doctors say it is still 'patent' (open) and they can hear the blood flow from the aorta to the pulmonary artery all the time, This can be heard as a continuous murmur.

Symptoms: Abnormal heart sounds.

Investigations: Chest X-Ray; Echocardiogram or cardiac ultrasound; electrocardiogram (ECG); cardiac catheterization and angiography (contrast X-Ray of the blood flow through the heart and the blood vessels in the heart).

Treatment – Heart surgery if there is a defect which causes serious problems or which may lead to damage later on.

23. *Hernia* – Occurs when the contents of the abdominal cavity protrude through a weakness in the wall of the abdomen. Commonly found near the tummy button (*umbilical hernia*) or in the groin (*inguinal hernia*).

Cause: Weakness in the abdominal wall; sudden build-up of pressure inside the abdomen, e.g. sneezing, pushing, heavy lifting.

Symptoms: Slight bulge by tummy button or in the groin.

Investigations: Hernia can be felt (like a lump).

Treatment: Sometimes hernias heal by themselves (spontaneously); sometimes surgical repair is necessary, especially if the contents of the abdomen get stuck in the opening of the hernia and cause further problems.

24. *Impetigo* – Also known as (*School Sores*) *are boils* (skin infections).

Causes: Usually caused by a type of skin bacteria called *staphylococci* (*staph* for short).

Symptoms: Areas on the skin become red, painful and swollen. Pus may form in the centre.

Investigations: Physical examination.

Treatment: Antibiotics; antiseptic soap and nasal cream to kill the staphylococci on the skin and in the nose.

25. *Leukemia* – Literally means 'white blood' (too many immature white blood cells in the blood). In children, the most common form of leukemia is acute (sudden) lymphoblastic leukemia. In this type of leukemia, the bone marrow produces too many lymphoblasts (immature young lymphocytes). Lymphocytes are a type of white blood cell which are involved in fighting infection. Another form of leukemia called myeloid leukemia usually occurs in slightly older children (see Chapter 20, page 208).

Causes: Ionizing radiation (nuclear energy); exposure to certain chemicals, pesticides; solvents; electromagnetic fields.

Symptoms: Infections; paleness and tiredness; enlarged liver, spleen and lymph glands. Children may also have anemia (lack of red blood cells) and a shortage of platelets, leading to a tendency to bleed.

Investigations: Blood tests; bone marrow test.

Treatment: Chemotherapy to kill the leukemic cells; blood transfusions, platelet transfusions; antibiotics; bone marrow transplant (usually using healthy bone-marrow from a compatible donor); radiotherapy to head and spine to prevent leukemic cells 'hiding out' in those places. Once the child is 'in consolidated remission' (no leukemic cells in the blood for a while), maintenance treatment is given for another couple of years.

26.   *Measles* – Viral infection in childhood.

Cause: Virus infection spread by airborne droplets.

Symptoms: Fever; runny nose; red and watery eyes; *intolerance of light*; cough; small white spots in the mouth (Koplik's spots); red *rash* all over body, starting from forehead and behind ears and soon spreading all over body. May lead to complications such as *viral pneumonia; encephalitis* or *secondary bacterial infection*s e.g. *bronchopneumonia* or middle ear infections.

Investigations: Physical examination; history.

Treatment: Keeping child home for 10 days.

27.   *Meningitis* – Infection of the meninges, the protective layer surrounding the brain.

Cause: Virus or bacterial infection.

Symptoms: Fever; headache and neck stiffness; drowsiness; floppiness; refusing feeds; high-pitched cry when changing diapers; unconsciousness; restricted movement of the head (e.g. impossible to lower the chin onto the chest; raising the legs hurts); meningitis rash.

Investigations: See Chapter 17, Page 173).

Treatment: Good nursing for viral meningitis; hospital admission and immediate course of intravenous antibiotics for bacterial meningitis.

28.   *Mumps* – Viral infection affecting the parotid gland

Cause: Virus infection.

Symptoms: Painful swelling of the parotid gland (which produces saliva) just in front of the ear; slight fever. Can lead to complications such as viral pancreatitis; orchitis (painful swelling and inflammation of the testicles); viral meningitis

Investigations: Physical examination; history.

Treatment: No specific treatment, child is usually okay after about 2 weeks.

29.   *Pyloric Stenosis* – See Chapter 26

30.   *Rheumatic Fever* – An immune response in which symptoms mimic rheumatic condition but may also involve heart valve damage. In some people, a strep throat (throat infection by special strain of Streptococcus bacteria) is followed by inflammation of joints and heart valves. In these people, the bacteria also cause antibodies to 'attack' the body's own joints and heart valves. Occasionally, Rheumatic Fever involves myocarditis (inflammation of heart muscle).

Cause: A very aggressive type of streptococcus ('strep') bacterium.

Symptoms: Sore throat, which may be followed by fever; joint pains (arthritis); carditis (inflammation of the heart); palpitations; heart murmur; chest pain; high temperature; a high ESR (indicating inflammation); sore joints the heart valves have been damaged, they may get tired on exertion. May lead to complications including heart valve disease (usually the mitral valve, sometimes also the aortic valve, the tricuspid valve and the pulmonary valve).

Investigations: Blood tests to check for streptococcal infection/antibodies; throat swab (to test for streptococcal infection); ESR (Erythrocyte Sedimentation Rate); ECG (electrocardiogram); Chest X-Ray; echocardiogram (to check for valve defects)

Treatment: Bed-rest until ESR and temperature are normal; Regular antibiotics to prevent repeat infection especially before dental treatment and before surgery; some patients may need heart valve replacement surgery penicillin before surgery and before dental treatment.

31.   *Rubella or German Measles* – Airborne infection caused by a virus.

Cause: Virus infection spread by airborne droplets.

Symptoms: Very light rash. Birth defects to the unborn child if the mother is infected within the first three months of pregnancy.

Investigations: Physical examination.

Treatment: Keeping child home for a few days. All children are normally immunized against rubella; all girls should be immunized to prevent them from contracting rubella when they get pregnant later on in their lives.

32.   *Scarlet Fever* – An acute infection of the throat.

Cause: Special strain of *Streptococcus* bacteria (*Streptococcus Pyogenes*).

Symptoms: Cough; sore throat; fever; enlarged tonsils; all over body rash, starting behind the ears and spreading all over skin. Can lead to middle ear infection; sinusitis; rheumatic fever and acute glomerulonephritis (infection of the *glomeruli*, the tiny blood filters in the kidneys).

Investigations: Throat swab.

Treatment: Antibiotics.

33.　*School Sores* – Please see Impetigo, Chapter 13, Page 134.

34.　*Seizures* (*convulsions*) – Uncontrolled shaking and jerking of body, arms and legs.

Causes: High fever; sudden increase in body temperature; epilepsy; cerebral palsy (if brain damage present); brain tumor.

Symptoms: Shaking and jerking of body; rigid face; no response when child is called by name.

Investigations: Find out cause and treat accordingly.

Treatments: Depending on cause, e.g. reducing body temperature in febrile convulsions.

35.　*Tonsillitis* – inflammation or infection of the tonsils, lymph tissue on either side of the throat.

Cause: Usually a bacterial infection

Symptoms: Sore throat; cough. May lead to *upper respiratory tract* infection.

Investigations: Throat swab to check for bacteria.

Treatment: Antibiotics; tonsillectomy (only if tonsils are constantly infected or very frequently infected).

36.　*Vomiting and diarrhea* – Often occur together, though not always.

Causes:
– Congenital blockage somewhere in the gastro-intestinal tract can be the cause in newborn babies in the first few days after birth
– Regurgitating food is usually of no significance, especially if only very small amounts of milk are brought up. Regurgitation can also be due to hiatus hernia – top of stomach does not close properly and food goes back into gullet (reflux)
– Pyloric stenosis, in which case there may be projectile vomiting
– Emotional upsets can lead to vomiting, especially if the child feels unable to talk about what is upsetting him/her
– Motion sickness when travelling by bus, boat, car
– Too much food (especially at birthday parties, etc)
– Gastro-enteritis – inflammation of the lining of stomach and bowels, which may be caused by a virus, or by food poisoning; stomachache and diarrhea
– Appendicitis – often starts with vomiting and pain around the tummy button; pain later moves to upper right-hand part of the abdomen

Diarrhea usually accompanies vomiting in gastro-enteritis or in food intolerances (e.g. lactose intolerance; *gluten* (a wheat protein) intolerance in *coeliac disease*). Both can lead to dehydration and a disturbance of the electrolyte balance

Symptoms: Throwing up feeds; runny stools.

Investigations: Checking fluid balance; taking a stool sample.

Treatment: The main complication of diarrhoea and vomiting is *dehydration* and a change in the body's *electrolyte balance*. A lot of children around the world still die of dehydration as a result of vomiting and diarrhoea. This is why vomiting and diarrhoea should always be taken seriously in children. Parents should make sure the child still passes good amounts of urine, and should give the child *rehydration fluid*. This can be bought from the chemist or made at home. In serious cases children will be admitted to hospital and given *intravenous fluids*.

Summary of main points

This chapter has offered a brief overview of:

- Neonatal Intensive Care Units and common reasons for newborns to be admitted to such units
- Equipment encountered in Neonatal Intensive Care settings
- A large range of common childhood health problems, with symptoms, causes, investigations and treatment options

---

Chapter 14

Speech Language Therapy

By Dr Linda Hand, University of Auckland

In Speech Language Therapy (SLT) the focus is on identifying problems in communication rather than to enable communication. Professionals involved in SLT include Neurologist and Speech Language Therapist. Speech Language Therapists are also known as Speech Pathologists or Speech Therapists.

1.   Common terminology

aphasia	(Literally means no-speech) disorder of ability to speak, read, write or understand language
articulation	How speech organs are involved in producing sounds and speech
CVA	Cerebrovascular Accident (stroke)
dysarthria	Motor speech disorder resulting from a neurological injury. (dys = diffcult; arthr- = articulating)
dysphagia	Swallowing problems
dyspraxia	The brain has problems coordinating movement of the body parts needed for speech (lips, jaws, tongue)
phonology	Study of the sound systems of a language
semantics	Study of meaning
Speech Language Pathologist	Specialist in communication and swallowing disorders. In some countries SLPs are known as Speech Language Therapists (SLT)
Speech (Language) Therapist	See SLP above
syntax	Study of the sentence structure of a language
TBI	Traumatic Brain Injury, brain damaged as a result of an accident

2. Communication disorders

Communication disorders can occur from birth to old age and may include:

- Speech/Phonological (e.g. 'dutty' for 'cup'; 'tie' for 'sky'; seen in- dysarthrias)
- Voice (quality of the voice)
- Stuttering (also called dysfluency)
- Swallowing
- Augmentative and alternative communication systems

Language disorders are also a form of communication disorder and may arise for a range of reasons and can include many and varied features. Common causes for language disorders include damage to the brain (e.g. TBI, brain injury or CVA), congenital disorders and developmental disorders (including autism). 'Symptoms' of language disorders may include speakers

- getting words around the wrong way (e.g. *'the horse big'* where you would expect *'the big horse'*).
- getting words muddled (*"the trelly smash"* instead of *'the smelly trash"*).
- getting the wrong words, or cannot find words (*"it's the – oh, whaddya call it – the – um – thingy – you know – corner – no no – come- come – oh what is it?"*).
- appearing to understand what is said (nodding, smiling), but being unable to follow instructions.
- giving responses that have nothing to do with the question (this can be because they have not understood, but sometimes they do understand but are unable to formulate a relevant answer). Such answers may be inappropriate (e.g. too loud, too soft, include swearwords and insults); endlessly repetitive; or be giving the wrong emotional response, such as laughing at a sad story (may again be a comprehension problem, but can be at the level of emotional or empathic grasp rather than language comprehension per se).

3. Assessment

Assessment is a dynamic process, which involves the SLP or SLT gathering information about the client from various sources. Interpreters may be asked to interpret during:

- History taking/discussing the problem
- Formal tests
- Informal assessments/functional tasks

- Conversation (to provide data on the person's language and speech)
- Intervention (speech and language therapy)
- Feedback and discussion (with patient and his/her significant others)

4.   Therapy

Therapy (treatment) can be aimed at the level of impairment or at trying to fix the body part, or body function, that is creating the speech or language problem. Therapy often involves repeated practice of discrete tasks in order to develop new/different muscle or neural pathways and may involve:

- How to produce sounds
- Parents taking an active role by talking to their children in certain ways that will help their child's language development. Likewise spouses and other family members can have an active role to play in therapy for adults
- Playing games that require speech sounds, language structures, or words

"Cup, *cup*... Please pick up the cup..."

Figure 14.1. Speech language therapy

5.   Some notes for interpreters and translators

> "Speech Pathologists should be able to assess, diagnose and intervene with communication disorders in a language they do not speak – with the essential help of interpreters".
>   (Hand 2007)

Interpreting in the area of SLT differs from other types of interpreting in that, rather than conveying *what* the speaker is saying, the interpreter may also need to convey *how* things are being said. In other words, the interpreter may also be expected to provide metalinguistic information, i.e. information about speech and language.

Speech language therapists work with clients who have language and or speech disorders and interpreters need to be able to somehow 'reproduce' or comment on the way their clients communicate (Langdon 2002; Langdon & Cheng 2002; Merlini & Favaron 2005, p. 264). This requires a very precise use of vocabulary, starting with the words 'language' and 'speech', which are used in very specific meanings by Speech Language Therapists. One interpreter erroneously translated "Tell me about your child's language" as "How well does he speak?", a question with a completely different and much narrower focus.

The speech language therapist will need to know these speech and language 'features', and it may be important to know how much, and in detail, rather than generally. Langdon (2002:7) stresses the importance of *verbatim translation* of the patients' utterances during assessment sessions by saying: "do not edit what is said, and do not change sounds". Yet Langdon (2002:7) also urges interpreters to *explain to speech pathologists what is said versus what should have been said*, thereby helping them recognize the extent and causes of the language impairment and provide appropriate feedback. Gentile et al. (1996: 125–135) further clarify that the interpreter's metalinguistic descriptions may refer to *syntax, phonology and semantics*." (italics added) (Merlini & Favaron 2005, p. 265).

In addition many formal SLT tests are not appropriate to be interpreted because they are normally very specific to one particular language. This should be accounted for by the SLP or SLT, if not the interpreter should convey why a test is inappropriate or will not work.

When interpreting during formal tests, interpreters need to make sure they avoid:

- Changing the length, structure, kind of vocabulary (e.g. easier for more difficult terms) or references to pictures
- Explaining tasks
- 'Helping' the client; for instance by tapping the picture, looking at the picture ('eye pointing'), adding gestures the SLT did not use, repeating words, instructions (where the SLP only gave them once), rephrasing

When interpreting during informal or functional assessment tasks, interpreters should avoid:

- Not realizing the significance of what might look like 'chat' (but is actually 'data collection')
- Reverting to 'explaining the meaning'

Likewise when interpreting a client's history or discussing the client's problems, interpreters need to make sure they use the correct terms and reflect the open (non-directive) nature of the SLT's questions and avoid being sidetracked into discussions with the clients ('what she meant was …').

During conversation interpreters need to convey what the client says, and what is unusual about it.

During feedback and discussion, interpreters should be able to cope with the problem of the meaning of terms and should convey concerns back and forth (i.e. don't try to meet them yourself).

Summary of main points

- say exactly what the SLT says, with the exact gesture and/or reference to materials
- convey back exactly what the client says, letting the SLT adjust what they say if needed
- avoid explaining to the client
- explain to the SLT if needed
- if asked questions by parents/family members, convey to SLT to answer

---

Chapter 15

Mental health

Mental Health Interpreting can be a difficult field to work in. It may be difficult to interpret for clients who suffer from mental health problems which give them a limited or distorted view of what is going on. Clients suffering from episodes of paranoid psychosis may accuse the interpreter of twisting their words or of 'being out to get them' and of conspiring against them with the medical staff.

Cultural differences may lead the patient to make references to beliefs or practices which are not shared by mental health professionals in the country the patient finds himself in. The patient may have to clarify these during (de)briefing sessions. Aside from involving issues of a crosscultural nature, mental health interpreting in refugee settings may place an additional load on interpreters due to them having to interpret the trauma story – in the first person singular (Bot 2005, 2007; Crezee, Jülich, Hayward, in press).

In other cases, interpreting assignments may pose a problem due to the fact that the client is depressed to the extent of being totally withdrawn and unwilling or unable to communicate. In some cases, the client may be abusing the interviewer and/or the interpreter. Again, it is important to interpret whatever the client says. The fact that the client is swearing, and even the exact nature of the swearwords, may give the mental health professional an important indication of what is going on in the client's mind.

With regard to the terminology used it should be said that, even though psychiatric textbooks do not make easy reading due to all the specialized terms, interviews between mental health professionals and clients often involve simple, everyday language, such as: "How are you feeling?" and "I cannot sleep, because they are out to get me". Hence the main aim of this chapter is to ensure the interpreter is familiar with some of the mental health issues clients may be struggling with, so as to enable them to understand the background of any mental health interviews they may be involved in.

This chapter will give a very brief overview of some of the most common types of mental illnesses and personality disorders. Please note that these terms will usually not be used in the interviews themselves, i.e. the psychiatrist is not very likely to tell the client "You have a schizoid personality disorder with paranoid components". The overview merely serves to give interpreters some background information as to the disorders, the better to understand some of the patient's utterances and responses.

Finally, mental health professionals rely quite heavily on the interview with the client for assessment and diagnosis. They cannot simply order an X-ray or blood test to find out additional information. Therefore, the golden rule is, once again, to interpret whatever the patient says, no matter how odd this may sound to the interpreter.

1.   Latin and Greek roots

auto	self
bi	two
bipolar	two extremes (two opposite poles)
delude	to make someone/yourself believe something that is not true
delusion	false personal belief
delusional	having false personal beliefs; believing things that are not true
depress	to push down
hallucinate	to feel/hear/see things which are not there
hallucination	feeling/seeing/hearing things which are not there
idio	own; individual
psyche	mind
phrenos	brain
schizo	split
	Please note: schizophrenia does not equal 'split personality'; the word schizophrenia is therefore somewhat misleading
therapy	treatment

2.   Briefing and debriefing

It is important that the mental health professional take the time to (de)brief the interpreter. During the briefing session the professional may talk to the interpreter about the objective of the interview, the client's history/background and any crosscultural issues. During the debriefing session, the professional may ask the interpreter if there was anything else the interpreter noted about the client's choice of words, intonation, or pitch that may have carried meaning. It may be appropriate for the interpreter to comment on certain non-verbal aspects of communication, such as gestures, posture, physical space and facial expressions.

The health professional may also ask the interpreter to give him/her some general information on the client's cultural background. The interpreter should emphasize that he or she can only provide some very general cultural background information, and from the interpreter's own point of view. The interpreter should also stress that no two individuals are quite the same and that factors such as personality, age, gender, religion, amount of exposure to other cultures, length of time in the new country and individual life experiences may have shaped the individual to a large extent. Hence the interpreter should phrase his cultural clarification by first stating: "What I am going to say will be objective, a lot will depend on the patient's age, religion, …(etc), however, in general …". (Health Media 1988).

3.   Behaviors and their implications for the interpreter

Some conditions are associated with behaviors and speech patterns which may confuse the interpreter. It may help the interpreter to know that certain behaviours and utterances are commonly observed in certain conditions. The interpreter should interpret everything that is said exactly as it is said.

- *Psychosis.* Psychotic patients may show signs of paranoia as well; they may also feel that they are receiving special guidance from above. They may say "A voice told me to take the next street, because he wanted to protect me." Again, it is important to interpret this faithfully.
- *Schizophrenia and psychotic episodes.* Sometimes schizophrenic or psychotic patients hear voices and talk back to them. These clients may seem to listen to 'voices' in different corners of the room and reply to those voices, looking in the directions the voices appear to be coming from. The interpreter should simply interpret what they say.
- *Suicidal patients.* If the patient is thinking about different ways to kill himself or herself, the interpreter should interpret these utterances faithfully. The interpreter should NEVER decide to not interpret these suicidal thoughts simply because the interpreter is against suicide or believes suicide is bad. It is absolutely essential that the professional be aware of these suicidal thoughts, so that the patient can be given all due care and attention.
- *Disorganized thought patterns.* Sometimes clients can go on and on, expressing seemingly nonsensical thoughts. Such clients may talk non-stop and may not appear to make any sense. They may talk about pigs singing beautiful songs and voting for the conservative party in green underpants on tropical islands, drinking coffee from beer mugs. It is important that the interpreter interpret this stream of consciousness (any seemingly unconnected thoughts that come up) exactly as they are voiced. It may be best to interpret simultaneously, as it is difficult to interpret disorganized thinking consecutively, precisely because it does not make sense and is therefore difficult to remember. Interpreting thoughts accurately may offer the health professional important insights as to what is going on inside the client's mind.

4. Some mental health professionals

Psychiatrist. Medical doctor who has specialized in mental illnesses or psychiatry; psychiatrists are able to prescribe medication.

Psychologist. Not a medical doctor, but someone who has studied the workings of the human mind and completed a (Master's or Ph.D.) degree in psychology at university; psychologists are *unable to prescribe medication.*

Licensed Professional Counselor. Counselor who has completed Master's or Ph.D. studies and who is licensed to practise independently in the US (regulations will vary per state); a similar system exists in some other countries.

Counselor. This is not a protected profession in some countries. Counselors may have studied psychology or counseling, or may be experienced registered nurses specializing in counseling.

Psychiatric and Mental Health Nurse Practitioner. Advanced Nurse Practitioner specializing in mental health.

Psychotherapist. A psychotherapist may have a Master's or doctoral degree; Graduate diploma in Psychotherapy (some countries).

Behavior analyst. A behavior analyst may hold a Master's or Doctoral degree in behavioural psychology.

5. Some common therapeutic approaches

- *Classic psychotherapy* also called Psychodynamic therapy -therapist and a client talk about the client's problems, often going back to the client's childhood to find out where problems have come from.
- *Cognitive Behavioural Therapy* (*CBT*) – tries to help people understand how (irrational) thoughts can influence the way they behave, and changing these thoughts can change their beahaviour. CBT is often used to treat extreme fears (phobias), anxiety, depression and addictions.
- *Dialectal Behavioural Therapy* (*DBT*) – aimed at teaching clients skills for coping with stress, managing emotions and improving relationships with others. DBT involves skills training, acknowledging thoughts that are normally avoided, cognitive therapy and amending behaviour. Mindfulness (being aware of where you are and what your body is doing without having any particular feelings about this) is an important part of DBT.
- *Humanistic Therapy* – focuses on the innate goodness of human beings and their ability to overcome a fixed pattern of unhelpful behaviours (based on their past lives) into a more helpful pattern of behaviours.
- *Mindfulness* – focuses on living in the moment.

6.   Common reasons for counseling

Common reasons for counseling may include grief counseling (following a loss, change or death); relationship counseling (families, marriages, partnerships) and addiction counseling (Internet addiction, gambling, sex addiction; substance abuse).

7.   Some commonly used pharmaceutical drugs

Anticonvulsants. These may be given to calm and stabilize the person's moods.
Mood stabilizer. Drugs that act to stabilize mood; these may include tranquilizers and anticonvulsant medication.
Antidepressants. These include Serotonin Selective Reuptake Inhibitors (SSRIs); Tricyclic Anti-depressants (TCAs); Serotonin and Noradrenaline Reuptake Inhibitors (SNRIs); MAO Inhibitors MAOIs (by tablet or patch, to reduce side-effects)
Antipsychotics. Tranquilizing medication which works against psychotic symptoms such as hallucinations and delusions.

8.   Mental illness

The WHO defines mental health as 'a state of well-being in which an individual realizes his or her own abilities, can cope with the normal stresses of life, can work productively and is able to make a contribution to his or her community' (WHO, n.d.).

Most mental health professionals follow the American Psychiatric Association's (APA) Diagnostic and Statistical Manual of Mental Disorders (DSM-IV-TR 2000). The DSM-IV distinguishes between a large range of mental disorders, including:

1. Anxiety disorders – including: Generalized Anxiety Disorder (GAD); panic attacks; Obsessive Compulsive Disorder (OCD); Phobias.
2. Affective disorders – disorders which affect the patient's emotions, including depressive and manic disorders and Bipolar (formerly Manic Depressive) Disorder.
3. Personality disorders
4. Psychotic disorders – including Psychosis/Psychotic Episode and Schizophrenia
5. Dementias – loss of memory and other mental functions, e.g. in Alzheimer's disease

Interested readers are referred to the DSM-IV-TR (American Psychiatric Association 2000) or the DSM-V (American Psychiatric Association 2013) which uses a multidimensional approach including clinical syndromes, developmental disorders and personality disorders, physical conditions, severity of psychosocial stressors and highest level of functioning.

9.   Some mental health disorders

For ease of use, only some of the more common disorders are listed here in alphabetical order, rather than under their APA classification. Developmental disorders such as Autism spectrum disorders (ASD) and Attention Deficit Hyperactivity Disorder (ADHD) have been included in Chapter 13, because they are often first diagnosed in childhood.

1.   *Acute Stress Disorder*
As for PTSD, but symptoms last for less than 30 days.

2.   *Anxiety disorders*
See under Generalized anxiety disorder and panic disorder below.

3.   *Bipolar (Affective) Disorder*
Formerly known as Manic Depressive disorder.

What happens. This is a major psychological disorder which is characterized by extreme mood swings, ranging from mania (feeling *invincible*) to depression (feeling *down*) to feeling elements of both these moods. Moving from *high* to *low* is known as cycling.
      People with bipolar disorder may move from one extreme to the other, or feel a little bit of both extremes at the same time.

Symptoms:
      Manic phase. Feeling 'on top of the world', show exaggerated emotions and feelings of extreme happiness; in this phase patients seem to have boundless energy, do not seem to need any sleep and may be agitated, hyperactive and very talkative;. They cannot concentrate very well and may have inflated self-esteem and delusions of grandeur ('I am a champion'). Sometimes patients are hypomanic (less severe than manic).
      Depressive phase. This phase is the opposite of the manic phase; the patient feels sad, lonely, unworthy, guilty and has very low self-esteem. He or she cannot seem to get anything done and is apathetic and listless.

Causes: Range of environmental, biologic, genetic, psychological and interpersonal factors.

Treatment: Mood stabilizing medication such as lithium, anti-psychotic medication, anti-depressants and sometimes also anticonvulsant drugs.

4.   *Brief psychotic episode* – see under *Psychosis*

5.   *Depression* – comes from a word that literally means: 'pushing down'.
Please note: depression is a very general term which can cover a very wide range of moods and situations

What happens. Clinical depression can be an abnormal emotional state with exaggerated feelings of sadness, worthlessness, emptiness and hopelessness. Depression can be a normal response of sadness and despair following a loss.

Causes of major depression: Depression can be triggered by a wide range of factors, including traumatic life experiences; genetic disorders; nutritional disorders (e.g. a Vitamin B deficiency); medication; disorders of the central nervous system (e.g. Parkinson's Disease); disorders of the endocrine system (e.g. hypothyroidism); obesity; infections; cancer.

Symptoms: Depressed people may be apathetic (literally: no feelings) and withdrawn; they may either overeat or lose all interest in food.

Types of depression
As with many other mental illnesses, clients may show a mixture of symptoms.

In *neurotic depression*, the individual is being very hard on himself. This can be an exaggerated response to a stressful situation (such as being left by a loved one).

In *psychotic depression*, the individual may not be able to separate the 'real' from the 'unreal' and have hallucinations, delusions and confusion.

Postnatal depression – some researchers suggest this is triggered by a rapid drop in the female hormone progesterone after childbirth. Postnatal depression is either treated with antidepressants, talk therapy, support or with natural progesterone. In serious cases, the woman may develop puerperal psychosis, which means she may lose all sense of reality and be at risk of harming herself or her child.

6.   *Eating disorders*
What happens:
In *anorexia nervosa*, patients starve or purge themselves (laxatives; induced vomiting) out of an untrue belief that they are overweight; weight may drop to dangerously low levels.

In *bulimia*, patients binge eat followed by purging; otherwise similar to anorexia.

Treatment: Therapy (e.g. CBT); closely monitored food intake.

7.   *Generalized Anxiety Disorder (GAD)*

What happens: Ongoing and sometimes disabling anxiety about life in general.

Cause: Unknown, although this disorder tends to run in families.

Symptoms: Constant worrying; mild heart palpitations; dizziness.

Treatment: Talk therapy (revisiting childhood); CBT.

8.   *Obsessive Compulsive Disorder (OCD)*
What happens. Disorder of checking and doubting. Patients are constantly troubled by obsessions and carrying out repetitive acts to reduce their anxiety (e.g. constant handwashing or cleaning).

Cause: Unknown; tends to run in families.

Symptoms: Performing the same repetitive acts over and over again, thereby wasting a lot of time.

9. *Phobias*
What happens. Intense and paralyzing fear of situations, e.g. an intense fear of mice, spiders, dogs. Some phobias include:

Agoraphobia. An intense fear of leaving the safety of one's house, unless accompanied by a 'safe person'

Social phobia. An intense fear of not being able to cope in social situations

Body dysmorphia. Untrue beliefs about (shape of) own body

10. *Panic attacks*
What happens: People worry that if they face a particular situation they will panic and lose control. They may avoid driving across bridges, going up escalators, walking past dogs.

Symptoms: Heart palpitations; disordered breathing; tingling around mouth and fingers; chest pain.

Treatment: CBT or DBT; breathing exercises (short breath in, long breath out, so carbon monoxide cannot accumulate and make symptoms worse).

11. *Post Traumatic Stress Disorder* (*PTSD*)
What happens: Type of anxiety disorder that may affect people who have seen or experienced a traumatic event involving (the threat of) injury or death; very common in war veterans, survivors of rape and assault.

Symptoms: (i) Reliving the traumatic event: recurrent intrusive thoughts, nightmares, flashbacks; (ii) Avoiding any possible reminders of the traumatic event: feeling numb, flat, detached, not interested in normal activities; (iii) Hyper arousal – startling easily, concentration problems, irritability, sleeping problems, hyper-alertness. Depression, alcohol and drug abuse are common.

Treatment: Talk therapy, support groups.

12. *Psychosis*
What happens: During a psychotic episode, the person is unable to distinguish the 'real' from the 'unreal' and unable to separate normal thoughts from abnormal thoughts; delusions and hallucinations (e.g. hearing voices) may occur.

Factors: Stress; childhood trauma; (early) cannabis use; changes to brain and brain chemicals (especially dopamine).

Treatment: Antipsychotic drugs.

13.   *Schizophrenia*
What happens: Frequent psychotic episodes, but symptoms last longer than 6 months. Men are often first diagnosed between the ages of 15 and 25, while women are usually affected in their twenties or thirties.

Symptoms include:

Disorganized thinking. Thoughts may come and go so quickly that the patient is unable to get 'a grip on them'. Patients may be easily distracted and 'jump' from one topic to the next; others may find it totally impossible to follow these thought processes

Delusions. False and illogical beliefs; feelings that 'people are out to get me' OR feelings of grandeur ('I am a champion")

Hallucinations. Hearing voices, seeing people or things; feeling fingers touching the body.

Treatment: Medication such as anti-psychotic drugs; individual psychotherapy; learning social skills; problem solving; learning independent life skills; family therapy (stable family environment is important).

Summary of main points

This chapter has given a brief overview of interpreting in mental health, including:

- the importance of briefing and debriefing
- health professionals involved
- commonly used thereapies
- some common mental health disorders

Chapter 16

Oncology

Proof read by Dr J. Crezee, Academic Medical Center,
University of Amsterdam

Oncology is the branch of medicine that deals with various types of cancer. Oncologists are doctors who specialize in the treatment of cancer.

The word cancer still has a lot of negative connotations. The fact that people still, rightly or wrongly, associate cancer with death, can make interpreting in this area very difficult. In fact, there are many different types of cancer and both treatment and outlook can vary enormously. It is important to understand these differences and the variations in outlook.

This chapter will attempt to give some general background information on cancer, investigations, typing and staging as well as treatment options.

1. Cancer

Throughout our body the cells in different organs are designed to do a particular job(s). e.g. lung cells are different from skin cells. The centre of each cell contains a blueprint for new cells i.e. vital information as to exactly what new cells should look like and on how they should behave.

Sometimes, and for reasons unknown, something goes wrong and different new cells start to grow. These cells do not look like the normal cells and do not function like normal cells. They can be benign (not cancerous) or malignant (cancerous).

Cancerous cells usually grow and multiply very fast (compared to normal cells). This is a problem because they spread and take over the organ affected, pushing the normal cells out of the way and interfering with their normal functioning.

By way of analysis, cancer cells may be compared to weeds, because like weeds, they grow very fast and are not useful. If weeds are not removed or destroyed with 'weed-killer' they can take over the whole garden and choke the normal plants. Similarly, if cancer cells are not destroyed, they can take over the body and 'choke' the normal cells.

Cancer cells can spread in two ways, by:

–   *Invasion*, where cancerous cells grow into neighboring tissues and organs. This may be compared to someone having some weeds in his garden, close to the boundary line, and these weeds invade or grow into the weed-free neighboring property,

or:

–   *Secondaries* involve new 'colonies' starting up: Cancer cells can spread through the blood or lymph system. This may be compared to 'a river carrying weeds downstream', which then start to grow somewhere else. It may also be compared to birds carrying seeds over to another area. These new growths are known as *metastases*.

2.   Investigations

–   *History* – Investigations will usually start with a thorough history. The health professional will ask the patient about symptoms including pain; appetite; weight loss; bleeding; vomiting; coughing; history of employment; social background, family history, etc.
–   *Physical examination* – Doctors may feel for lumps, size of organs, fluid retention and swelling of lymph nodes. They will judge the patient's appearance and listen to the patient's heart and lungs.
–   *Tests* – A number of tests may be ordered, including blood tests.
    Blood tests: In recent years cancer specific blood tests (tumor markers) have been developed which can give the doctor an indication of whether the patient might have a specific form of cancer. Some better known tumor markers include PSA (prostate specific antigen) and Ca-125 (may give an indication of whether the patient might have ovarian cancer). Other tumor markers have been patented for other types of cancer.
–   *Imaging* – The patient may be referred on to a specialist or outpatients' clinic for further investigations, including X-Rays and contrast X-Rays. Contrast X-Rays may include IVU's (for imaging of the urinary system) or ERCP's (for imaging of the gall-duct system).
    A number of increasingly sophisticated scanning methods can be used for precise imaging. These include PET scans; total body scans; VQ Scans; CT scans (also called CAT scans where C(A)T stands for Computerized Tomography or Computer Aided Tomography); ultrasounds; Doppler tests; mammogram, thermograms and so on. MRI scans (Magnetic Resonance Imaging) can also produce very detailed images of the body, including the soft tissues.

- *Endoscopies* – Endoscopies are procedures where the doctor has a look inside an organ(s) by inserting a fiber optic tube. Tubes may be inserted through existing body openings. Types of endoscopies include:
  Bronchoscopy. Tube inserted through the windpipe into the bronchi.
  Colonoscopy. Tube inserted through the rectum into the large intestine or colon.
  Colposcopy. Tube inserted through the vagina to look at vagina and cervix.
  Cystoscopy. Tube inserted through the urethra into the bladder.
  Esophagoscopy. Tube inserted into the gullet.
  Gastroscopy. A flexible tube is inserted through the gullet, down into the stomach, to allow the professional to have a look at the inside of the stomach.
  Hysteroscopy. Tube inserted through vagina and cervix, into the womb.
- *Laparoscopy* – In other cases, the surgeon may need to create a small hole not unlike a key hole and insert the tube through this. This is done in a laparoscopy (procedure where the doctor looks inside the abdominal cavity).
- *Open surgery* – Sometimes open surgery is performed to confirm a suspicion of cancer. The surgeon makes an incision to open the body and have a look inside.
- *Biopsy* – Act of taking a tissue sample. Biopsies can be done by way of fine needle biopsy; hook wire biopsy; during endoscopy or laparoscopy; Smear test (some cells are scraped away from the surface (e.g. the surface of the cervix).

3.   Diagnosis – Typing and staging

The diagnosis 'cancer' is usually reached on the basis of history, i.e. on what the patient tells the doctor and a number of tests. Tests are primarily aimed at typing (finding out what type of cancer cell is involved) and staging (finding out what stage the cancer is at, how far it has spread).

Typing involves obtaining a sample of the cancer cells, typically obtained by means of biopsies (removing some living cells, refer above). An operation or endoscopy may be needed to remove some living cells. Examples of endoscopy (looking inside) are listed under Investigations above.

Once the sample of cells has been removed, it is sent to a pathologist (histologist, a tissue specialist or cytologist, a cell specialist) who looks at the cell under the microscope to see if there are any cancer cells and, if so, what type of cells they are. Typing of the cells is important, because it influences the approach/treatment as different types of cancer respond to different types of treatment.

In respect to staging, different types of staging or classification apply to different types of cancer, however a commonly used staging system is the 'TNM' classification. In this staging classificaton system 'T' describes the size of the tumor and whether it has invaded nearby tissue on a scale of 1 to 4, 'N' describes the degree of regional lymph nodes involvement on a scale of 0 to 3, and 'M' describes whether the tumor has metastasized (spread) ('0' = not and '1' is yes). For instance T4N0M0 stands for a tumor that has invaded neighboring organs but without regional lymph node involvement and without metastases.

For some tumor types specific or earlier staging scales are used, this may be confusing. Bowel cancer, for example, is usually staged according to the Dukes classification (Dukes A, B, C, D with A, meaning that the cancer is confined to the lining of the bowel and D indicating that there are metastases elsewhere, for example in the liver). Lymphomas may be classified as Stage I, II, III or IV, depending on the spread of the cancer.

The classification of cervical cancer can be confusing, as two different stages are also distinguished, with the earliest pre-cancerous cell changes are described as CIN-1, CIN-2 and CIN-3, while developments beyond these (very early stages) are described as cervical cancer stage I to IV.

It is very difficult to take a general approach to staging, as a lot depends on the condition of the patient, the type of cell involved, the success of previous treatment, and so on.

4.   Treatment

Treatment may be *curative* (aimed at achieving a cure) or *palliative* (aimed at lessening the patient's suffering only), and these terms can be very difficult to interpret.

When the patient is terminally ill (when death seems inevitable), health professionals will decide on the best palliative approach, which may involve radiotherapy, to shrink the tumor, or sustained release morphine, to control the pain.

While researchers around the world are still working on new approaches to cancer, some of the most common treatment options to date include:

– *Surgery* – To surgically remove cancer cells. Surgery is often no longer an option when the tumor has invaded neighboring organs.
– *Radiotherapy* – Concentrated dose of radiation is applied to a specific area. Radiotherapy may also be used to shrink benign tumors. Radiotherapy may cause side-effects like nausea and irritated skin.
– *Chemotherapy* – Treatment of cancer by chemicals which are intended to 'search and destroy' predominantly cancer cells. Chemotherapy may have certain side-effects such as hairloss and gastro-intestinal complaints such as vomiting and diarrhea.
– *Hormone therapy* – Some cancers are very sensitive to hormones and shrink when treated with appropriate hormones (e.g. prostate cancer is sometimes treated with estrogen). In other cases doctors may withhold hormones, e.g. estrogen may be withheld if the patient is suspected of having breast cancer.

- *Brachytherapy* – Radio-active sources may be temporarily or permanently implanted in the area where the tumor is in order to destroy the cancer from close by. In order to prevent radiation from affecting health professionals and visitors, these patients are often nursed in isolation.
- *Hyperthermia* – Overheating cancer cells in order to destroy them and also to help maintain the effects of radiotherapy. Hyperthermia is now also combined with chemotherapy, where chemotherapy is inside little balls of fat which are placed where the cancer is. Hyperthermia is then used to melt the fat so the chemotherapy medicine can work directly on the cancer.
- *Immunotherapy* – The use of agents to boost the immune response of the body against the cancer cells.
- *Laser treatment* – Using laser to burn away cancer cells, allowing new cells to grow up from the basal membrane.
- *Cryotherapy* – To freeze off cancer cells, e.g. liquid nitrogen treatment for superficial skin cancers.

5.   Common forms of cancer

1. *Bowel cancer (colon cancer)* – Cancer of the large intestine (colon) or rectum.

Cause: Unknown. Risk factors may include age, dietary factors and family history.

Symptoms: Bowel cancer is usually staged according to the Dukes classification (Dukes A, B, C, D with A meaning that the cancer is confined to the lining of the bowel and D indicating that there are metastases elsewhere, for example in the liver).

Early signs include blood in stool; changes in bowel habits (diarrhea or constipation); slight bleeding. Later signs include feeling of discomfort of fullness in abdomen; pain; anemia; weight loss.

Investigations: barium enema using barium as a radio opaque contrast; colonoscopy; biopsy.

Treatment: Surgery; radiotherapy; chemotherapy.

2. *Breast Cancer* – Cancer cells in breast tissue which can form a lump, cause discharge from a nipple, or cause puckering of the skin (making it look like the skin of an orange), sometimes seen in Paget's disease of the breast.

Cause: Unknown. Often found in close relatives (with breast cancer) i.e. mother; sister; maternal aunt or grandmother.

Symptoms: Painless lump found during self-examination of the breast; dimpled skin; inward turning nipple; discharge (fluid) from the nipple.

Investigations: Mammogram; CT scan; breast ultrasound scan (recommended if breast tissue is dense; MRI scan; breast biopsy (needle biopsy; hook wire biopsy).

Treatment: Lumpectomy; mastectomy plus reconstruction (breast removed leaving skin and inserting artificial breast); followed by radiation therapy; chemotherapy; hormone treatment (often: Tamoxifen®). Follow-up including regular mammograms; chest X-Rays; bone scans; total body scans.

3.   *Cervical cancer* – Abnormal cells growing on the cervix or neck of the womb.

Cause: Risk factors include *Human Paplloma Virus* (*HPV*) (wart virus strains) infection; starting sexual intercourse before body's immune system is mature (before age 18); smoking.

Symptoms: Spotting in between menstrual periods; bleeding after intercourse.

Investigations: Smear tests; colposcopy; cone biopsy.

Treatment: Laser surgery; LEEP or diathermy loop treatment; cryosurgery; cone biopsy; hysterectomy: radiation therapy; chemotherapy – all depending on the stage

Please see Page 158 of this chapter for the classification of cervical cancer which can be confusing It is clear that the interpreter understands these classifications.

4.   *Colon cancer* (refer Bowel cancer above)

5.   *Lung cancer* – Abnormal cells growing in lung tissue. Differing types including small cell (also called oat cell) and squamous cell carcinoma (often seen in (former) heavy smokers); adenocarcinoma or broncho-alveolar carcinoma (seen in non-smokers); epithelioma (often seen after asbestos exposure).

Cause: Often related to smoking (active or passive) or inhalation of irritant gases such as asbestos.

Symptoms: Dry cough; coughing up blood; chest pain; wheeze; breathlessness; frequent chest infections or asthma attacks; weight loss. If spread the patient may have headaches or bone pain.

Investigations: Chest X-Ray; needle biopsy or bronchoscopy and biopsy; tomogram of chest; VQ Scan; perfusion lung scan; CT scan of body (to check for spread); ventilation lung scan (inhaling gas as a contrast medium); blood test; sputum test.

Treatment: Surgery; radiation therapy; chemotherapy.

6.   *Leukemia* – Refer to Chapter 20, Page 208.

7. *Lymphoma* – Any cancer which starts in the lymph glands. Includes Non-Hodgkin's lymphoma (including Burkitt's lymphoma) or Hodgkin's lymphoma. Many different types depending on the type of cell involved (mantle cell; T-cell; B-cell).

Cause: Damage to the DNA of the lymph cells. Exposure to chemicals may play a role.

Symptoms: Painless lumps on lymph glands.

Investigations: Biopsy; CT scan; MRI scan.

Treatment: Radiotherapy; chemotherapy; prednisone – treatment depends on the stage and the type of cell involved.
See Chapter 24 for more information.

8. *Melanoma* – A cancer which starts from the pigment cells (melanocytes) in the outer layer of the skin.

Cause: Unknown, but risk factors include exposure to UV light; fair skin; moles; family history; previous skin cancer.

Symptoms: A change in existing freckles or moles, including irregular edges, change of colour (including black, blue and red or light grey); also moles or freckles which itch, bleed, or are tender or form a crust.

Investigations: Surgical excision and biopsy; measuring the depth; body scanning.

Treatment: (Wide) surgical excision and biopsy depending on the depth of the melanoma (measured in millimeters); the thinner the melanoma, the better the outlook; radiation therapy; chemotherapy.

9. *Myeloma* – cancer starting from the bone-marrow cells

Symptoms: Severe bone pain and spontaneous fractures; often occurs in ribs, vertebrae, pelvic bone and flat bones of the skull.

Treatment: Radiation.
See Chapter 20 for more information.

10. *Ovarian Cancer* – Cancer of the ovary/ovaries.

Cause: The exact cause is unknown, but risk factors include: Gene mutations; family history of particular types of cancer; hormonal factors including: early start of menstrual periods, late menopause, never having had children, never having used contraceptive pill.

Symptoms: Symptoms are typically late and include discomfort in abdomen; lump or swelling on ovary*; abnormal vaginal blood loss; sometimes ascites (fluid collection in the abdomen) or swelling of the legs.

Investigations: CT scan; Pap smear; laparoscopy or laparotomy; biopsies; Ca125 tumor marker test.

Treatment: Total abdominal hysterectomy with removal of both ovaries (bilateral oophorectomy); irradiation of the pelvis; chemotherapy; iridium treatment (localized radiation through implanted iridium rod].
*different from an ovarian cyst

11. *Pancreatic cancer* – Cancer of the pancreas

Cause: Smoking; diabetes; exposure to PCBs (polychlorinated biphenyl compounds).

Symptoms: Loss of appetite: weight loss; flatulence; pain around mid-stomach or in the back; jaundice; sudden onset of diabetes.

Investigations: Laparoscopy; imaging.

Treatment: Partial pancreatectomy (surgical removal of part of the pancreas) plus surgical removal of part of small intestine and stomach; chemotherapy; radiotherapy.

12. Prostate Cancer – Abnormal cells in the prostate;

Cause: Unknown. Risk factors may include age, dietary factors and family history.

Symptoms: Prostate cancer may be classified as stage A, B, C, D, where A means that the cancer is confined to the 'capsule' of the prostate and D indicates that there are metastases. Symptoms include lump in the prostate; problems with urination (urge; slow start; slow stop; weak stream or trickle).

Investigations: PSA blood test (Prostate Specific Antigen); rectal examination; biopsy; body scanning.

Treatment: Depends largely on the stage of the cancer, the patient's age and general condition. Treatment may include transurethral resection of prostate (TURP); radical prostatectomy; radiation; chemotherapy; brachytherapy; hormone treatment.

13. *Sarcoma* – Refer to Chapter 21, Page 217.

14. *Stomach cancer – gastric carcinoma* – Cancer cells in the lining of the stomach. For more information refer to Chapter 26, Page 162.

Cause: Unknown, but helicobacter pylori bacteria are thought to play a role as do genetic mutations in some families.

Symptoms: Aversion to meat; nausea; swallowing problems; lack of appetite.

Investigations: Barium swallow (contrast X-ray where patient swallows barium); gastroscopy and biopsy; CT scan; PET scan.

Treatment: Surgery (gastrectomy).

15.   *Skin cancer* – Uncontrolled growth of abnormal cells on the skin. Various types including basal cell carcinoma (BCC), squamous cell carcinoma (SCC), melanoma (see there).

Cause: Often result of sun exposure; often seen in farmers, outdoor workers; vehicle drivers (left or right arm).

Symptoms: Sores or changes in the skin that do not heal; crater-like lesions; change in colour; bleeding; itching; pain. Sometimes people get patches of *actinic keratosis*, (rough grey-pink scaly patches) as a forewarning that they may be at risk for skin cancer. Can recur or spread.

Investigations: Regular 'spot checks'; biopsy; total body scan (to check for spread).

Treatment: Removal by burning off the patches (*cauterizing*); freezing off the patches with liquid nitrogen (*cryo-surgery*); *radiation* or *excision* (cutting out); may be followed by chemotherapy or radiotherapy.

16.   *Testicular Cancer* – Abnormal cells in the testicles (balls), usually in men between 15 and 45 years of age.

Cause: Unknown, but risk factors include undescended testicle (see Chapter 27).

Symptoms: Swelling or lump; heavy feeling; nipples may feel large and tender.

Investigations: Biopsy.

Treatment: Chemotherapy. Prognosis very good if detected early.

17.   *Uterine Cancer – also known as endometrial cancer or cancer of the womb –* Abnormal cells in the uterus (womb) in women after menopause.

Cause: Unknown, but risk factors involve hormonal factors, especially unopposed estrogen, (estrogen that is not balanced out by natural progesterone); as an example, overweight women may produce more estrogen in their fat tissue (even after menopause), without producing progesterone.

Symptoms: Vaginal bleeding (after menopause).

Investigations: Hysteroscopy; Biopsy.

Treatment: Hysterectomy (surgical removal of the womb); radiotherapy.

6.   Some notes for interpreters and translators

As mentioned in Chapter 2, interpreters need to be aware of the need to convey all information accurately and the need to not censor or leave out information. Interpreters must tell the health professional if they feel unable to convey all information accurately due to cultural or personal restraints.

Interpreters need to be aware of the various ways in which patients may respond to bad news. They need to be aware that patients may deny that the doctor (or interpreter) has ever given them 'the bad news', that patients may get angry and abusive, or may get depressed and withdrawn. They need to know that all these responses are natural and that the health professional understands this. Most importantly, perhaps, the interpreter needs to realize that it is the health professional, not the interpreter, who needs to deal with these responses and who is in control of the interview. Occasionally interpreters may feel obliged to admonish the patient for his aggressive responses or withdrawn behaviour. Sometimes, the health professional, ignorant of interpreting ethics, may even ask the interpreter to 'get the patient to talk', or to comfort the patient. Neither are appropriate. In some cultures it is not acceptable for patients to be told their real diagnosis and families may exert pressure on the interpreter to not interpret accurately. In this situation, the interpreter needs to remind a patient's relatives that he needs to adhere to the interpreter code of ethics. They may want to add: 'Please tell the doctor how you feel about this and I will be happy to interpret between you and the doctor. However, please do not ask me to breach my professional code of ethics, which requires me to maintain accuracy and impartiality.'

Summary of main points

This chapter has given a brief overview of oncology, including:

- common investigations used for diagnosis (determining type and stage of cancer)
- health professionals involved
- commonly used treatment methods
- some commonly encountered forms of cancer

PART III

Healthcare specialties

Chapter 17

Neurology

Nerves and the nervous system

The Central Nervous System (CNS) is literally the control centre of the body. The workings of the CNS are very complicated but to enable interpreters to have a good general understanding of what the neurosurgeon or neurologist is talking about when they are explaining the patient's condition to the patient, or patient's relatives, the CNS is broadly explained in this chapter.

Some patients require rehabilitative services after suffering neurological events such as strokes. Please refer to Chapter 7 for health professionals involved in rehabilitative services. First, let us look at the Latin and Greek roots that come up frequently in terminology to do with the CNS.

1. Latin and Greek roots

cerebellum	part of the brain behind the brain stem (Latin: *small brain*)
cerebro-vascular	to do with the blood vessels in the brain
cerebrum	brain
cervix	neck (*cervical* region – C1–C8)
dura	one of the outer linings of brain and spinal cord
encephal-	brain (tissue)
epi-	on top of
epidural	on top of the dura
lumbar puncture	spinal tap (taking a sample of cerebrospinal fluid for testing)
lumbar	lower back (*lumbar* region: L1–L5)
meninges	membranes covering the brain and spinal cord
neuro(n)	nerve cell
para-	alongside; beyond
paraplegia	paralysis affecting lower half of the body

paresis	weakness
peripheral nerves	nerves outside of the Central Nervous System (i.e. **not** in brain and spinal cord)
plegia	paralysis
quadru	four (4)
quadruplegia	paralysis affecting four limbs
sacrum	tailbone (sacral region: S1–S5)
spina	backbone; spine
sub	under
subdural	under the dura
tetra	four (4)
thorax	chest (thoracic region: T1–T12)
vertebra (plural: vertebrae)	one of many bones forming the backbone

2. Anatomy of the CNS

The CNS consists of the brain and the spinal cord.

2.1 The brain

Structures inside the brain include the cerebrum, cerebellum and ventricles.

Ventricles are chambers filled with cerebrospinal fluid inside the brain, which circulates through these ventricles and down the spinal cord.

Spaces and membranes around the brain include:

- subarachnoid space
- subdural space (*sub* being under the dura)
- dura mater (*dura mater* being hard mother)
- epidural space (*epi* being on top of)
- meninges (outer coverings)
- inner meninges (*pia mater* or soft mother)
- middle meninges

2.2 The spinal cord

The function of the spinal cord is to transmit messages from the body to the CNS and vice versa, including reflexes. The spinal cord is enclosed by the vertebral canal (behind the vertebral column).

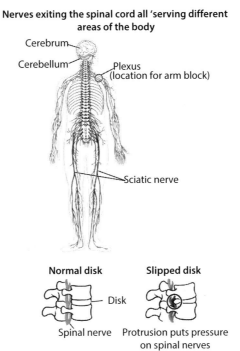

Nerves exiting the spinal cord all 'serving different areas of the body

Cerebrum

Cerebellum

Plexus
(location for arm block)

Sciatic nerve

Normal disk   **Slipped disk**

Disk

Spinal nerve   Protrusion puts pressure
on spinal nerves

Figure 17.1. Spinal nerves

3.   Function of the CNS

The CNS has two main functions, firstly it stimulates movement and secondly it maintains normal body balance and health (e.g. breathing; digestion; blood pressure; temperature).

These two functions are achieved through the millions of nerve cells that make up the CNS. These nerve cells pass signals (information) onto each other in two directions, from the CNS to the body (down the spinal cord and along the 'peripheral nerves') and from the body to the CNS (along the peripheral nerves and up the spinal cord).

The CNS also involves hormonal messengers, which are covered in Chapter 25 (endocrinology).

A number of things can go wrong in the transmission of signals from one nerve cell to the other. Most nerve cells have very long arms called *axons*. The axons are protected by myelin, a sort of rolled-up pancake like sheath. If the myelin gets inflamed (as in Multiple Sclerosis) and or damaged, nerve signals can not be transmitted.

In other illnesses (e.g. Parkinson's Disease), there is something wrong with the 'transmission fluid' in the space between the nerve cells which stop signals from being properly transmitted.

When someone breaks their neck or back (backbone) and the spinal cord (the bundles of nerves going down the backbone) is damaged, the person can be paralysed as a result, because signals from the brain to the muscles can no longer be transmitted. Likewise signals to do with sensation and pain can no longer be transmitted to the brain.

4. Health professionals

Neurologist – physician specializing in disorders of the nervous system.
Neurosurgeon – surgeon specializing in surgery involving the nervous system.

5. Disorders of the nervous system

Some common disorders affecting the Central and Peripheral Nervous System are:

1. *Alzheimer's Disease* – see Dementia below.

2. *Brain tumor* – Any growth in the brain. Tumors can cause pressure and interfere with normal brain activity. A brain tumor can be benign (not cancerous) or malignant (consisting of cancer cells)

Causes: 20–40% are secondaries to cancers elsewhere in the body (e.g. breast, lung, stomach, bowel, kidney or melanoma). Associated factors may include exposure to vinyl chloride and immunosuppressant drugs.

Symptoms: Headaches, nausea, vomiting, seizures, loss of movement or sensation, changes to eyesight; sometimes personality changes.

Investigations: Brain scan (i.e. CAT/MRI/PET scan) and or biopsy through craniotomy (making opening in the skull).

Treatment: Surgery and or radiotherapy. Note chemotherapy is not an option due to the blood-brain barrier – the barrier between the blood circulation and the circulation of cerebro-spinal fluid, which inhibits treatment effects.

3. *Cerebral Palsy* – A group of disorders affecting the CNS, ranging from mild to severe forms of motor control.

Causes: Damage to motor areas in the developing brain occur during pregnancy, at birth or not long after birth due to a lack of (or low levels of) oxygen or infection (e.g. rubella).

Symptoms: Floppy muscles, young babies sitting and walking late; *scissors gait* when walking; involuntary movements of face and hands; slurred speech; spastic finger movements; problems seeing/hearing.

Treatment: Physiotherapy; braces, crutches or wheelchairs; speech therapy; surgery; muscle relaxants; anti-convulsants.

4.   *Coma* – A deeply unconscious patient, who is unable to communicate/respond to any stimuli.

Causes: Brain injury; stroke; poisoning; bleeding into the brain; brain tumor, and many other possible reasons.

5.   *Cerebro-Vascular Accident* (*CVA*) or *stroke* – A incident affecting the blood vessels in the brain.

Causes: A CVA can be caused by either a bleed (brain *hemorrhage*) or a blood clot (*embolism*) in the arteries which bring oxygen to the brain.

Symptoms: This depends on which part of the brain is affected i.e. does not get (enough) oxygen. The CVA can affect the motor centre (which sends signals to the muscles) which can result in hemiparesis (weakness down one side of the body) or hemiparalysis (paralysis down one side of the body). In other cases, the speech centre may be affected, which affects the person's ability to speak and understand language (aphasia). The CVA is often preceded by a TIA (Transient Ischemic Attack) or warning stroke.

Treatment: Physiotherapy; occupational therapy; speech therapy; drugs to dissolve clots or to prevent further clotting (if the CVA was caused by a blood clot); sometimes *endarterectomy* surgery to open up the carotid arteries, if these are narrowed/blocked.

6.   *Dementia* – This involves parts of the brain associated with memory, learning and decision making which no longer function properly. There are different forms of dementia including Alzheimer's disease (large percentage of cases), Lewy Body dementia and Multi-infarct dementia.

Causes: Signs of dementia can be due to diseases, like Parkinson's or Huntington's, which cause a loss of brain cells, but can also be due to multiple small infarcts in the brain; alcohol or drug abuse; head injury; lack of certain B Vitamins, anemia, brain tumors; or infections (e.g. AIDS, Creutzfeldt-Jakob's disease).

Symptoms: Memory loss (especially short term memory); confusion; disorientation; personality changes; loss of social skills.

Treatment: Some types of dementia can be treated by treating the cause (e.g. benign brain tumor, lack of Vitamin B12); other forms cannot currently be treated, however research continues into prevention.

7. *Epilepsy* – Sudden bursts of electrical activity in the brain.

Epilepsy involves sudden and recurrent seizures and is thought to affect 1–2% of the population.

There are many different subtypes of epilepsy, all characterized by a lack of control on the part of the person having the episode. Some subtypes are broadly classified as focal seizures or partial seizures, which affect just one part of the brain. The person may experience strange sensations or movements, and partial seizures may become generalized. Generalized seizures, in comparison, affect both halves of the brain. The person may lose consciousness (sometimes only very briefly).

Patients may get an aura or a feeling that they are going to have an episode.

Causes: Too much electric activity in the brain, causing brain messages to become muddled up. This can be caused by severe head injuries; CVA; a brain tumor; chemical imbalances; infection in the brain; genetic conditions and drug abuse. If the cause of the epilepsy is known, we talk about symptomatic epilepsy, if there is no known cause we talk about idiopathic epilepsy.

Symptoms: These can vary from person to person, depending on the type of episode. Symptoms may include seizures (formerly called fitting); loss of consciousness and incontinence; clenching teeth; being mentally *absent* for a very short while; picking at clothes, staring into space, clenching fists, smacking lips.

Investigations: An EEG, which records the electrical activity of the brain.

Treatment: Anti-epileptic drugs; some patients have a support dog (seizure-alert dog), which can sense an oncoming episode and can warn the person so they are able to get themselves into a safe place before an episode.

8. *Guillain Barré Syndrome* – see Chapter 22, Page 227.

9. *Hemorrhage* – Blood 'bursting forth'

This is bleeding from ruptured blood vessel into the brain, or in the space surrounding the brain. The bleeding leads to increased pressure on the brain and the patient may lose consciousness or go into a coma. Sometimes premature babies also bleed into the brain, which may cause brain damage or cerebral palsy.

Sites of bleeding can include: *subdural* (often slow, signs may occur days after the accident); *epidural* (often arterial, signs will develop very quickly); *arachnoid* (congenital malformation of blood vessels in the brain), and *cerebral* (*in the brain itself*).

Causes: Brain injury, high blood pressure, aneurysm (weaking in blood vessel); blood vessel abnormality; bleeding disorder; brain tumor; liver problem (affecting blood's ability to clot).

Symptoms: Severe headache; loss of consciousness.

Investigations: CT Scan; cranial ultrasound.

Treatment: Often neurosurgical to relieve pressure on the brain.

10.   *Headache* – Pain in the head

Causes: Headaches can have many different causes: one of the more common being muscle tension (tension headache), migraines (see below) or cluster headaches (these come in clusters followed by long headache-free periods). Hangover headaches are caused by dehydration when a person has drunk too much alcohol. Other causes may include Extra-cranial, such as infection (eyes/ears/sinuses); influenza or tension, and Intra-cranial, such as tumors; meningitis or damage (e.g. swelling) to the brain.

Investigations: History; imaging.

Symptoms: Throbbing, pounding or dull pain in the head, depending on the cause.

Treatment: Muscle relaxants; painkillers.

11.   *Meningitis* – An infection/inflammation of the membranes protecting the brain and spinal cord. Meningitis can cause deafness and brain damage, and life-threatening septic shock (if caused by bacteria, which can multiple rapidly).

Causes: Bacterial or viral infection (e.g. through cup sharing).

Symptoms: Headache; neck stiffness; fever; chills; rash (small spots of bleeding under the skin); drowsiness; nausea; vomiting; child screams when legs are lifted for diaper change (pull on meninges).

Investigations: Lumbar puncture to test cerebrospinal fluid.

Treatment: Immediate high-dose antibiotics for bacterial meningitis.

12.   *Migraine* – A throbbing headache, which is usually one-sided.

Causes: Migraines are the end result of a chain of events in the brain, and may be triggered by certain foods (e.g. wine, chocolate, coffee), hormones, or stress, however the root cause of migraines is still unknown.

Symptoms: A sensitivity to light; nausea, vomiting. Patients may feel a migraine coming on (aura).

Treatment: Anti-migraine drugs.

13.   *Motor Neurone Disease* – see Chapter 22, Page 228.

14. *Multiple Sclerosis* or *MS* – A destruction of the protective *myelin sheaths* around the *axons* (long arms) of nerve cells, which results in nerve messages not being passed on.

Causes: Unknown, perhaps genetic predisposition and/or a virus or environmental factors. Autoimmune (the body's own immune cells attack the nervous system).

Symptoms: In MS, attacks alternate with remissions. The disease may lead to a progressive loss of function, which may become fatal if breathing muscles become paralysed.

Treatment: Medication to control symptoms.

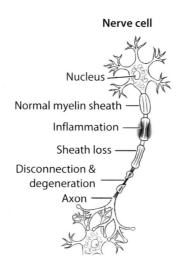

Figure 17.2. Myelin sheath

15. *Myasthenia Gravis* – see Chapter 22, Page 228.

16. *Poliomyelitis* – see Chapter 22, Page 229.

17. *Parkinson's Disease* – A degeneration of (the *substantia nigra*) part of the brain which leads to lower levels of *dopamine* (neurotransmitter), which consequently means that nerve signals can not be transmitted properly.

Causes: Unknown.

Symptoms: Mask-like facial expression; wide-eyed, unblinking stare; drooling, open mouth; difficult to start movement; tremor (trembling hands); depression.

Treatment: Physiotherapy; anti-Parkinson drugs (to encourage production of dopamine).

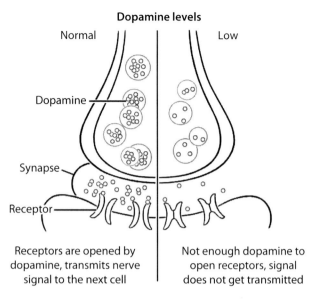

Figure 17.3. Parkinson's Disease schematic

18. *Persistent Vegetative State* – A situation in which a patient who was previously in a coma, now seems to be awake, but is not able to respond or to communicate. The patient needs to be fed and toileted.

19. *Sciatica* – Severe pain along the sciatic nerve.

Causes: Slipped disk (see below); irritation due to osteo-arthritis (wear and tear) of the vertebrae (see under bone disorders); back injuries/exertion.

Symptoms: Severe pain (sometimes also weakness) down the lower back and leg.

Investigations: X-Ray; CT scan; MRI scan.

Treatment: This is dependent on cause, but can include anti-inflammatory drugs; physiotherapy; surgery.

20. *Shingles* – Inflammation of the nerves caused by the herpes zoster virus. This virus lays dormant in the body of those who have had chickenpox in the past, and is mostly seen in people over 50 years of age, those in a weakened condition due to illness, stress or poor nutrition, or in people who are *immunosuppressed* (have low immunity) e.g. those who are *HIV positive*.

Causes: Reawakening of the herpes zoster virus.

Symptoms: Pain, blisters and redness along the path of the nerve.

Treatment: Sometimes medication (e.g. Acyclovir).

21.   *Slipped disk* – Also known as a *herniated disk, ruptured disk* or *prolapsed disk*. Occurs when the nucleus of an intervertebral disk pops out and presses on the spinal nerves. Can happen in the neck and lower back.

Causes: Due to incorrect lifting or other sudden injury.

Symptoms: Nerve pain (e.g. sciatica); pins and needles; weakness.

Investigations: MRI scan; CT scan.

Treatment: Rest; strenghtening exercises; surgery (e.g. percutaneous transforaminal endoscopic discectomy.

22.   *Spinal Cord Injury* – A fractured spine or broken back(bone) in which various nerves of the body are injured and result in a loss of movement/function of parts of the body.

Causes: Typically due to an accident (e.g. being thrown clear off a car; contact sports like American football or rugby; diving into shallow water; falling from a height).

Symptoms: Loss of movement/function in the body, the degree of this loss depends on the level of the injury.
   Quadruplegia – Injury to nerves which serve the body from the neck down; the patient may suffer loss of feeling/sensation and paralysis from the neck downwards; this may also affect the patient's breathing muscles.
   Paraplegia – Injury to the nerves which serve the lower half of the body; the patient may suffer loss of feeling/sensation and paralysis from the middle of the body down.

Treatment: Wheelchair with/without neckbrace; physiotherapy for passive move-ments; to prevent 'contractures'; may need in-dwelling catheter; pressure area cares (to prevent pressure sores).

23.   *Syphilis* – A venereal disease (sexually transmitted disease) which eventually attacks the central nervous system.

Causes: Sex with an infected person.

Symptoms: There are three stages and related signs: (1) Chancre, open sore; (2) Joint aches, rash (latent stage: blood test positive Wassermann Test), and (3) Organ deterioration. We speak of neurosyphilis when the illness has affected the central nervous system, with symptoms possibly including meningitis; memory loss; loss of coordination; personality changes.

Treatment: Antibiotics (including partners).

24.   *Whiplash* – Also refered to as *Cervical Acceleration Decelaration (CAD)*, is an injury of neck which occurs when the head snaps forwards and then back very fast, such as in a car accident.

Causes: A very sudden snapping movement of the head.

Symptoms: Headaches; pain in shoulders; pins and needles in arms.

Treatment: Depending on severity may include NSAIDS, muscle relaxants, cervical collar; physiotherapy, cervical traction.

6.   Some common drugs

analgesics	pain killers
anticonvulsants or *anti-epileptic drugs*	sometimes used as tranquilizers
hypnotics	sleeping drugs
muscle relaxants	reduce pain by relaxing tense muscles
psychotropics	have an effect on the mind
sedatives	calming drugs

7.   Some common investigations

-   *CT Scan* – Computerised tomography scan using radiation to produce clear 'sliced' images of a certain part of the body.
-   *EEG* – Electro-encephalo-graphy, where by leads are attached to the head to test the electrical activity of the brain.
-   *Lumbar puncture* – Procedure in which CSF (cerebrospinal fluid) is collected for testing from the lumbar region under local anesthetic using a hollow needle and syringe.
-   *Spinal tap*- As for lumbar puncture
-   *MRI scan* – Type of scan which uses magnetic fields to produce very clear images

---

Summary of main points

This chapter has given a brief overview of neurology, including:

-   a brief overview of anatomy
-   Latin and Greek roots
-   health professionals involved
-   some commonly encountered conditions relating to the nervous system, together with common investigations and treatment methods

Conditions affecting the nervous systems can affect level of consciousness (LOC), speech, perception, sensation and movement among others.

Chapter 18

Cardiology

Heart and the circulatory system

The heart is one of the most vital organs in the body (the other two being the brain and the lungs). When the heart stops, circulation stops, and the bodies tissues do not receive any more oxygen. Tissue death will start after 5 minutes.

People who suffer a cardiac arrest (where their heart stops beating) are increasingly at risk of brain damage if their heart does not start pumping again within 5 minutes. For this reason cardiopulmonary resuscitation (CPR), which is a combination of the artificial respiration and heart massage, is very important.

In order to gain a better understanding of the heart and how it works, it is good to have a look at the hearts structure and function. Firstly though lets look at the Latin and Greek roots for related terminology.

1. Latin and Greek roots

angiography	X-Ray examination of the blood vessels, using a radio-opaque fluid, which is injected into the blood stream
angioplasty	blood vessel repair, using a thin cardiac catheter with a balloon (and a stent) on it
arrhythmia	irregular heartbeat (literally: no rhythm)
cardiac catheterization	examination of the heart by introducing a thin catheter into an artery and passing it into the coronary arteries
cardiac surgeon	heart surgeon
cardiologist	doctor specializing in the heart
cardiology	special branch of medicine dealing with the heart (card = heart)
cardiomegaly	enlargement of the heart (megalos: big)
cardioversion	an electric shock delivered to the heart to stop abnormal heart rhythms, in the hope that the heart's own pacemaker (the sinus node, see below) will become the pacemaker again and the heart will get back to 'sinus rhythm'.

carditis	inflammation of the heart
chemical cardioversion	attempts to restore normal heart rhythm by administering medication
coronary artery	artery which takes blood rich in oxygen to the heart muscle itself
Coronary Care Unit or CCU	special care unit for patients with heart problems
coronary	like a crown (corona: crown)
defibrillator	machine for applying electrical shocks to the heart to stop fibrillations (abnormal heart rhythms) or to 'jump start' the heart again
EKG or ECG	Electrocardiogram, a procedure used to measure the electrical activity of the heart muscle
endocarditis	inflammation of the inner lining of the heart (endo: inside)
fibrillations	irregular heart rhythm where the heart is not contracting properly (bit like quivering)
infarction	death/damage due to lack of oxygen
ischemic	no blood (i.e. no oxygen)
myocarditis	inflammation of the heart muscle
palpitations	fluttering of the heart, abnormal heart rate or abnormal heart rhythm
radio-opaque	chemical compound that resists radiation and becomes highly visible in X-rays (so blood vessels filled with the dye show up on X-rays)
sinus rhythm	heart rhythm originating in the sinus node, the natural pacemaker of the heart
thoracic surgeon	surgeon who operates on the thorax (chest)
myocardial	heart muscle (Myo = muscle)
cyanosis	looking blue due to lack of oxygen (cyan = blue)

2. Anatomy of the heart

The heart consists of four compartments or chambers. The top two chambers are called the atria, atrium being the Latin word for the vestibule or ante-chamber where people used to wait before being admitted to the main room. The lower two chambers are called the *ventricles*.

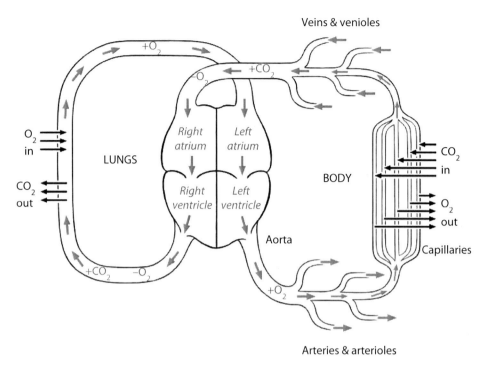

Figure 18.1. Schematic representation of the heart

There are valves between the atria and the ventricles. The valve between the right atrium and the right ventricle is called the tricuspid valve, because it has three (tri) leaves. The valve between the left atrium and the left ventricle is called the mitral valve, because it has two leaves and looks like a bishop's hat (mitre).

The heart has two other valves, one valve between the left ventricle and the aorta (called the aortic valve), the other between the right ventricle and the pulmonary artery (called the pulmonary valve). Memory aid: mitraL – Left; tRicuspid – Right.

NB Figure 18.1 is a schematic diagram only and not a picture of what the heart really looks like.

3. Function of the heart

The hearts function is to supply the body with oxygenated blood full of nutrients, and to remove de-oxygenated blood full of waste products (waste products of cell metabolism).

The heart pumps blood full of oxygen into the aorta. The aorta branches off into arteries which supply various organs and areas of the body. Arteries are strong, elastic, muscular blood vessels as they have to with stand high pressure.

Arteries branch off into *arterioles* and finally into *capillaries*, the smallest blood vessels in the body. Oxygen is supplied to the tissues, and the tissues in turn dump their 'waste' into the bloodstream.

The capillaries change into small veins, which drain into venioles. Veins contain blood which is low in oxygen (*de-oxygenated*) and which contains various waste products. Veins direct this blood to the right atrium of the heart. This blood goes through the lungs to 'pick up' new oxygen for delivery around the body.

The blood passes from the right atrium through the first valve (tricuspid valve) into the right ventricle. From there it passes through the pulmonary valve into the pulmonary artery into the lungs.

Blood rich in oxygen (*oxygenated*) leaves the lungs and flows into the left atrium. From the left atrium it goes through the *mitral valve*, into the left ventricle. From the left ventricle, the blood is pumped through the *aortic valve* into the aorta, for delivery around the body.

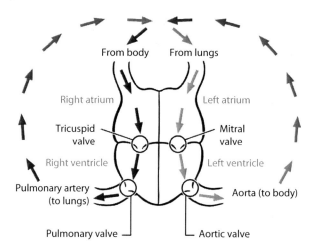

Figure 18.2. Schematic representation of the heart valves

The heart = pump, pumps blood around the body and around the lungs:

right atrium → (tricuspid) valve → right ventricle → (pulmonary) valve →

pulmonary artery/lung →artery → blood to lungs →

→ oxygen in/CO_2 out → to left atrium → (mitral) valve → left ventricle →

→ aortic valve → aorta → arteries → small arteries → capillaries →

oxygen out and CO_2 in, nutrients and wastes exchanged – *you may compare this to a truck doing deliveries to individual houses and picking up their waste for taking to the dump.*

→ small veins → large veins (venioles) → large vein → right

atrium of heart → right ventricle → lungs → heart → body → heart →

lungs → heart → body → heart → and so on...

In addition to the various organs and body tissues that require oxygen to function, the heart muscle itself also needs oxygen to function properly. The very first arteries to branch off the aorta are called the coronary arteries which run around the heart, as if forming a crown around the heart ('corona' means crown). It is these coronary arteries that bring blood that is rich in oxygen to the heart muscle itself.

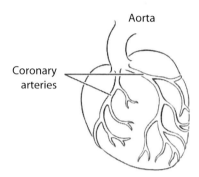

Figure 18.3. Heart and coronary arteries

4.   Health professionals

Cardiologist – Physician specializing in heart disorders
Cardiosurgeon – Surgeon specializing in heart surgery
Cardiothoracic surgeon – Surgeon specializing in heart and lung surgery

5.   Disorders of the heart

Broadly speaking heart problems can be classified into four main types:

1.   *Problems with the coronary arteries*
This affects oxygen supply to the heart muscle and is often refered to as Coronary Artery Disease (CAD) (formerly known as Ischemic Heart Disease). *Ischemic* literally means 'no blood'. Obviously a lack of blood equals a lack of oxygen supply, and without oxygen the heart muscle cannot do its job.

In people with CAD there is damage to, or narrowing of, the coronary arteries which supply the heart muscle with blood. As a result, the heart muscle does not get enough oxygen, resulting in chest pain. This chest pain is known as *angina pectoris*, literally meaning a 'tightening of the chest'.

Patients may have chronic and ongoing CAD but they may also present with Acute Coronary Syndrome (ACS), i.e. with acute coronary artery problems such as heart attacks (myocardial infarctions) or unstable angina. This is discussed further below.

2. *Problems with the heart valves*

People may be born with valve defects or may develop problems with their heart valves following infections somewhere else in the body. Heart valves may start to leak and doctors will hear an abnormal heart sound called a murmur, which may be a sign that blood is leaking back (*regurgitation*). Leaky valves may lead to an enlarged heart and heart failure, depending on the valves involved and depending on what caused the leaky valve. Heart valves can now be replaced through non-invasive procedures, although in some countries surgeons still prefer open heart surgery.

3. *Problems with the heart's role as a pump*

People may develop problems with their heart not being able to pump the blood around efficiently anymore. This is known as heart failure. Patients often experience shortness of breath and swelling of the ankles. See page 187 for more information.

4. *Problems with conduction of electrical activity in the heart*

So how does the heart muscle know when to contract? The heart is self-sufficient. The sinoatrial node (SA node), the heart's own pacemaker found at the top of the right atrium, gives the signal. The SA node sends an electrical impulse directly to the atrioventricular node (or AV node), which sends a message to the atria to contract. The signal then passes through the septum, the central heart wall dividing the heart into left and right. The two branches branching off into the left and the right side of the heart then spread the message into the ventricle muscle, which synchronises a ventricular contraction (i.e. make both ventricles contract simultaneously).

6. Some common disorders of the heart

1. *Acute Coronary Syndrome (ACS)* – ACS can relate to either unstable angina (see angina below) or a heart attack.

Causes: See under Angina and heart attack.

Symptoms: See under Angina and heart attack.

Investigations: Blood test to look for elevated levels of cardiac enzymes, which signal major damage to the heart muscle (these would not be present in unstable angina or Non-STEMI heart attacks).

Treatment: Doctors will need to work out whether ACS patients are experiencing unstable angina or a heart attack, and if a heart attack, what kind of heart attack they are having i.e. STEMI or nonSTEMI. Please see under Heart Attack below.

2. *Angina* – From Angina Pectoris meaning 'tightening of the chest'. Angina occurs when there is narrowing of the coronary arteries. As a result, the arteries cannot

supply the heart muscle with enough oxygen, especially during exertion. This results in chest pain.

Doctors distinguish between stable angina and unstable angina. In unstable angina there are unstable plaques in the walls of the arteries which may break off and cause a blockage of the artery without warning, e.g. at rest or at night. In stable angina there are partial blockages of the artieries, but they are stable. Stable angina is more common and is also (as the name suggests) more predictable in that the pain usually comes on with physical exertion or emotional stress.

Unstable angina is less common, less predictable and more dangerous. Symptoms can be unpredictable as platelets can suddenly collect on existing plaques in the walls of the arteries. Unstable angina can be the cause of sudden death through a sudden heart attack.

Causes: Being overweight or obese; diabetes; high blood cholesterol; smoking; lack of exercise; 'predisposition' through family history.

Symptoms: *Stable angina (more predictable):* Pain or tightness in the chest, especially on exertion or following a heavy meal, or when stepping out into the cold. *Unstable angina (unpredictable):* Pain or tightness in the chest at rest or at night.

Investigations: ECG (EKG); exercise ECG or stress test; blood tests; angiography.

Treatment: Medication (sprayed under the tongue it helps to open up the coronary arteries so more oxygen can be supplied to the heart); oxygen; Coronary artery by-pass surgery; angioplasty a balloon or a stent (which is a small mesh tube used to keep the artery open); drugs to stabilize the plaques in the walls of the coronary arteries. Cholesterol control (by diet or medication or both).

3.   *Conduction Problems* – Occurs when the hearts electrical signal is not conducted properly.

Causes: This may be causes by an:

– *Incomplete heart block*
– *Complete heart block*
– *Heart Flutter*

There are different types of heart flutter:

1.   *Atrial Flutter:* Heart rate beats at 240–360 beats per minute. Caused by damaged heart muscle.

2.   *Atrial Fibrillation* or *AF* involves very fast atrial contractions resulting in the heart being unable to pump properly. AF patients are at risk of complications associated with clots which can form in the atrium and travel around the body, causing embolisms, thrombosis or a stroke.

3. *Ventricular Fibrillation* is where the heart is not pumping, only quivering, so there is no circulation which leads to death. Ventricular fibrillation is very dangerous because it usually leads to cardiac arrest where the heart stops completely.

*Treatment: A*trial flutter and atrial fibrillation treatment includes cardioversion; drugs (e.g. Amiodarone, digoxin); anti-clotting treatments. For ventricular fibrillation CPR is performed (a combination of artificial respiration, either mouth to mouth, or with an Ambu bag, and heart massage), and a defibrillator may be used (two *paddles* are placed on the chest and a shock is delivered) to try and get the heart's own pacemaker (the SA node) working again and the heart pumping in normal sinus rhythm again.

4. *Congenital Heart Defects* – Heart disorders that children are born with. Septal defects or a 'hole in the heart' are probably the most common, being cuased by an opening in the wall (septum) between the heart chambers. In an Atrial Septal Defect (ASD*) there is a hole between the atria. In a Ventricular Septal Defect (VSD) the hole is between the ventricles. In ASD blood which is low in oxygen flows through the hole in the wall between the atria from left to right atrium. As a result, blood which is low in oxygen is mixed with blood which is rich in oxygen and blood with less oxygen goes into the body. In VSD blood which is low in oxygen keeps passing through the hole in the wall from the left ventricle back into the right ventricle.

Causes: There are a number of Congenital Heart Defects, ranging from single conditions such as Patent Ductus Arteriosus (PDA – see Chapter 13, Page 133), ASD and VSD, to complex heart defects such as Transposition of the Great Arteries (TGA), and Tetrology of Fallot (TOF) (which includes a narrow pulmonary valve, a hole in the wall, an over-riding arorta as well as hypertrophy of the right ventricle), Double Outlet Right Ventricle or DORV (where the aorta comes out of the right ventricle), Valve Atresia (valve narrowing or blockage), AV Canal Defects (combination of septum defects and valve problems).

Symptoms: Very often one of the first things that nurses and parents notice is that the baby looks 'dusky' and seems out of breath when feeding. In ASD the baby will be tired and not feeding well, and as a result the baby will not be growing well either. The baby may also have frequent chest colds. In VSD the baby may have fast shallow breathing; frequent chest colds; sweating; not be feeding well and or growing normally and be irritable.

Treatments: There is a lot of excellent material (including animations) on Congenital Heart Defects available on the internet. Surgical techniques are continually being improved and updated.

*Please note the abbreviation ASD may also be used to refer to Autism Spectrum Disorder, so please doublecheck before interpreting or translating this abbreviation.

5.   *Congestive heart failure* also called *Heart Failure* – Occurs as a result of faulty pump action whereby the heart cannot pump sufficient blood and oxygen around the body to meet the body's needs.

Causes: Previous heart attack or CAD; heart valve problems.

Symptoms: Due to this faulty pump action, some body parts do not get enough oxygen and or retain fluid. This fluid retention may show in swollen ankles and shortness of breath (fluid retained in blood vessels in the lungs). Some patients may have to sleep sitting up, to avoid shortness of breath at night; some are short of breath when speaking.

Treatment: Medication including anti-arrhythmic drugs to help maintain normal heart rhythm and *diuretics* to get rid of excess fluid; drugs to strengthen the heart muscle. Low-salt and low-fat diet; fluid restriction to avoid overloading the heart. Exercise to maintain fitness and health.

6.   *Myocardial Infarction (MI) or Heart Attack* – Occurs when there is a partial or complete blockage of a coronary artery, which can lead to part of the heart muscle being starved of oxygen and dying. Doctors currently distinguish between two types of MI, the more 'common' ST segment elevation myocardial infraction (STEMI) and the less common Non-STEMI. In a STEMI the coronary artery is completed blocked by a blood clot and a large part of the heart muscle will start to die. This means the heart cannot pump anymore and the patient may die quite suddenly. In a non-STEMI there are unstable plaques in the walls of the coronary artery, and platelets are collecting and sticking to this plaque. As a result the coronary artery becomes partly blocked. Because there is less damage to the heart muscle, the heart can continue to pump adequately, which means there is less risk of sudden death.

Causes: Blockage of an (already narrowed) coronary artery by a thrombus (clot) or by a plaque which has broken of from the wall of the artery. Damage to the arteries can be caused through high blood cholesterol levels (blood fats); smoking; diabetes; high blood pressure; also predisposition through family history; gum disease (*gingivitis*); lack of physical activity; obesity.

Symptoms: Shortness of breath; a crushing feeling in chest which *radiates* to arms and or jaw (note some people only have pain in their arms (either left or right)).

Investigations: 12 lead-EKG or ECG; 5-lead EKG or ECG; angiography; an elevated CPK (Creatine Kinase) blood test may indicate damage to the heart muscle; other enzyme tests may also go up after a heart attack.

Treatment: Depends on the type of heart attack. If the EKG shows ST elevation, there is a big blood clot that needs to be dissolved because it is completely blocking a coronary artery. If there is no ST elevation, there are plaques in the wall of the coronary artery that need to be stabilized to prevent them from causing further blockages. Treatment also includes managing several possible complications, including cardiac arrest (heart stops because heart muscle is so damaged that it cannot contract anymore); systemic embolism; pulmonary edema (swelling in the lung circulation) and shock.

For STEMIs treatment includes (urgent) angioplasty; clot-dissolving drugs (such as Streptokinase®) and fibrinolytics (drugs which help to dissolve fibrinogen). Other drugs include aspirin, clopidogrel, betablockers and statins (blood cholesterol lowering drugs). The patient may also require oxygen; cardiotonic drugs (to strengthen the heart muscle); drugs to stop irregular heartbeat; pain killers; sedatives; laxatives (to prevent extra strain on the heart) or coronary artery by-pass surgery (CABG). See Figure 18.4. In a CABG a vein from the patient's legs may be used to create a bypass from the top of the aorta 'downstream' past a narrowed area of the coronary artery. Implanting a stent has become a very popular procedure; stents are implanted using a heart catheter. See Figure 18.5. After discharge treatment includes a rehabilitation programme involving physiotherapy; gentle exercise; limiting caffeine; stopping smoking.

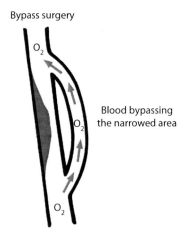

Figure 18.4. Coronary Artery By-Pass Graft (CABG)

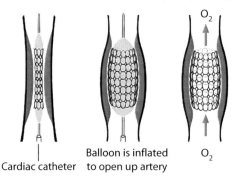

Figure 18.5. Stent in coronary artery

7. *Valve defects* – Occurs when one of the heart valves is not working properly, or is damaged/narrowed so that blood leaks back (regurgitation). Valve defects can affect the mitral valve (between left atrium and left ventricle), tricuspid valve (between right atrium and right ventricle), aortic valve or pulmonary valve.

Causes: Rheumatic fever; valves damaged by strep bacteria; other infections, e.g. gingivitis; high blood pressure.

Symptoms: Heart murmur; sometimes symptoms as for heart failure.

Treatment: Medication to control symptoms of heart failure; valve repair or valve replacement.

7. Some common drugs

anginine	drug against angina (tablet placed under the tongue, so it can be absorbed directly into the bloodstream)
vasodilator	widens up the blood vessels/arteries
antiplatelets	aspirin, clopidogrel – these drugs stop platelets from sticking together
antifibrinolytics	heparin
betablockers	drug used to slow the heart so it does not have to work too hard
digoxin	drug used to strengthen the pump action of the heart (in heart failure or in problems with irregular heart beat)
diltiazem	used against angina and high blood pressure
nitrolingual sprayor GTN spray	medication sprayed under the tongue, where it is directly absorbed into the bloodstream; used for relief of *angina*: vasodilator; arteries widen, resulting in more oxygen to the heart (and hence less pain)
amiodarone®	drug used to correct irregular heartbeat
diuretics	drug used to help reduce fluid retention (e.g. in patients with heart failure)
ACE inhibitors	drug used to correct hypertension. ACE inhibitors reduce your body's supply of angiotensin II. Angiotensin makes blood vessels contract and narrow
calcium channel blockers	Calcium channel blockers (CCBs) slow the movement of calcium into the cells of the heart and blood vessels. Calcium causes stronger heart contractions, so CCBs ease the heart's contraction and relax the blood vessels
Angiotensin Receptor Blockers or ARBs	ARBs block receptors for angiotensin

8. Some common investigations

– *Blood pressure* – Blood pressure can tell the health professional a lot about the pump action of the heart. Blood pressures can be taken while the patient is sitting, lying or standing.
   Blood pressures can be taken manually with a sphygmomanometer and stethoscope. Some departments use a cuff attached to a machine which inflates the cuff automatically every 15 or 30 minutes. The reading will show up on a screen.
– *Arterial blood pressure monitoring* – In special care units, blood pressure is often monitored through a line in the patient's artery (arterial line) which is connected to equipment which shows the reading up on a monitor screen.
– *Central Venous Pressure* – Doctors may want to monitor the central venous pressure, by inserting a special line into the neck vein or into the upper hollow vein which drains blood from the body back into the (right atrium of the) heart.
– *Swan Ganz Catheter* – If the doctors are interested in measuring pressures in different areas in the heart, they may insert a Swan Ganz Catheter in the large subclavian vein just above the heart to monitor these pressures and to measure cardiac output.
– *Cardiac Catheter for Angiography or Angioplasty or PTCA* – The patient is taken to the *Cath Lab* and *ECG* leads are attached. Then a catheter (a long narrow tube) is inserted either through the patient's artery in the left groin (if the doctors want to examine the coronary arteries) or through a vein in the left groin (if the doctors want to examine the right side of the heart and the pulmonary artery).
   The long tube is then slowly pushed up the aorta and then into the coronary arteries. The patient stays awake.
   The doctor will want to do an *angiogram* (a special X-Ray of the blood-vessels) and inject some contrast dye so that he will be able to get a good picture of the blood vessels on the screen. The angiogram will show up any narrowing or blockages of the arteries.
   The angiogram is filmed for later study by the heart surgeon prior to surgery.
   If there is narrowing in one or two arteries due to fatty deposits on the walls of the arteries, the patient may be asked to come back to the Cath Lab for a PTCA or angioplasty. In some cases the angioplasty is done immediately following the angiogram, but this is always discussed with the patient first.
– *PTCA* – Percutaneous (through the skin) transluminal (across the diameter [of the bloodvessel]) coronary (in the coronary artery) angioplasty (repairing the blood-vessel).
   The coronary arteries are approached with a catheter (see under cardiac catheter), and pushed into that part of the coronary artery which is narrowed. The balloon around the catheter is then inflated to squash the fatty plaque in the artery, thus opening that part of the artery up again.

The ECG is watched all the time for signs that the heart muscle is suffering from lack of oxygen.

The stent method often helps to open up arteries for longer periods. Sometimes stents are put in areas where there is severe narrowing to open up the artery at that point. Stents are like little 'mesh' tubes.

– *EKG or ECG or Electrocardiogram* – The electrical activity of the heart can be monitored by means of an ECG (a recording of the electrical activity of the heart). In a twelve lead EKG, ten electrodes are placed on the skin (six around the heart and four on arms and legs). For monitoring in a Coronary Care Unit or for telemetry (monitoring from a distance), three or four electrodes are placed on the skin around the heart. Experienced professionals can read ECGs and tell whether everything is normal, or whether the person is suffering from certain disorders.

– *Exercise EKG – also called Stress Test or Treadmill Test* – Exercise EKGs are done to see how the heart copes with exercise. The patient walks on a treadmill, while the EKG leads are attached to their chest. The exercise EKG (sometimes called stress test or treadmill test) may help the doctor to diagnose whether the patient has ischemic heart disease. As the patient continues to exert themselves, the ECG may start to show signs that the patient's heart is not getting enough oxygen (so-called ischemic changes).

Summary of main points

This chapter has given a brief overview of the heart, including:

– a brief overview of anatomy
– health professionals involved
– some commonly encountered conditions relating to the respiratory system, together with common investigations and treatment methods

In adults, heart problems usually affect one of the following:

– arteries
– heart muscle
– conduction of electrical activity
– heart valves

In babies heart problems usually affect the anatomical structure of the heart, e.g. hole in the wall between left and right side of the heart.

Chapter 19

The respiratory system

The respiratory system controls our breathing. Any problems with this system can threaten our survival in the short term. The respiratory rate (the number of breaths per minute) is one of the vital signs observed by health professionals in the Emergency Room or in Intensive Care Units.

It is important that interpreters understand terminology used when health professionals discuss common breathing problems such as asthma or the breathing problems experienced by premature babies.

1. Latin and Greek roots

alveolus	little air sac (plural: *alveoli*)
apnea	no breathing
bronchi (plural)	breathing tubes (*bronchus*: single)
dyspnea	difficulty in breathing/abnormal breathing
eorex	out
expiration	breathing out
inspiration	breathing in
larynx	voice box (containing the vocal cords)
pharynx	throat
pneu/pnea	to blow (Greek)
pneumon	lung (Greek)
pulmon	lung (Latin)
pulmonary artery	blood vessel going from the heart to the lung (to pick up oxygen)
re-	repeated; again and again
respiration	breathing (in/out)
spirare	to blow (Latin)
trachea	windpipe

2. Other important terms

gas exchange   breathing in *oxygen* (O_2) and blowing out *carbon dioxide* (CO_2)

mucus   slime

sputum

or phlegm   the slimy substance that is coughed up from the lungs; spit

3. Anatomy of the respiratory system

Mouth

pharynx/throat

epiglottis

larynx/voice box and vocal cords

trachea/windpipe

bronchi

bronchioli (literally: 'smaller bronchi').

alveoli or air sacs

respiratory centre in the brain

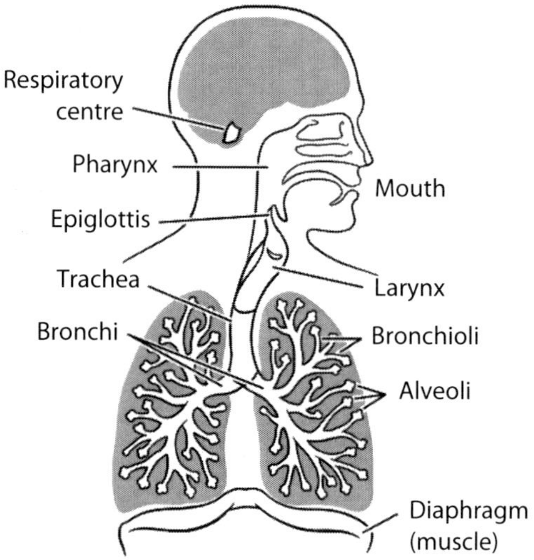

Figure 19.1. Cross-section of the airways

4. Function of the respiratory system

The respiratory centre in the brain ensures that there is an ongoing exchange of O_2 and CO_2 between the blood and the lungs. The respiratory centre in the brain stem sends a signal to the breathing muscles. The breathing muscles, which run down from the neck to the upper ribs, tighten and pull the chest up and out. At the same time, the large muscle below the lungs, (the diaphragm) contracts and the chest cavity becomes bigger. As a result of a change in air pressure in the lungs, air is sucked into the chest cavity. This is inspiration or breathing in. After inspiration, the breathing muscles relax, the elastic fibers in the lung contract, pressure builds up in the diaphragm below the lungs, and air is pushed out. This is called expiration or breathing out.

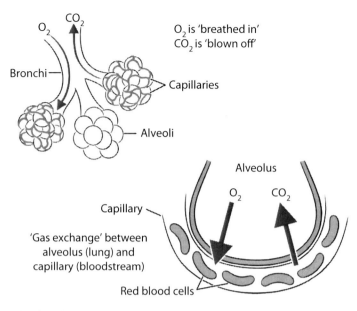

Figure 19.2. Alveoli and gas exchange close-up

In most people the respiratory centre in the brain is stimulated by high levels of CO_2 in the blood, however for those with longstanding lung problems (such as emphysema) it may be stimulated by low levels of O_2 in the blood.

The diagram below may help you understand the mechanism of breathing:

Control: respiratory centre in the brain → breathing muscles tighten → inspiration
→ breathing muscles relax → expiration

O_2 inhaled → attached to hemoglobin in the wall of red blood cells → transported around body

CO_2 is blown off

In many cases, patients with breathing difficulties will find it difficult to breathe when they are lying down flat. They will find it easier to breathe when they are sitting up.

Brain injury or drugs which affect the respiratory centre in the brain can also adversely affect breathing. In this case, a ventilator or breathing machine may be used to help patients breathe.

5. Health professionals

Respiratory specialists – doctors specializing in disorders of the respiratory system.

Clinical respiratory physiologists (CRPs) – health professionals who carry out a wide range of respiratory function tests, including sleep studies.

Sleep physiologists – Health professionals who carry out sleep monitoring tests (including oxygen saturation and heart rate).

Sleep technologists – See Sleep physiologists.

6. Disorders of the respiratory system

1. *Asthma* – A long term condition where the airways are inflamed and narrowed (*bronchospasm*), which may lead to attacks of wheezing, or coughing, and difficulties in breathing out.

Causes: Many asthma patients are hypersensitive to wheat, dust, pollen, (airborne) or to certain drugs. Sometimes taking deep breaths (when stressed or after exertion) or breathing in cold air may trigger (bring about) an asthma attack. This hypersensitivity causes the muscles in the wall of the bronchi (airways) to tighten so the airways become narrowed. At the same time, the membranes in lining of the airways swell up and produce a lot of mucus, leading to a clogging up of the airways.

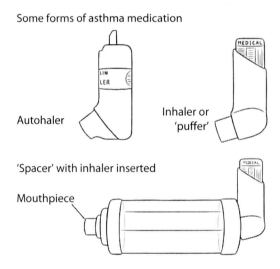

Figure 19.3. Some forms of asthma medication

Symptoms: The patient finds it very difficult to breathe out and may wheeze when breathing out, producing a sort of whistling sound. Children often cough when they get an asthma attack. Other symptoms include chest tightness; shortness of breath; use of accessory breathing muscles.

Investigations: Spirometry (lung function test); using a peakflow meter (to see how much air the patient can still blow out).

Treatment: Preventers (often steroid inhalers) to stop ongoing inflammation and prevent asthma attacks; bronchodilators (given as inhalers or through nebulisers) (see Figures 19.3, 19.4, 19.5) to open up the airways by relaxing the muscles around the bronchi; oxygen; prednisone in tablet form or injected intravenously (into the vein); avoiding triggers; sometimes breathing exercises.

It should be noted that asthma attacks can become life-threatening within a very short space of time, and an ambulance should be called if a person is having real difficulty breathing and speaking. Children in particular may die if they become exhausted with the effort of pushing the air out.

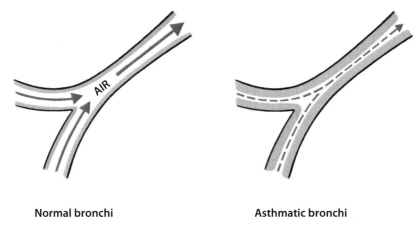

Normal bronchi   **Asthmatic bronchi**

Swelling and narrowing of bronchi
resulting in 'wheezing' (a whistling sound)

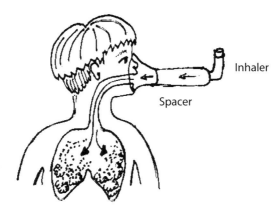

Inhaler

Spacer

Figure 19.4. Bronchi during an asthma attack

Note: Nebulizers are devices which help patients to inhale medication in spray form. In hospitals nebulizers are usually connected to oxygen supply to help carry the medication into the lung. The nebulizer may have a mouth piece or a mask to fit around the patient's nose or mouth.

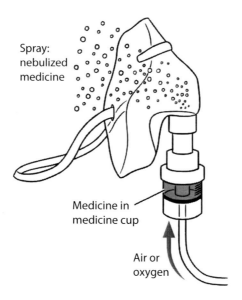

Spray:
nebulized
medicine

Medicine in
medicine cup

Air or
oxygen

Figure 19.5. Nebulizer spray

2. *Bronchiectasis* – Air passages become dilated (widened) and distorted (mis-shapen).

Causes: An infection leads to distortion of the airways. Phlegm collects in pouch-like widening in the walls of damaged bronchi.

Symptoms: Recurrent chest infections, which in turn lead to further damage to the walls of the airways; slightly raised temperature; feeling unwell during an infection.

Treatment: Assistance to help patient to cough up the phlegm (e.g. postural drainage); antibiotics for airway infections.

3. *Bronchitis* – Inflammation of the bronchi.

Cause: *Acute bronchitis* is usually caused by a virus (90% of cases) or bacterial infection (10% of cases), while *chronic bronchitis* (i.e. ongoing) may be due to smoking, or working in a dusty, polluted environment.

Symptoms: Coughing up phlegm; raised temperature.

Investigations: X-Ray; Sputum specimen sent to lab to test for bacteria.

Treatment: Non-steroidal anti-inflammatory drugs; drugs to loosen (and cough up) phlegm.

4. *Cancer of the larynx* – Cancer cells on the vocal cords or on the wall of the voicebox.

Causes: Smoking is a risk factor.

Symptoms: Chronic hoarseness; (later) lump on neck; earache; sore throat.

Investigations: Laryngoscopy or micro-laryngoscopy (looking inside the voicebox).

Treatment: Laryngectomy (removal of voicebox) and creation of a stoma (opening in the larynx); radiotherapy; chemotherapy; speech therapy; patient learns to talk again through the stoma.

5.   *Cancer of the lung* (see lung cancer)

6.   *Chronic Obstructive Pulmonary Disease* (*COPD*) or *Chronic Obstructive Respiratory Disease* (*CORD*) – Damage to the alveoli (tiny air sacs).

Causes: Respiratory illness (such as asthma, chronic bronchitis, bronchiectasis or emphysema); smoking.

Symptoms: Wheezing; tight feeling in the chest; constant cough with lots of phlegm; tiredness; weight loss; frequent colds ; *cyanosis* (purplish blue colour) of fingernails and lips; *oedema* (swelling) due to fluid retention.

Investigations: Pulse oximeter (testing oxygen levels); Spirometry (a type of lung function test); Chest X-ray.

Treatment: Oxygen; bronchodilators; corticosteroids; lung training (pursed lip breathing); BiPAP mask (bi-level positive airway pressure mask that helps COPD patients keep their airways open).

7.   *Emphysema* – from the Greek: *blown up, inflated*. Alveoli become permanently enlarged, small bronchi collapse and the lungs lose their elasticity making chest and lungs appear permanently blown up.

Causes: Long-term exposure to smoking, pollution, industrial dust and fumes.

Symptoms: Severe shortness of breath; lack of oxygen.

Treatment: Oxygen; bronchodilators; corticosteroids; physiotherapy: breathing exercises; antibiotics for infection.

8.   *Cor Pulmonale* – Sometime refered to as 'fluid on the lungs'. Occurs as a result of an increase in pressure in the arteries in the lungs. As a result the right side of the heart enlarges because it has to work harder to pump the blood through.

Causes: Ongoing lung conditions such as emphysema or COPD.

Symptoms: With increased blood pressure in the lung arteries, breathing becomes increasingly difficult; swollen ankles.

Investigations: Chest X ray; Electro Cardiogram; echocardiogram.

Treatment: Stop smoking (smoking cessation); oxygen therapy; medication for heart failure.

9.   *Hay Fever* – (*Allergic rhinitis*) – An allergic reaction to substances.

Causes: Various substances including plant pollens, dust, dustmites), pets (fur/hair).

Symptoms: Runny, itchy nose, watery eyes, sneezing, stuffy feeling in nose; lack of energy.

Investigations: Physical examination. Sometimes skin test for allergies.

Treatment: Anti-allergy drugs; nasal sprays.

10.   *Hyaline Membrane disease* (see Infant Respiratory Distress Syndrome below)

11.   *Infant Respiratory Distress Syndrome* (*IRDS*) or Neonatal Respiratory Distress Syndrome – Occurs in premature babies, with babies of diabetic mothers also at risk (see Chapter 13).

Causes: If a baby is born before 28–32 weeks of pregnancy, its lungs are still premature and not ready for breathing. These babies' lungs lack surfactant and the little air sacs (alveoli) may easily collapse.

Symptoms: The babies breathing is difficult and laboured (grunting). Other signs may include flared nostrils and indrawing of the chest.

Treatment: The baby is admitted to Neonatal Intensive Care Unit and given surfactant into the lungs. The baby is put on a ventilator and Positive End-Pressure Ventilation (PEEP) or Continuous Positive Airway Pressure (CPAP) may be used to help keep the baby's alveoli open. Preventive treatment can also include giving the mother a course of steroids antenatally, which help the baby's lungs mature.

12.   *Lung carcinoma/Cancer of the lung/Lung cancer* – Cancer cells take over normal lung tissue. There are different types of lung cancer (small cell vs non-small cell) and also different stages (limited – one lung; extensive – spread to both lungs. In lung secondaries or metastases cancer cells have spread to other parts of the body).

Causes: In most cases lung cancer is caused by smoking. Other causes may include passive smoking or breathing in other irritating substances (such as asbestos, coal dust, nickel, petroleum, radon gas).

Symptoms: Chronic coughing or wheezing; blood in phlegm; weight loss; fatigue.

Investigations: Chest X-Ray; (Spiral) CT scanning; angiography or VQ Scan (to look at the blood vessels in the lung); bronchoscopy and biopsy; needle biopsy; sputum or phlegm samples. Cancer cells will be checked under the microscope to decide what type of cancer it is (see Chapter 16).

Treatment: The cancer cells may spread to other areas, such as the brain, bone marrow, liver. Where the cancer spreads and whether the cancer spreads largely depends on the type of cancer. Treatment depends on cell type and spread (stage). This may include surgical treatment such as pneumectomy (removal of entire lung) or lobectomy (removal of one lung lobe). However surgery is only useful if the cancer has not spread. Non-surgical treatment includes radiotherapy; chemotherapy and targeted therapies.

13.   *Pneumonia* – Infection/inflammation of alveoli (see Figure 19.3).

Causes: Infection (often bacterial) causing the alveoli swell up which makes it difficult for oxygen to pass through the wall of the alveoli into the bloodstream.

Symptoms: Tiredness and shortness of breath (due to lack of oxygen); fever.

Investigations: Chest X-Ray (may show a *whiteout* – area of no air movement at all); oxymetry (percentage of oxygen saturated blood).

Treatment: Bed rest; oxygen; physiotherapy; antibiotics (intravenously).

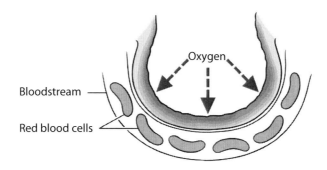

Inflammation and swelling: Difficult for oxygen to enter the bloodstream

Figure 19.6. Swelling and inflammation of the alveoli

14.   *Sleep Apnea* – Also called *Obstructive Sleep Apnea* (*OSA*) occurs when a persons windpipe collapses repeatedly during sleep, obstructing the airway.

Cause: Windpipe keeps blocking off the passage of air to the lungs; often in obese individuals.

Symptoms: Snoring; waking up to take a breath (leading to disrupted sleep, lack of deep sleep stages, and waking up feeling very tired).

Investigations: Sleep study in Sleep Lab (with video and continuous pulse oxymetry overnight).

Treatment: Continuous Positive Airway Pressure (CPAP) mask/machine to keep airways open; sometimes by By-Face Positive Airway Pressure (PAP) mask (not continuous).

15.   *Tuberculosis (Tb)* – Infection with Tb bacilli.

Causes: Mycobacterium tuberculosis (bacteria) spread through airborne droplets (coughing, sneezing, laughing). Tuberculosis may be *walled off* and lie dormant in body for long time (during this time the Tb is called inactive). Another infection (including HIV) may reactivate the Tb by allowing it to 'break out of the walls'. Active Tb is infectious to others.

Symptoms: Cough; tiredness; fever; weight loss; night sweats; blood in sputum

Investigations: Chest X-Ray; Mantoux test; The *Ziehl-Neelsen (Zn) AFB stain test*; LED-FM (see page 203) eyesight test (visual acuity).

Treatment: Depends on whether the patient has inactive tuberculosis or active tuberculosis. Also depends on whether the patient has a drug resistant strain of Tb (common in South East Asia, Africa). *Inactive tuberculosis* can be treated with an antibiotic (INH) to prevent active Tb. *Active tuberculosis* can be treated by INH plus a combination of other drugs. Tb drugs can have side-effects affecting eyesight, liver function or hearing, so visual acuity (eyesight) and audiometry (hearing) tests may be done during treatment. Patients on treatment for Tb should not drink any alcohol. For cultural reasons, some interpreters interpret 'No alcohol' as 'No alcohol – this includes beer'.

Possible complication: Disseminated tuberculosis: Tb has spread from the lungs to other parts of the body through the blood or lymph system.

NOTE: Interpreters should wear a mask when interpreting for patients with <u>*infectious*</u> *tuberculosis.*

7.   Some common drugs

anti-cough	prevent too much coughing, by suppressing the inclination to cough (often using codeine).
anti-histamines	drugs which prevent allergic reaction by preventing release of histamine.
bronchodilators	drugs which open up the bronchi (given as inhalers or through nebulizers).
corticosteroid drugs	may lessen symptoms in life-threatening situations.
expectorants	drugs which make it easier to cough up phlegm/sputum from air passages.
mucolytics	drugs which help dissolve mucus, making it easier to cough up.
preventers	drugs to prevent asthma attacks; often inhaled corticosteroids.

8. Some common investigations

- *Arterial blood gases (ABGs)* – Blood taken from the patient's artery then sent to the lab for precise measurement of levels of oxygen and carbon dioxide (also pH and a few other indicators).
- *Bronchoscopy* – The doctor pushes a flexible fibre-optic tube into the patient's bronchus and examines the lining, taking biopsies if needed. A bronchoscopy may be done if it is difficult to reach a diagnosis in any other way. Sometimes the patient may have washings of the bronchi and alveoli (lavage). These washings or biopsies may show up Tb bacilli.
- *Chest X-Ray (CXR)* – An X-Ray of the chest area, taken in two directions – one with the patient facing the X-Ray machine, one with the patient standing sideways to the X-Ray machine. The Chest X-Ray can give valuable information on the structures in the chest (heart, lungs, windpipe) and any abnormalities (air, blood or fluid in the chest; thickenings in the lungs; enlarged heart, etc).
- *CT scan* – Computerised Tomography imaging.
- *Light Emitting-Diode Fluorescence Microscopy (LED-FM)* – A type of smear microscopy (microscopic examination of sputum specimen), more sensitive and less time-consuming than the standard Ziehl-Neelsen AFB stain.
- *Lung function test* – Series of tests done in the pulmonary lab, measuring, amongst other things, oxygen uptake on exercise (6-minute walk test) and amount of oxygen inhaled and exhaled.
- *Mantoux test* – Skin test whereby a small amount of tuberculin is injected just under the skin. The test is 'positive' for tuberculosis if the injection site becomes red and raised two to three days after the test.
- *Oximetry* – Monitors oxygen saturation of the blood (normally 96–98% on air).
- *Peak flow meter* – Tube with mouthpiece which measures the amount of air the patient is still able to breathe out (or to 'shift'). The patient takes a breath in, places their mouth around the mouthpiece (sealing it off), and 'huffs' into the peak flow meter.
- *Pulse oxymetry* – Oxygen saturation measured by means of a device placed on the nail of the patient (see Figure 11.2, page 104).
- *Spirometry* – Checking the air capacity of the lung with the aid of a machine
- *Sputum specimen (sputum spec)* – Patient coughs up some phlegm into a sterile container, which is sent to the laboratory for testing (infection, tuberculosis).
- *Transbronchial biopsies* – Biopsies taken by using bronchoscopy.
- *Ziehl Nielsen Acid Fast Bacteria Stain Test (AFB)* – Traditional test on sputum for tuberculosis bacteria, which will stain (show up) when touched with an acid dye.

Summary of main points

This chapter has given a brief overview of the respiratory system, including:

- a brief overview of anatomy
- Latin and Greek roots
- health professionals involved
- some commonly encountered conditions relating to the respiratory system, together with common investigations and treatment methods.

Chapter 20

Hematology

Blood and blood disorders

Blood flows through our bodies through a complicated system of blood-vessels. This system of blood-vessels is described in more detail in the chapter on the circulation. This chapter will deal with the blood itself, its components and with the various types of blood vessels.

1. Blood

1.1   Latin and Greek roots

albumin	blood protein
anemia	lack of blood (no blood)
athero	fat(ty)
arterio-	arterial; to do with the arteries
arteriosclerosis	hardening of the arteries
atherosclerosis	fatty hardening of the arteries
capillary	to do with the finest (hair-like) blood-vessels (capilla: hair)
coagulation	clotting (literally: clumping together)
cyte	cell
embolus	big blood clot
embolism	blockage of a blood vessel by a blood clot (or air bubble)
emia	see: hemia
erythro	red (erythrocyte: red cell)
fuse	to pour (liquids)
-gram//graphy	image; recording (grafein: to write)
haem-	see: hem-

hematologist	doctor specializing in the treatment of blood disorders
(h)emia	in the blood (e.g. *leukemia*)
hem-, hemo-, /hemato-	blood (from the greek: *haimos* or *haimatos*)
hemoglobin	protein in red blood cells that allows them to carry oxygen
hemorrhage	bleed (blood bursting forth)
heparin	anti-clotting agent (hepar: liver)
infusion	to pour in
leuko	white (*leukocyte*: white cell)
lymphocyte	lymph cell
lymphoma	lymph cancer (oma: growth, tumor)
-penia	lack of (e.g. thrombocytopenia: lack of platelets)
plaques	deposit; patch (e.g. *atheromatous plaque*: fatty deposit)
plasma expander	helping to increase the volume of the plasma
thrombo	clot
thrombocyte	platelet; (clotting cell)
thrombosis	occurrence of clots (-osis: condition, state)
transfuse	to pour (fluid) across

1.2 Anatomy of blood

Blood consists of formed elements and fluid:
– Formed elements: Red blood cells (oxygen; hemoglobin); White blood cells (immune system; fight infections)
– Platelets (clotting)

Fluid (serum):
– Salts (electrolytes: Na; Cl; Ca; K, etc)
– Oxygen and CO_2
– Food (sugar, fat, proteins), vitamins and minerals
– Hormones (chemical messengers)
– Proteins
   – Albumin
   – Globulin
   – Fibrinogen
– Wastes (removed via kidneys or lungs)

1.3   Function of blood

Red blood cells live for around 90 to 120 days. If a person loses a lot of blood, it will take a few months before they have replaced the lost blood cells.

If a blood-vessel gets cut, blood will start to clot in order to stop the bleeding and start the repair process. Clotting (coagulation or 'clumping together') is a very complicated process, involving a chain reaction of many different coagulation factors. Put in a nutshell:

damage → platelets clump together → clots form → bleeding stops

Sometime, unwanted clotting occurs. This often happens to people who already have a damage to the walls of their blood vessels. This damage can be due to fatty deposits, cigarette smoking or many other factors. Unwanted clotting can also be a result of other disorders. Unwanted clotting can be dangerous because it can lead to clots block-ing arteries. The medical word for a small clot is thrombus. Thrombosis is a condition where people have clots in their blood-vessels. A large clot (consisting of many small clots, sticking together) is called an embolus. When large clots cause a major blockage this is called embolism.

In short:

plaques in walls of blood vessels may lead to unwanted clotting (thrombosis; embolisms)
thrombus → less oxygen to cells
embolism → less or no oxygen to cells   →   lung embolism in the lung;
                                                      OR   CVA (in the brain);
                                                      OR   heart attack (in the heart)

1.4   Health professionals

Hematologist – Doctor specializing in blood disorders.
Phlebotomist – Health professional specializing in taking blood samples.

1.5   Disorders of the blood

1.   *Anemia* – There are not enough red blood cells in the blood, or there is not enough hemoglobin, or the volume of red cells is low; often a sign of underlying illness.

Causes: Blood loss through heavy blood loss (hemorrhagic anemia), heavy menstrual periods; occult (unnoticed) bleeding in stomach or bowels; cancer; sickle cell anemia; inability to absorb iron from food; decreased red blood cell production (e.g. in kidney failure); or *hemolytic anemia* (involving the breakdown of red blood cells), e.g. in malaria, blood transfusion reactions or Rhesus disease.

Symptoms: Feeling cold, weak, tired, irritable; short of breath.

Investigations: Full Blood count (FBC); Red Blood Count (RBC); Hb (hemoglobin) Ht (hematocrit); gastroscopy; colonoscopy (to check for blood loss from the digestive tract); CT Scan.

2. *Hemophilia* (bleeder disease) – A hereditary bleeding disorder where either Clotting Factor VIII (hemophilia A) or Clotting Factor IX (hemophilia B) are missing, so clotting time is longer than normal.

Causes: Inherited from carrier mother, *mostly* males only are effected.

Symptoms: Bruising very easily; bleeding does not stop.

Investigations: Clotting test.

Treatment: Transfusion of the missing clotting factors to prevent bleeding. Transfusions can lead to complications such as brain hemorrhage or developing antibodies to transfused Factor VIII.

3. *Leukemia* (Greek: white blood) – Cancer affecting the white blood cells. Normally stem cells in the bonemarrow develop into different types of healthy white cells, red cells and platelets; in leukemia the bonemarrow produces lots of immature white cells called *blasts*; the blood is flooded with immature white cells (*white blood*), but there are not enough red cells, platelets or healthy white cells.
    There are several types of leukemias Acute Myeloid Leukemia; Acute Lymphoid Leukemia; Chronic Myeloid Leukemia (CML); Chronic Lymphoid Leukemia (CLL). Acute leukemia develop very quickly while chronic leukemia develops slowly and symptoms may be less pronounced.

Causes: Exact cause is unknown, but risk factors include high levels of radiation; exposure to chemicals; chemotherapy.

Symptoms: Tiredness; weight loss; looking pale; fever; sweats; repeated infections; enlarged lymph glands; enlarged liver and spleen; abdominal discomfort (large spleen). Patients can also have anemia, as well as bleed easily and develop infections because the *blasts* cannot fight these infections.
    Leukemia may also lead to internal hemorrhaging, which may be fatal (lead to death). Likewise high fever, due to uncontrolled infection, can also be fatal.

Investigations: Bone marrow aspirate (sample); blood test (white cell count); biopsy of lymph gland(s).

Treatment: Chemotherapy; radiation; allogeneic bone marrow transplant (transplant using bone marrow from another person). Bone marrow transplants can have complications, graft-versus-host disease (see Chapter 24), whereby the healthy donor bone marrow attacks the sick body of the person receiving it.

4. *Malaria* – Parasite infection of the liver and red blood cells.

Cause: Bite by infected mosquito.

Symptoms: Fever with chills; headache; hemolytic anemia and jaundice. Can result in brain damage leading to coma and death.

Treatment: Preventing mosquito bites in tropical countries; oral medication.

5. *Myeloma* – Cancer of the blood which develops in the bone marrow.

What happens: Myeloma cancer cells in spine, ribs, pelvic bones; these can destroy the bone

Causes: Exact cause is unknown.

Symptoms: Severe bone pain; soft spots in the bone; spontaneous fractures (breaks of the bone).

Investigations: CT scan; MRI scan; bonemarrow biopsy; kidney function tests; blood tests for abnormal monoclonal (M) protein (produced by the myeloma cells).

Treatment: Chemotherapy.

6. *Rhesus disease* – See Chapter 29 for specific information on Rh disease.
Please note: A person (most people) can be positive for Rhesus factor (Rh+), which means they have this factor on the surface of their red blood cells. Others may be Rh negative (Rh−), which means they do not have it. If a Rh− person receives Rh+ blood, that person will start to make antibodies against the Rh factor.

7. *Sickle cell disease* – An inherited blood disorder. During an attack of sickle cell anemia, red blood cells take on a rigid 'sickle' shape after giving up their oxygen. Sickle shaped cells cannot fit through the narrow capillaries resulting in blood supply to that part of the body being blocked.

Causes: Genetic/inherited. Sickling attacks are more likely to occur when the patient is in a cold environment or doing exercise.

Symptoms: Sickling attacks are very painful, because parts of the body are deprived of oxygen and therefore send out pain signals. If sickling occurs in the bone, bone may die off.

Investigations: Blood test; if *sickling* occurs in the lungs, an X-ray may show a complete whiteout, meaning that whole areas of the lungs are no longer involved in oxygen exchange.

Treatment: Treatment of symptoms only. Genetic counselling is advised for carriers of sickle cell anemia wishing to have children.

8. *Thalassemia* – An inherited condition where the body makes abnormal hemo-globin and many red blood cells are destroyed, resulting in (severe) anemia. There are several types, including Alpha thalassemia, Beta thalassemia and Hb Barts. Common in South East Asia, the Pacific Islands and countries around the Mediterranean. The term thalassemia major refers to a severe form of the condition, whereas the term thalassemia minor refers to a less severe form.

Cause: Genetic

Symptoms: These range from nothing to mild to severe anemia. Carrier mothers may experience recurrent miscarriages and stillbirths if unborn baby has inherited a severe form of thalassemia.

Investigations: Blood tests.

Treatment: Treatment of symptoms only. Genetic counselling is advised for carriers of thalassemia wishing to have children.

9. *Transfusion reaction* – The body's response to receiving non-compatible blood (e.g. wrong blood group, wrong Rhesus factor).

Cause: Non-compatible blood transfusion (e.g. in emergency medicine).

Symptoms: Lower back pain; chills; low blood pressure; sometimes kidney failure (blood in urine); shock; death.

Investigations: Blood test.

Treatments: Stop transfusion; manage symptoms.

1.6   Some common drugs

anticoagulants	drugs used to prevent clotting
antifibrinolytics	drugs used to break down and dissolve blood clots
heparin	anticoagulant (given by injection or intravenous drip)
vasodilators	drugs used to widen the blood vessels
Vitamin K	helps to stop bleeding (given to newborns as they tend to be low on Vitamin K)
Warfarin®	anticoagulant; effects are monitored by regular blood tests.

1.7   Some common investigations

–   *Bleeding time* – Testing how long it take before the bleeding stops (earlobe and blotting-paper).
–   *Blood grouping* – Test done to see what blood group a person has, *Type A, B, AB* (universal receiver) or *Type O* (universal donor); *Rhesus factor*, Rh+ (rhesus positive) or Rh– (Rhesus negative);

- *Group and hold* – Checking blood group and keeping blood on standby.
- *Clotting time* – Test done to see how soon blood clots.

2. Blood vessels

2.1 Latin and Greek roots

angio	blood-vessel
angiography	process of producing an image of the blood-vessels (using contrast dye)
angioplasty	blood vessel repair (see also Chapter 18)
angiogram	image of the blood vessels following angiography
aorta	largest body artery with smaller arteries branching off to take oxygen to specific areas (comparable to a main road with many side-roads branching off)
arterial	relating to arteries
arteries	strong muscular blood-vessels transporting blood rich in oxygen
cardiovascular	to do with heart and blood vessels
claudication	narrowing of leg arteries, causing patients to stop frequently when they are walking due to severe pain (in legs) caused by lack of oxygen in leg muscles
Cholesterol	blood fats
cyanosis	looking blue (due to lack of oxygen)
endarterectomy	removal of fatty plaques from the wall of artery (endo: inside; arter: artery; ek: out: tomy: cut)
fem-pop or femoropopliteal	relating to (arteries) in upper and lower leg
hematoma	bruise (literally: blood swelling)
hemorrhage	bleed
occlusion	blockage
occluded	blocked
phlebitis	inflammation of the veins
sclerosis	hardening
thrombectomy	procedure to remove a big blood clot from the body either by surgically removing it or by dissolving it and sucking it out through a catheter (thin tube)
thrombophlebitis	inflammation of blood vessel with formation of (small) clots
vascular	relating to blood vessels
venous	relating to veins

2.2 Anatomy of blood vessels

There are three main types of blood vessels:

- *Arteries* – Strong, muscular blood-vessels which take blood that is rich in oxygen (bright red) around the body, distributing oxygen and nutrients to all the body cells.
- *Capillaries* – Very fine, hair-like blood-vessels, which form the link between the tiniest end arteries and the tiniest little veins.
- *Veins* – Wide blood-vessels which take blood low in oxygen, but high in carbon dioxide (a waste product) back to the heart. This blood looks dark-red.

2.3 A word about cholesterol

There are two types of cholesterol, High Density Lipoprotein (HDL) or 'good cholesterol', which removes cholesterol from the blood vessels and Low Density Lipoprotein (LDL) or 'bad cholesterol', which can build up fatty plaques in the walls of the arteries.

Cholesterol is measured in two different ways. In the UK, Canada, Australia and NZ cholesterol is measured in millimols per liter (mmol/L), but in the US it is measured in milligrams per deciliter (mg/dL).

Some people suffer have high cholesterol levels as an inherited condition called *hyperlipidemia* (high fats in the blood). The following approximate levels are recommended for healthy people (at the time of writing):

Table 20.1. Recommended cholesterol levels

	US	UK, Canada, Australia, NZ
Total cholesterol	< 200 mg/dL	< 5 mmol/L
LDL	< 70 mg/dL	< 1.8 mmol/L
HDL*	> 60 mg/dL	> 1.5 mmol/L
Triglycerides	< 150 mg/dL	< 1.7 mmol/L

*the higher the more protective

2.4 Disorders of the blood vessels

1. *Aneurysm* (Greek: widening) – Local widening of blood vessels, usually in brain, abdomen or chest. There are different types of aneurysm. A dissecting aneurysm occurs when blood seeps through a length-wise tear between layers of the wall of the artery. The layers come apart and swell and the artery becomes shaped like a balloon. An abdominal aortic aneurysm (AAA) is a widening in the aorta in the abdomen. Complications can arise as a result of a rupture and bleed which can lead to death.

Causes: Sometimes congenital weakness in blood vessels, but can also be due to injury; smoking; atherosclerosis.

Symptoms: Sometimes abdominal discomfort, sometimes no symptoms.

Investigations: Auscultation (murmur); Doppler; ultrasound.

Treatment: Watchful waiting; repair by vein graft or surgical clipping or by inserting a coil.

2. *Deep Vein Thrombosis (DVT)* – A big blood clot in a deep vein, usually the lower leg.

Causes: Being immobile for a long period of time (e.g. bed-rest; paralysis); cancer; drugs (e.g. birth control pills); injury/damage to veins (e.g. intravenous needle or canula); varicose veins; old age; previous DVT.

Symptoms: Swelling; pain; warm and tender limb with discolored skin. This condition can lead to a lung embolism (big blood clot stops blood from entering lungs to pick up oxygen) which may be fatal.

Investigations: Doppler; ultrasound, CT scan.

Treatment: Anticoagulants.

3. *Narrowing of arteries* – When arteries are narrowed or blocked, oxygen cannot get through to the tissue, resulting in pain. If no oxygen gets through at all, cells start to die.

Causes: Artery walls may be damaged due to smoking, high blood pressure or high levels of insulin or glucose. Fat may also be deposited on artery walls due to high blood fats (cholesterol).

Symptoms: Narrowed or blocked arteries can lead to a number of conditions, depending on where the blockages are:

    Eyes – Narrowing of the tiny arteries at the back of the eye (in the *retina*) may lead to loss of vision.

    Heart – Coronary artery narrowing may lead to angina or heart attacks (see Chapter 18, Pages 184, 187).

    Neck – Carotid artery narrowing may lead to TIAs or CVAS (see Chapter 17, Page 171).

    Legs – Narrowing of the femoral arteries (groin and upper leg) may lead to peripheral vascular disease which may lead to claudication (being able to walk only a small distances before severe pain comes on), or to leg ulcers that do not heal, or gangrene (tissue dying off and going black).

    Kidneys – Narrowing of the tiny arteries in the glomeruli, which may lead to kidney failure (see Chapter 27, Page 276).

Investigations: angiography; arteriography; Doppler; ultrasound; CT scan.

Treatment: Lifestyle changes such as stopping smoking, exercise and cholesterol lowering diet; cholesterol lowering drugs; angioplasty with stent; balloon angioplasty (see Chapter 18, Page X); endarterectomy (removal of fatty plaques); by-pass surgery using vein graft (blood vessel replaced with vein from patient's own leg) or manmade graft. Where there is narrowing of leg arteries treatment may include femoropopliteal (*fempop*) bypass surgery to by-pass narrowed section of leg arteries and improve blood supply to the leg or amputation of (part of) the leg.

4.   *Thrombophlebitis* – Inflammation, usually in superficial vein.

Cause: Damage to the vein (e.g. through an intravenous needle or canula); long periods of immobility (e.g. long flight); birth control pills, especially in women who are older or who smoke. Complications can arise if the clot breaking off and causes a blockage elsewhere (e.g. in heart, lungs or brain).

Symptoms: Swelling, redness, tenderness.

Investigations: Doppler; ultrasound; CT scan.

Treatment: Anti-coagulants; compression stockings; elevating legs; exercise.

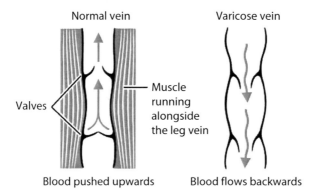

Figure 20.1. Varicose veins

5.   *Varicose veins* – Bulging, twisted, swollen veins, often in legs.

Causes: Standing for long periods of time; pregnancy; constipation; family history; being overweight. Complications can arise whereby leg circulation can be affected and leg ulcers can occur.

Symptoms: Itching around veins; swelling in legs; aching legs; throbbing pain; muscle cramps; pain behind knee.

Investigations: Doppler; ultrasound.

Treatment: Exercise; elastic support stockings; sclerotherapy (which entails injecting veins with sclerosing solution to close them down); stripping (surgical removal of veins).

Summary of main points

This chapter has given a brief overview of blood and blood vessels, including:

- a brief overview of the composition of the blood
- a brief overview of the main blood vessels and their functions
- Latin and Greek roots
- Health professionals involved
- some commonly encountered conditions relating to blood and blood vessels, together with common investigations and treatment methods.

Chapter 21

Orthopedics

The skeletal system

The skeletal system is the supporting framework of the body. It consists of 206 bones in total, including the small bones in the ear. Some of these bones are known only by their Latin names. The list below includes the parts of the skeleton most commonly referred to.

1. Latin and Greek roots

ankylo	stiff
arthro	joint
inter-	in between
-itis	inflammation
osteoarthritis	inflammation of bone and joint
intervertebral	in between the vertebrae
myelum	bonemarrow
osteo	bone
porosis	porous; brittle
sarcoma	cancer of the connective tissue (*sarc* – connective tissue; *oma* – tumor or swelling)
spondylos	vertebra
therapy	treatment
vertebrae	33 small bones that make up the spine

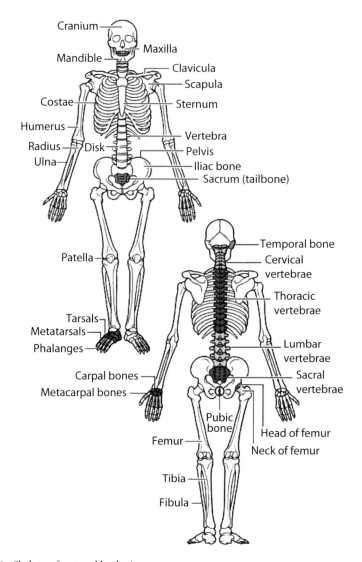

Figure 21.1. Skeleton front and back view

2.   Anatomy of the skeletal system

2.1   Head

cranium	skull; 'brain box'
temporal bone	bone on the side of the skull, above the ear
maxilla	upper jaw
mandible	lower jaw

2.2   Torso

Vertebrae	there are 33 vertebrae in the spine, separated by intervertebral disks
cervical	(vertebrae) at neck level
thoracic	(vertebrae) at chest level
lumbar	(vertebrae) at lower back level
sacral	(vertebrae) at the level of the tailbone
clavicula	collar bone
scapula	shoulder blade
costae	ribs
intercostal	between the ribs
sternum	breast bone
pelvis	area between the hip bones
iliac bone	hip bone

2.3   Arms

humerus	upper arm
radius and ulna	two bones of the forearm
metacarpal bones	small bones in the hand

2.4   Legs

femur	thigh bone
neck of femur	neck of the thigh bone
head of femur	head of the thigh bone
patella	knee-cap
meniscus	small crescent-shaped piece of cartilage in the knee joint in the knee joint
fibula	one of two long narrow bones in the lower leg
tibia	shin bone
metatarsal bones	small bones in the foot

3.   Function of the bones

The bones have various functions:

- support of the body
- protection (e.g. ribs protecting heart and lungs)
- leverage (movement)

– production of blood cells (in the bone-marrow)
– storage of minerals (calcium; phosphorus)

Bone has an excellent blood supply and is constantly changing and developing depending on circumstances (e.g. during weight-bearing exercise, bone gets stronger). Bone is made up of minerals and collagen fibres. Healthy bone requires protein, Vitamin D3, calcium and phosphorus. Excessive consumption of soft drinks containing phosphorus (and inadequate intake of calcium) may lead to an imbalance in the body, causing bone loss.

The bone marrow (soft centre) of some flat bones (hip bones, breast bones) is involved in the production of blood cells.

4. Health professionals

Chiropractor – Health professional who has completed studies in the area of musculo skeletal disorders; often specializing in manipulation of the spinal column.

Orthopedic surgeon – Medical doctor specializing in orthopedic surgery.

Osteopath – Health professional specializing in trying to eliminate structural problems of the skeletal system, and especially in manipulation of the spinal column.

Physical therapist or Physiotherapist – Health professional who has completed a studies in the treatment of muscular disorders; physiotherapists are often involved in treatment of sporting injuries, rehabilitation of patients (e.g. following surgery or strokes) or in helping prevent breathing problems (e.g. patients with chronic lung disorders). See also Chaptes 7 and 22.

5. Disorders of the bones and joints

1. *Ankylosing spondylitis* (also called *bamboo spine* or *poker spine*) – Ongoing inflammation and stiffness of the spine and pelvic joints. Eyes, heart, lung and bowels may also be involved. Eventually the joints involved start to fuse together. The spine becomes rigid. Usually occurs in men between 20 and 40 years of age.

Causes: Autoimmune disease.

Symptctoms: Worsening pain and stiffness in the lower back.

Investigations: Blood tests.

Treatment: Nonsteroidal anti-inflammatory drugs (NSAIDs).

2. *Anterior cruciate ligament rupture* – Rupture of ligament that runs across the front of the knee.

Cause: Twisting force to the knee while foot firmly on the ground, during sports or motor vehicle collision.

Symptoms: Pop and severe pain when injury happens; initial instability, extensive swelling.

Investigations: Physcial examination (patient cannot fully straighten the leg); MRI.

Treatment: Surgery

3. *Curvatures of the spine* – Spine curves to the left or right side – the most common type of curvature is scoliosis (from the Greek, meaning *crooked*).

Causes: Unknown.

Symptoms: Depends on curvature.

Investigations: X-ray.

Treatment: Back brace; surgery in severe cases.

4. *Bone Cancers* – A fast growing tumor in the bone and/or the connective tissue, in the leg or in the upper arm. Can be a primary bone cancer (starting in the bone) or secondary (cancer started somewhere else, then travelled to the bone) source. There are many different types of primary bone cancer, osteosarcoma is one of these. Secondary bone cancer refers to cancer spread (to the bone) from somewhere else. Common in breast, prostate or lung cancers.

Causes: Unknown.

Symptoms: Pain; problems with movement; fracture.

Investigations: X-ray, MRI scan, bone scan, bone biopsy. For secondary forms investigations include CT scan.

Treatment: Limb-sparing surgery with bone graft or prosthesis; amputation; radiotherapy, chemotherapy, palliative treatment. For secondary forms treatment can include surgery; chemotherapy; radiotherapy.

5. *Fractures* – Broken bones. There are several types of fractures: Open fracture (bone sticking out through the skin), closed fractures/simple fractures skin is not broke and greenstick fractures (incomplete fractures). Children's bones, in particular, are a bit like young green twigs and often bend rather than break completely. Fractures can also be displaced (bone pieces are out of place and need to be put in place again because

they have been displaced), non-displaced bone pieces are still in place or comminuted (bone has been broken into more than two pieces).

Some common fractures include: a fractured neck of the femur (#NOF) (especially in older women), dinner fork fracture (when radius and ulna are broken close to the wrist); spine (which may cause injury to the spinal cord, see Chapter 17), and fractured tibia and fibula (#tib fib).

Causes: Impact of some kind.

Symptoms: Depends on the fracture, please see above.

Investigations: X-Rays.

Treatments: General treatment methods for fractures include repositioning (putting it back in place) or reducing the fracture (bending it back into position); collar-and-cuff; sling; plaster cast; sometimes traction (pulling it into alignment using a weight and pulley system) is used for broken thigh-bones. Surgical treatment may include total hip replacement for a broken neck of femur (NOF); screw and plate; dynamic hip screw; pin; external fixation (bone supported by metal rods from outside of the body.

For open fractures the skin wound will not be closed so as to not lock in bacteria (anaerobic bacteria thrive if there is no oxygen) which may cause gas gangrene under the skin. Complications such as compartment syndrome can arise when plaster casts become too tight, blocking blood flow or putting pressure on the nerves. Symptoms of compartment syndrome may include pain; tingling; 'pins and needles'; numbness; patient is unable to move their toes or fingers (flex, extend). In this case the cast will need to be split, to relieve the pressure and restore the blood flow.

6.   *Hydrocephalus* (from the Greek meaning: water on the brain) – Cerebro Spinal Fluid (CSF) is not absorbed, leading to too much fluid in the ventricles (cerebrospinal fluid spaces) in the brain. Hydrocephalus may also result from brain injury (including stroke).

Causes: (In infants) not well understood. In older people: brain injury.

Symptoms: In infants, the skull will grow bigger to accommodate the fluid.

Investigations: CT or MRI scan.

Treatment: Shunt (or other surgery) to drain away excess cerebrospinal fluid.

7.   *Osteoarthritis* – '*Wear and tear*' of joints/spine.

Causes: Overweight; too much jarring exercise.

Symptoms: Stiffness; tenderness; deformity; difficulty moving.

Investigations: X-ray; arthroscopy; ESR blood test *to exclude* Rheumatoid arthritis and other conditions.

Treatment: Weight loss; corticosteroid injections into joint; NSAIDS; physiotherapy; knee brace. Surgical treatmentmay include total hip/knee replacement; osteotomy (to realign bone).

8.   *Osteomalacia* – Referred to as rickets in children and osteomalacia in adults.

Cause: Malabsorption of calcium in the gut (either because there is not enough calcium in diet, or because of a lack of vitamin D) or because of a phosphate deficiency (because phosphate is lost through kidneys).

Symptoms: In rickets children's bone may become soft and bowed. In osteomalacia bones in the arms, legs, ribs and or lower back are painful. Other symptoms include muscle weakness; waddling (ducklike) gait; chronic fatigue; bones lose their shape.

Investigations: X-Ray; bone density scan.

Treatment: Exposure to sunlight (Vitamin D); diet with calcium and or phosphorus; Vitamin D supplements; avoid fizzy drink.

9.   *Osteomyelitis* – Inflammation or infection of bones and bone-marrow.

Causes: Usually from infection elsewhere in the body (e.g. pneumonia or an urinary tract infection); open wound over bone (e.g. small heel wound) or open fracture.

Symptoms: Pain; fever; chills.

Investigations: ESR; CT or MRI scan.

Treatment: Immobilizing affected bone (e.g. brace, splint); high dose of IV antibiotics; surgery.

10.   *Osteoporosis* (also *brittle bone disease'*) – Bones become thinner, lighter, more brittle and break more easily.

Causes: Lack of Vitamin D3; lack of (weightbearing) exercise; poor diet (not enough calcium, too much fizzy drink); certain drugs (e.g. long-term use of corticosteroids); loss of estrogen protection after menopause; family history of osteoporosis; smoking; excessive alcohol intake.

Symptoms: Bones break easily.

Investigations: DEXA scan (bone density scan).

Treatment: Increase calcium intake; weightbearing exercise; Vitamin D; hormone replacement therapy.

11. *Rheumatic Fever* – see Chapter 13, page 136.

12. *Rheumatoid Arthritis* (RhA) – A connective tissue disorder involving inflammation of the connective tissue in joints, tendons and other parts of the body.

Cause: Not known; auto-immune disease – some link it to gluten intolerance.

Symptoms: Patients often feel ill, painful and stiff; (small) joints may be swollen or deformed.

Investigations: Blood tests: ESR (erythrocyte sedimentation rate) and C-reactive protein (CPR) are high, indicating inflammation; Rheumatoid Factor is positive in the blood; X-Rays; family history.

Treatment: Disease modifying anti-rheumatic drugs and biologic drugs (such as Humira®); some patients benefit from a diet that is gluten-free and high in fish oil. Surgery: Joint replacement may be considered (total hip replacement; total knee replacement; finger bone replacement).

13. *Slipped disk*
See Chapter 17.

14. *Whiplash*
See Chapter 17.

Summary of main points

This chapter has given a brief overview of the skeletal system, including:

– a brief overview of anatomy of bones and joints
– Latin and Greek roots
– health professionals involved
– some commonly encountered conditions relating to the bones and joints, together with common investigations and treatment methods.

Chapter 22

Muscles and the motor system

The motor system involves both nerve cells and muscle cells.

Within the motor system the brain coordinates and controls movement by sending signals to the muscles, that is the brain sends signals to the muscles, the muscles then contract and movement results. The cerebellum ensures that movement is smooth and coordinated.

Please note: Alcohol influences the cerebellum, resulting in movement that is less smooth and coordinated.

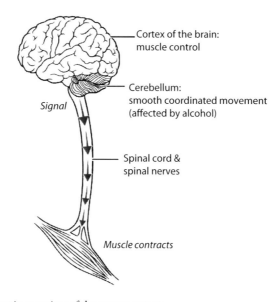

Figure 22.1. Schematic overview of the motor system

1. Latin and Greek roots

atrophy	absence of growth (muscle atrophy)
a	not; without
ab	away from
ad	towards (NB *adc…* often changes into *acc…*)
-algia	pain

anti	against
bi	two (biceps = two headed)
chondro-	cartilage-
con	together
contract	pull together
duct	lead
dys-	bad; difficult; painful
dystrophy	abnormal growth
fascia	bundle
hernia	broken
-lysis	destruction of –; loosening of –; freeing of –
malacia	softening
myalgia	muscle pain
myo	muscle
neuromuscular	to do with both nerves and muscles
-oid	resembling (e.g. deltoid muscle – resembles a (river) delta)
ortho	straight
para	beside/alongside; beyond; accessory to (e.g. paramedic)
pathos	sick/diseased
ped-	child; grow
plasty	repair
sarco-	connective tissue
syn	together
tonus	tone (muscle tone)
tract	route; pull
tri	three (triceps = three-headed)
trophy	growth

2.   General terminology in relation to muscles

EMG	electromyography (-electrical stimulation of muscle to measure strength of muscle contractions)_
lesion	damage; injury; wound
ligament	band of fibrous tissue binding joints together
physical therapy	literally: physical treatment, also physiotherapy or physio
	– active movement
	– passive movement
posture	way somebody holds their body (e.g. stooped; hunched shoulder)

RICE	Rest; Ice; Compression; Elevation treatment for injuries
ROM	range of movement exercises
sphincter	circular band of muscle fibers around natural orifices (openings)
sprain	traumatic injury to muscle, tendon, ligament around joints: pain, swelling
strain	damage (usually muscular) due to excessive physical effort (overdoing it)
tendon	strong fibrous cord attaching muscle to bone
torn muscle	tear in muscle fibers

3. Anatomy of the muscles

There are three main types of muscle in the body:

– *cardiac muscle* – muscle in the wall of the heart. The cardiac muscle (myocard) responds to the heart's own pacemaker, the sinus node.
– *skeletal muscle* – role is to provide movement (voluntary; automatic or reflex) of skeleton (e.g. breathing; walking; grasping)
– *smooth muscle* – involuntary muscle in hollow organs and blood vessels that play a role in digestion and circulation.

4. Function of the muscles

In general muscles provide movement; maintain posture and produce heat (e.g. when someone with a high fever gets the *chills* because the 'thermostat' in the brain has been reset and the person feels cold.

5. Health professionals

See Chapter 21, Page 220.

6. Disorders of the motor System

1. *Guillain Barré Syndrome* – A virus infection leads to an antibody response where the body's immune system mistakenly attacks part of the nervous system, resulting in nerve damage.

Causes: Virus infection.

Symptoms: Weakness; muscle wasting; paralysis (may need ventilator); tingling; numbness. Mostly affects people between 20 and 50 years of age. NB: Guillain-Barré symptoms can worsen very quickly.

Investigations: Blood tests; lumbar puncture; MRI scan.

Treatment: Acute stage- rest; pain relief; physiotherapy; ventilator/respiratory support; Recovery stage – strengthening exercises.

2.   *Motor Neurone Disease (MND)* – Degeneration of nerve cells results in progressive muscle wasting; usually affects patients over 50 years of age (this condition is often fatal within 3–10 years). MNDs include Amyotrophic lateral sclerosis (ALS) (also called: Lou Gehrig's disease or classical motor neuron disease).

Causes: Toxins; inherited; viral and environmental causes have also been suggested.

Symptoms: Muscle wasting and weakness; spasticity; difficulty swallowing. Can lead to complications due to respirator infections.

Investigations: Electromyography (EMG); MRI scan; muscle biopsy.

Treatment: Physical therapy; occupational therapy; wheelchair.

3.   *Muscular Dystrophy (MD)* – Group of inherited disorders of the motor system, which lead to gradually worsening muscle weakness and muscle loss. One form of MD is Duchenne's Muscular Dystrophy, which only affects boys.

Causes: Genetic disorder; missing protein (in DMD).

Symptoms: Affected children may develop problems walking by age 6 and are usually in a wheelchair by age 12. Breathing may be affected by age 20.

Investigations: Electromyogram (testing muscle tone and strength).

Treatment: Braces; walker; wheelchair; ventilator support if necessary.

4.   *Myasthenia gravis* – An auto-immune disorder affecting the motor system. Antibodies attack the junction between nerves and muscles, and the nerve signal is not transferred to the muscles.

Causes: Auto-immune.

Symptoms: Drooping eyelid is often an early sign. Painless muscle weakness can progress to paralysis, which is dangerous if breathing and swallowing are affected.

Investigations: Repetitive nerve stimulation.

Treatment: Immunosuppressants; immunoglobulins; removing the thymus gland; stem cell treatment is being investigated.

5.   *Poliomyelitis* – Infection where the polio virus destroys the *motor nerves.*

Causes: Polio virus.

Symptoms: Sore throat, malaise; headache; fever (nonparalytic poliomyelitis); in paralytic poliomyelitis this is followed by muscle pain, muscle weakness, problems urinating; problems breathing and may lead to paralysis (if breathing muscles paralysed, it may result in death).

Investigations: Lumbar puncture (to distinguish it from meningitis); blood test for polio antibodies.

Treatment: Ventilator support if necessary; physical therapy, leg braces.

6.   *Polyneuropathy* – A *malfunction* of many peripheral nerves at the same time, leading to *degeneration* of those nerves.

Causes: Many different causes, including diabetes, alcohol abuse or infections such as *herpes zoster* or *Guillain Barré* (see Page 227).

Symptoms: Itchiness; 'crawling'; 'burning'; pain.

Investigations: Electromyogram; Nerve conduction velocity test (NCV).

Treatment: Painkillers; physical therapy.

7.   Disorders of the muscles

Disorders to do with the muscles proper are often related to either exercise, overuse, trauma, injury or infection. Patients will often see their primary doctor or physical therapist (see Chapter 7) for advice. Assessment will involve physical examination and history taking.

1.   *Carpal Tunnel Syndrome* – Increased pressure in the carpal tunnel (a narrow space inside the wrist) causes pressure on the median nerve.

Causes: Occupational overuse; writst injury; swelling during pregnancy or menopause.

Symptoms: Lead to numbness, pain and tingling or pins and needles in the hand and or arm.

Investigations: Physical examination; history.

Treatment: Wrist supports or splints; avoiding repetitive movements; steroid injections; surgery.

2.   *Groin Strain* – Adductor muscle in the inner thigh muscle stretched too far.

Treatment: Rest, stretching, ice, heat.

3.   *Hematoma* – Literally blood swelling. Blood leaks into the muscle tissue after injury, causing tenderness and bruising.

Treatment: Ice packs.

4.   *Myositis* – Inflammation of muscle tissue.

Treatment: Corticosteroids.

5.*Occupational Overuse Syndrome (OOS) (also known as Repetitive Strain Injury or RSI)* – Carpal tunnel syndrome and tendonitis are examples of OOS.

6.   *Shin splints* – Swelling or inflammation of muscles and tendons over the shin bone due to overuse or increased activity.

Treatment: Rest, ice; stretching, strengthening; orthotics; taping.

7.   *Ruptured Achilles Tendon* – Rupture of tendon at the back of the heel, pain, swelling, inability to walk.

Treatment: Cast or walking boot; surgery.

8.   *Sprain* – Stretch and/or tear of a ligament.

Treatment: RICE; immobilization and surgery if severe.

9.   *Strain* – Injury of a muscle or tendon.

Treatment: RICE; immobilization and surgery if severe.

10.   *Tendonitis* – Inflammation of the tendons (fibrous cords connecting muscles to bones) e.g.Tennis elbow; Achilles tendonitis; rotator cuff injury.

Treatment: RICE; anti-inflammatory drugs; physiotherapy.

8.   Common treatment methods for muscle injuries

Drugs	Anti-inflammatory drugs or gels; painkillers
Physical therapy or Physiotherapy	Physical therapy may include exercises; electrical stimulation; massage; taping (rigid sports tape; stretchy kinesiology tape); applying heat or cold (ice).

Summary of main points

This chapter has given a brief overview of the muscles and motor system, including:

- a brief overview of anatomy of the muscles and the motor system
- Latin and Greek roots
- health professionals involved
- some commonly encountered conditions relating to muscles and the motor system, joints, together with common investigations and treatment methods.

Chapter 23

The sensory system

The sensory system is the system that deals with the five senses:

- Eye-sight
- Smell and Taste
- Hearing
- Balance
- Touch

Impressions of the outside world (e.g. sights, sounds, smells, tastes and 'feels') are picked up by our eyes, nose, tastebuds, ears (and other receptors) and messages are sent to the brain as to what we are seeing, smelling, tasting, hearing or feeling.

1. The eye

Images enter the eye through the opening, the pupil. They then pass through the *lens* and are received by the nerve cells which are situated on the *retina*, at the back of the eye-ball. The nerve cells pass the messages along the *optic nerve* on to the brain.

2. Anatomy of the eye

This is a cross-section of the eye.

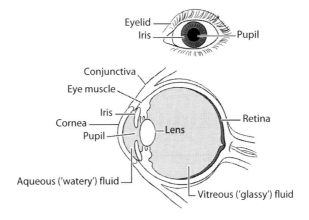

Figure 23.1. Cross-section of the eye

3. Different parts of the eye

conjunctiva	the inner lining of the eye-lids
cornea	the clear, dome-shaped, outermost layer of the eye
iris	the round disk which floats in the watery fluid between the cornea and the lens of the eye
lens	thin but tough see-through membrane in front of the eye-ball. The lens focuses the eye by changing its curve. When the curve of the lens changes, the light-rays passing through the lens are bent at a different angle
macula	the part of the eye that provides sharp, central vision, helping you see things clearly
optic nerve	takes images from the retina to the brain
pupil	hole in the middle of the iris. Muscles in the iris can make the pupil opening bigger or smaller. If there is not much light, the pupil opening will enlarge, to let more light in
retina	the nerve cells of the eye are situated on the retina, at the back of the eye-ball

4. Latin and Greek roots

astigmatism	blurry vision (cornea is not symmetrical) (a: no; stigma: mark)
blind spot	spot without nerve cells, where the optic nerve leaves the retina
cataract	cloudy, opaque lens
cochlea	(Greek: snail shell) hearing organ
corneal implant	artificial cornea
eardrum	see illustration
eustachian tube	tube connecting middle ear with nose-throat cavity
excimer laser	special type of laser used for eye-surgery
hyperopia/hypermetropia	farsightedness; condition where person has difficulty seeing things closeup
kerato-	cornea; to do with the cornea
- metrist	someone who measures
myopia	shortsightedness
ophtalmos	eye

opt-/optic	relating to the eye
photorefractive	light bending (rays)
photorefractive keratectomy	laser surgery to reshape the corneas to improve vision (less or no need for corrective glasses)
nystagmus	quick jittery movements of both eyes related to either loss of vision or loss of muscle control
retinoblastoma	tumor of retina (blast: immature cell; *oma*: growth)
strabismus	crossed eyes
tympanometry	checking how well the ear drum moves

5.   Health professionals

Ophtalmologist – Doctor specializing in eyes and eye-complaints.
Optometrist – Health professional specializing in testing our eye-sight.
Optician – Professional specialised in providing people with the right glasses or contact lenses.

6.   Disorders of the eye

1.   *Cataract* – Lens becomes increasingly cloudy or opaque.

Causes: Age; eye injury; diabetes; X-Rays; microwaves; UV light; long-term use of corticosteroids.

Symptoms: Blurry vision; 'grey film' covering the eye.

Investigations: Eye examination.

Treatment: Surgery to remove cloudy lens and insert an artificial lens; phacoemulsification where ultrasound used to break up lens into small pieces (which are then suctioned out).

2.   *Conjunctivitis* – (also called pink eye) is the result of infection or inflammation of the conjunctiva.

Cause: Viral or bacterial infection; irritation; allergy; chemicals.

Symptoms: Painful, swollen, red eyes; bacterial infection may cause yellow discharge.

Investigations: Swab; culture to see which bacteria has caused the infection.

Treatment: Anti-bacterial ointment; steroid or anti-histamine eye-drops for allergic conjunctivitis.

3. *Floaters* – Spots, flecks or 'cobwebs' in front of eye.

Cause: Bits of debris floating in the glassy fluid (vitreous humor) of the eye, due to ageing, injury or a bleed in the vitreous humor. Sudden increase in floaters with light flashes may be followed by retinal detachment (see below – medical emergency).

Symptoms: As above

Investigations: Eye test

Treatment: None.

4. *Glaucoma* – Too much pressure in the fluid in front of the lens, leading to pressure on lens. This pressure is transferred to the fluid in front of the retina (nerve cells) and may eventually lead to damage of the nerve cells. Different types of glaucoma, the two most common are open-angle glaucoma, which develops gradually (slow onset), and angle-closure glaucoma which can have an acute onset (start suddenly).

Cause: Risk factors include age; family history; myopia; diabetes.

Symptoms: Pain; reduced vision or even blindness; sudden loss of vision in one eye; halos around lights; often acute episodes with severe pain; nausea and vomiting.

Investigations: Regular eye-test; pressure test (puff of air blown against the eye (tonometry).

Treatment: Eye-drops: Surgery aimed at allowing fluid to seep away by enlarging drainage openings, e.g. laser treatment: laser iridotomy; laser trabeculectomy (filtration surgery).

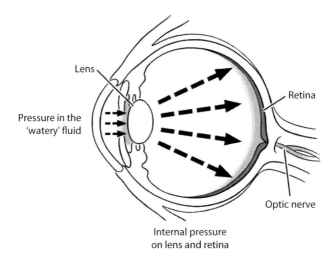

Figure 23.2. Schematic representation of glaucoma

5. *Macular degeneration also* age-related macular degeneration (AMD or ARMD) – a range of conditions affecting the macula, the central part of the retina. AMD is a leading cause of blindness.

There are two types of AMD: dry and wet.

Cause: Deterioration of the retina. Risk factors include age; smoking; light eye colour.
What happens: the macula deteriorates; especially in those aged 55 and older
Dry (atrophic) form: This type results from the gradual breakdown of cells in the macula, resulting in a gradual blurring of central vision. Single or multiple, small, round, yellow-white spots called drusen are the key identifiers for the dry type.
Wet form: Abnormal blood vessels grow under the center of the retina, leaking, bleeding and scarring, leading to a rapid loss of vision. Symptoms: Dry AMD: gradual blurring of central vision. Wet AMD: rapid loss of vision, usually in one eye first.

Symptoms: Blurry vision; blind spots.

Investigations: Visual field testing; special eye tests using contrast dye.

Treatment: Low vision aids; stopping smoking.

6. *Nystagmus* – Rolling or jerking eye-movements.

Cause: Some form of brain dysfunction; multiple sclerosis; use of alcohol or barbiturates (drugs causing sleepiness).

Symptoms: As above.

Investigations: Eye examination.

Treatment: Treating underlying condition.

7. *Retinal Detachment* – Retina comes away from the back of the eye.

Cause: Age, myopia.

Symptoms: Shower of sparkling spots and or floaters, followed by feeling as if a curtain is moving across the eye. Note this is a medical emergency, as it can lead to blindness.

Investigations: Eye examination.

Treatment: Immediate laser surgery to reattach the retina.

8. *Trachoma* – Type of conjunctivitis.

Causes: Contagious bacterial infection.

Symptoms: Pain; redness; swelling; scarred eyelids rub on eyeballs, can lead to blindness

Investigations: Eye examination.

Treatment: Urgent medical attention required including tetracycline (drug) and surgical repair of scarred eyelids.

7.   The ears

Sound waves enter through the outer ear and the ear canal until they hit the ear-drum.

The middle ear is situated between the ear-drum and the inner ear. In the middle ear, the sound waves are passed on by a number of small bones: hammer, anvil and stirrup, until they reach the inner ear.

The inner ear is the part of the ear that contains the cochlea, the hearing organ, which is shaped like a snail shell and lined with nerve cells. The inner ear also contains the balance organ. The nerve cells in the inner ear receive the sound message and send it on to the brain by way of the auditory nerve.

There is a tube called the Eustachian tube which leads from the nose-throat area to the middle ear. This tube is one reason why infections are easily transferred from the nose-throat area to the middle ear.

8.   Anatomy of the ear

The ear consists of three sections:

–   the outer ear – where sound is received and transferred to the eardrum.
–   the middle ear – where sound is transferred from the eardrum to the inner ear.
–   the inner ear – which contains the hearing organ and the balance organ.

The illustration shows a cross-section of the ear.

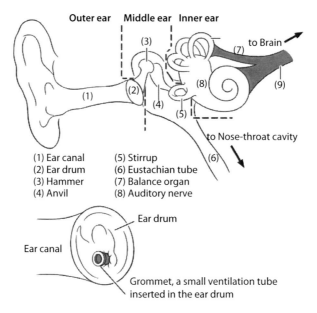

Figure 23.3. Cross-section of the ear

9. Health professionals

Audiologist – Health professional who diagnoses hearing or balance problems; may dispense hearing aids or recommend cochlear implants.
Audiometrist – Hearing tester.
Oto-Rhino-Laryngologist (ORL) specialist – See ENT specialist.
Ear/Nose/Throat (ENT) specialist – Doctor specializing in disorders of the ear, nose and throat. The *ENT specialist* also treat patients with disorders of the balance organ, as this is situated near the inner ear.

10. Disorders of the ear and balance organ

1. *Deafness* – Inability to hear (can be nerve deafness or conductive hearing loss).

Causes: Can be congenital; damage to auditory nerve through ongoing noise, drugs.

Symptoms: Hearing loss.

Investigations: Otoscopy; audiometry.

Treatment: Cochlear implant, a surgically implanted electronic device that provides a sense of sound. Cochlear implants comprise a microphone, a speech processor, a transmitter (behind the ear), a receiver and stimulator (placed in bone beneath the skin), and electrodes wound through the cochlea, which send nerve messages through to the brain. For this to be successful the patient needs a functioning auditory nerve; profound deafness in both ears; a wish to become part of the 'hearing' world.

2. *Ear Infection* (also *otitis media* or *middle ear infection*) – Bacterial infection of the middle ear whereby the middle ear fills up with fluid, causing 'pressing' or pressure against eardrum.

Cause: Cold blocking off the Eustachian tube; bacteria trapped inside middle ear (where they multiply causing infection). More common in young children as the Eustachian tube is floppier and blocks more easily.

Symptoms: Hearing loss; pain. Addition complications can arise for children if left untreated. Glue ear (gluey fluid remains in middle ear) leads to hearing loss which can affect (delay) speech.

Investigations: Checking ear for fluid with otoscope.

Treatment: Antibiotics; grommets if repeated ear infections.

3. *Impacted cerumen – impacted ear wax* – Ear wax blocks the outer ear so sounds cannot get through.

Cause: Ear wax (often pushed inside when cleaning ear with cotton buds).

Symptoms: Tinnitus (roaring sound in ear); hearing loss.

Investigations: History.

Treatment: Syringing or irrigating ear with lukewarm water.

4. *Glue ear* (see Ear infection).

5. *Meniere's Disease* – Fluid increases in the ear canals in the inner ear, which leads to more pressure in the inner ear, which disturbs the sense of balance.

Cause: Unknown; factors may include food allergy (including beans and legumes) or injury to middle ear.

Symptoms: Vertigo (dizziness) with sense of the room spinning; tinnitus (ringing in the ear); nausea, sweating. The increase in pressure can also damage the *cochlea* (hearing organ), leading to hearing loss.

Investigations: Audiometry; MRI brain scan.

Treatment: Drugs.

6. *Middle ear infection* (see Ear infection).

7. *Motion sickness* (also called seasickness or carsickness) – Motion of plane/car or ship makes person sick.

Cause: Very sensitive balance centre (inherited) in the inner ear.

Symptoms: Nausea and vomiting.

Investigations: History.

Treatment: Antihistamines; skin patch, worn close to the ear (and balance organ).

8. *Otitis media* (see Ear infection).

9. *Seasickness* (see Motion sickness)

11.   Drugs (for eyes and ears)

antihistamines	used for allergy relief; prevent the allergic reaction by preventing the release of histamine.
blocking agents	lower the pressure in the eye.
miotics	lead to narrowing of the pupil narrowed (treatment of glaucoma).
antibiotics	help the body fight bacterial infections.

12.   Touch

The skin contains many nerve endings. When we touch something, for example something hot, a message travels back from the nerve receptor, along a long path, back up along the spinal cord, to the brain. The brain then realizes that we are touching something hot and sends another message down along nerve paths to a muscle, saying: "Pull that hand back! Quick!" Those of us who have ever touched something very hot and pulled our hand back, will realize that these messages travel to and from the brain incredibly quickly.

13.   Disorders of touch

Disorders of touch/sensation will usually be investigated by the *neurologist* (nerve specialist).

1.   *Loss of sensation*

Cause: Many different factors may be involved, including nerve damage (please refer to Chapters 16 and 24) due to diabetes; a break in spinal cord; a nerve having been (accidentally) cut; swelling and pressure on the nerves (e.g. after having a plaster cast applied). Loss of sensation may also result from nerve cells not getting enough oxygen due to loss of blood supply to a certain area. Blood supply may be lost due to a blood clot blocking circulation, or may be due to the fact that the arteries are seriously narrowed and not enough blood can get through. Compartment syndrome may also be involved.

Symptoms: Loss of sensation.

Investigations: Neurological investigations.

Treatment: Treating the underlying cause.

2.   *Unusual sensation*

Causes: There may be pressure on a nerve either at the level of the spine (e.g. whiplash injury or prolapsed disk) or at another level, (e.g. on the nerve in the wrist in carpal tunnel syndrome or due to a cast which is too tight as in compartment syndrome).

Symptoms: Tingling; pins and needles; numbness.

Investigations: MRI scan; neurological investigations.

Treatment: Treating underlying cause.

Summary of main points

This chapter has looked at the sensory system, including:

- anatomy and physiology of the ears and eyes
- Latin and Greek roots
- health professionals
- common conditions affecting the sensory system.

Chapter 24

The immune and lymphatic system

The immune system is like the body's 'bodyguard'. It involves (amongst other things) the lymphatic system and special white blood cells called lymphocytes. During an infection the lymph nodes become large and tender because they are involved in fighting the infection. You may notice the doctor palpating (feeling) the lymph nodes during a physical examination.

1. Latin and Greek roots

antibodies	protein produced by the body's lymphocytes to identify and fight particular bacteria or viruses
antigen	from **anti**body **gen**erator, a substance in viruses or bacteria that generates or triggers an antibody response
auto-immune disease	where the body attacks its own cells (e.g. in *rheumatoid arthritis*)
foreign substances	substances from outside of the body which are alien to the body
immunocompromised	the immune system is not able to fight off infections very well
immunoglobulin	protein produced by the immune system to identify and fight foreign substances such as bacteria and viruses
immune deficiency	the immune system is not able to fight off infections, as in AIDS (Acquired Immune Deficiency Syndrome)
immune-depressant drugs	drugs which supress the immune system, making it less able to fight off infections
immunity	body's ability to overcome illnesses
immunization	immune system develops 'weapons' against foreign substances
active immunization	body is exposed to foreign substances and develops antibodies. Active immunization is long-lasting

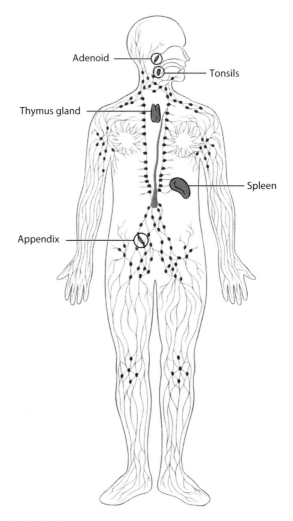

Figure 24.1. Lymph circulation system

passive immunization	Mother passes her immunity on to baby during pregnancy or whilst breastfeeding: Passive immunization does not last long
lymph tissue	lymph cells or lymphocytes (T cells and B cells)
lymphedema	swelling of a part of the body (usually an arm or a leg) due to lymph being 'collected' in that body part that cannot, or is unable to, drain away to rejoin the lymph vessels in the rest of the body (e.g. women who have had the lymph nodes in their armpit removed may develop lymphedema of the arm later on)

lymphocyte	special white blood cells that make antibodies against antigens
lymphoma	cancer involving the lymph cells
lymphatic ducts	network of lymph vessels that unite to form larger vessels called ducts
lymph nodes	lymph nodes filter the lymph, trapping foreign substances so the body can fight them
vaccination	Artificial active immunization (body is exposed to weakened component of bacteria or virus, so it starts to make antibodies)
	Artificial passive immunization – person is given serum containing antibodies (short-acting immunity)

2. Anatomy of the immune and lymphatic system

The body has two main circulation systems: the blood circulation system and the lymph circulation system. Not many people are aware of the second system and yet it plays a very important role. The lymphatic system consists of a system of lymph vessels and lymph nodes. The lymph nodes are like truck depots or bus stations, where lymph collects *en route*.

3. Lymphatic organs

appendix	lymph tissue in the GI tract; situated close to where the small intestine joins the large intestine close to where the small intestine joins the large intestine
bonemarrow	contains stem cells which develop into specialized blood cells (red and white blood cells and platelets)
gut or intestine	the lining of the gut contains a lot of lymphocytes which scan food to see if an immune response is warranted. Food is thought to play a much more important role in the development of (autoimmune) disease than previously thought
thymus	lymph tissue behind breast bone which generates T lymphocytes
tonsils and adenoid	lymph tissue in the throat

spleen	lies behind/under the stomach. The spleen breaks down old red blood cells; filters out damaged (old) blood cells; gets rid of bacteria and produces lymphocytes. *Sometimes the spleen is ruptured in accidents. This can result in a serious bleed leading to shock. A ruptured spleen is a medical emergency and must be removed immediately by a surgeon as it is too 'spongy' to be sutured.* *The spleen may also be larger than normal and prone to rupture in viral illnesses such as glandular fever, care needs to be taken in these cases as well.*

4.   Function of the immune and lymphatic system

The lymphatic system drains lymph fluid which has collected in tissue and takes it back to the blood circulation system (*fluid which contains protein and fats which have escaped from the blood circulation system).

The lymphatic system also produces lymphocytes (big white cells) which play a role in our immune system. Through our immune system our body's defense system develops i.e. we develop immunities. These include B lymphocytes which may grow into plasma cells (which develop antibodies), and T lymphocytes which destroy infected cells or bacteria and also have an effect on other parts of the immune system.

5.   Health professionals

Immunologist – Physician specializing in the immune system.
Hematologist – Physician specializing in the blood and related body systems.

6.   Disorders of the immune and lymphatic system

1.   *Acquired Immune Deficiency Syndrome (AIDS)* – Infection with Human Immuno-Deficiency Virus (HIV) which attaches itself to the CD4 helper T-cell lymphocytes so the body can no longer respond to infections. The virus can also stop B-cell lymphocytes from doing their job properly. Slowly, the CD4 cell count goes down and the immune system starts to fail.

Causes: HIV can only be transmitted through blood, semen, vaginal secretions and breast milk, i.e. through sexual intercourse, sharing of intravenous needles, breast-feeding by an HIV infected mother; or receiving organs from an infected donor.

Symptoms: Vary over the course of the disease. Those with blood (serum) which is positive for HIV antibodies may not show any symptoms of AIDS (sometimes for a long time). Early symptoms of HIV infection can include brief periods of illness (fever; chills; feeling unwell; headache); tiredness; oral thrush; weight loss; diarrhea. In full-Blown AIDS the patient has very low immunity and develops major infections characteristic of AIDS (e.g. Cytomegalovirus infection or CMV; tuberculosis; chronic herpes simplex virus infection or one of many others) or one of the secondary cancers characteristic of AIDS (e.g. Kaposi's sarcoma or Non-Hodgkin's Lymphoma).

Investigations: CD4 cell count below 350 cells/mm3; over the counter saliva testing kit.

Treatment: Highly Active Antiretroviral Therapy (HAART). *The patient will remain infectious even when on HAART*. Research is ongoing. AIDS can be prevented through practicing safe sex i.e. use of condoms, and using clean sterilized needles

2.   *Allergic reactions* – An overreaction of the body to foreign substances from outside the body (e.g. pollen or peanuts).

What happens: An allergen is any substance which causes an allergic reaction (e.g. nuts, eggs, shellfish, wasp or bee stings, pollen, antibiotics, latex). On first contact, the body makes the antibodies to the allergens. On second contact an antibody-allergen reaction takes place. Body cells are damaged and histamine comes out, causing the body's tissues to swell up. At the same time, blood vessels in the area widen, leading to redness.

   If this allergic reaction takes place in the airways, the breathing tubes become narrowed with swelling and the person produces a wheezing sound when trying to breathe out.

Symptoms: See Anaphylactic shock below.

Investigations: Skin test; history.

Treatment: Avoiding triggers; special diet; EpiPen autoinjector if necessary.

3.   *Anaphylactic shock* – *Anaphylaxis* means a severe allergic reaction which affects the whole body.

Symptoms: Blood vessels widen all over the body, leading to an enormous drop in blood pressure, which in turns leads to *shock*. There may be redness all over the body (an all-over body rash) as well as itching and swelling all over the body.

Investigations: Blood pressure; pulse; history.

Treatment: Epinephrine (adrenaline) injections must be given fast, preferably using an autoinjector such as the EpiPen®.

4.   *Elephantiasis* – (also known as *filariasis*) – A parasite infection leading to enlarge-ment of a limb due to blockage of lymph glands.

Causes: Tiny parasite (worm) found in tropical countries which are conveyed through the bites of mosquitoes infested with the parasites.

Symptoms: Enlargement of a limb due to obstruction/blockage of lymph glands.

Investigations: Finger prick test followed by checking blood smear under microscope.

Treatment: Drugs (diethylcarbamazine, also known as DEC); sometimes plastic surgery; bed-rest; tight bandages. Elephantiasis can be prevented thorough drugs (*DEC*) and avoiding mosquito bites.

5.   *Graft-Versus-Host-Disease (GVHD)* – Occurs when the healthy donor cells attack the weakened body of the host (the person receiving the donor cells or transplant).

Causes: Red rash; abdominal pain and cramps; nausea; dry mouth and dry eyes.

Investigations: Biopsy of skin or mucose of the mouth.

Treatment: Immunosuppressant drugs.

6a.   *Hodgkin's lymphoma* – Cancer of the lymphocyte.

Causes: Exact cause is not known.

Symptoms: Painless, enlarged lymph nodes (lumps), usually in the neck first then spreading to other lymph nodes; tiredness; night sweats; weakness.

Investigations: Biopsy of lymph nodes; body scan to check for spread.

Treatment: Combination of radiotherapy, chemotherapy; stem cell transplant (using healthy bone-marrow from patient); monoclonal antibodies. For young patients spe-cial measures are taken which include sperm storage for men prior to chemotherapy and hormone replacement therapy for young women following chemotherapy, as they may go into early menopause.

6b.   *Non-Hodgkin's Lymphoma* – Cancer of the lymphocytes which is not Hodgkin's lymphoma. Sixteen different types ranging from very slow growing to very aggressive, but usually B-cells and sometimes T-cells are affected.

Symptoms: Enlarged lymph nodes; tiredness; weight loss; (sometimes) enlarged spleen.

Investigations: Bone marrow biopsy; blood counts; CT scan.

Treatment: Chemotherapy; stem cell transplant (using healthy bone-marrow from patient); monoclonal antibodies; immunotherapy.

7.   *Lymphoma* – There are several types of lymphoma including *Burkitt's lymphoma* (a type of Non-Hodgkins Lymphoma, see above).

8.   *Lymphedema* (from: 'lymph edema') – Occurs when lymph cannot drain away as normal causing the affected body part to swell up.

Causes: Lymph nodes removed from armpit or groin following breast surgery or abdominal surgery; lymph drainage blocked for another reason, e.g. inflammation or blockage of lymph vessels, or patient does not have sufficient lymph vessels.

Symptoms: Arm or leg swells up; feels very 'tight'.

Investigations: History; physical examination.

Treatment: Sleeping with legs/arm elevated; elastic stockings; low salt diet (to reduce fluid retention); diuretics; sometimes surgery.

9.   *Systemic Lupus Erythematosus* or *(SLE)* – Autoimmune disease affecting connective tissue in any part of the body. SLE most often affects heart, joints, skin, lungs, blood vessels, liver, kidneys, and nervous system.

Causes: Exact cause is not known.

Symptoms: General malaise; fever; joint pains; butterfly rash on face.

Investigations: Blood tests.

Treatment: Immunosuppressants; disease modifying antirheumatic drugs.

10.   *Tissue rejection* – Occurs when antibodies are formed against strange tissues following a transplant. To prevent tissue rejection, tissue typing takes place before transplantation. The tissue typing is done in order to make sure that the tissues of the receiving person and the donor are very similar, so that, hopefully, the receiving person's immune system will not reject the donor organ. In addition, patients are given special immunosuppressant drugs to prevent rejection.

11.   *Tonsillitis* – Painful, red and swollen tonsils through bacterial or viral infection.

Causes: (Bacterial) infection of the throat.

Symptoms: Red, swollen tonsils. Can lead to complications including abscess and strep throat tonsillitis which may lead to rheumatic fever.

Investigations: Throat swab to check for bacteria.

Treatment: Antibiotics; chronic and recurrent episodes may require a tonsillectomy (tonsil surgically removed).

Summary of main points

This chapter has given a brief overview of the immune system, including:

– a brief overview of anatomy of the immune system
– Latin and Greek roots
– health professionals involved
– some commonly encountered conditions relating to the immune system, together with common investigations and treatment methods.

Chapter 25

The endocrine system

The endocrine system manages the bodys hormones (or chemical messengers). A number of organs and glands are involved in producing these chemical hormones and releasing them into the body. The following Latin and Greek roots form the basis of many medical words to do with the endocrine system.

1. Latin and Greek roots

acro	topmost; extreme
adrenals	hormone producing glands found *alongside the kidneys (ad-renal)*
diabetes	running through
ectomy	cut out; surgical removal of
endocrine	releasing internally
endocrinologist	doctor who specializes in the endocrine system
glycol	glucose, sugar
glycemic	sugar in the blood
hyper	too high, too much (compare *super*)
hyperthyroidism	hyperactive thyroid
hypo	too low, not enough (compare *sub*)
hypothyroidism	underactive thyroid
insipidus	tasteless (people with *diabetes insipidus* do not care what their drinks taste like, as long as they have something to drink!)
megaly	largeness (*megalos* – big)
mellitus	sweet as honey – in *diabetes mellitus* – fluid sweet as honey is running through the body (blood, urine)
parathyroid	alongside the thyroid
thyroid	shaped like a shield

2.   Overview of the endocrine system

Glands	Hormones include	Some selected functions
adrenal glands	corticosteroids	encourage the body to repair after injury
	aldosterone	helps the body retain water and sodium
	adrenaline (also called epinephrine)	helps the body's *flight-fight* response, increases heart rate and breathing rate
hypothalamus (in brain)	stimulating and inhibiting hormones	switch hormone secretion by pituitary gland on or off
ovaries	estrogen and progesterone	female sex hormones
pancreas	– enzymes for digesting food	
	– insulin (produced in cells called the Islets of Langerhans)	lowers blood sugar levels
	– glucagon	raises blood sugar levels
parathyroid gland (in the neck)	parathyroid hormone	regulates calcium levels in the blood and bone metabolism
pineal gland (in brain)	melatonin	sleep-wake patterns
pituitary gland (in brain)	Thyroid-Stimulating Hormone (TSH); Follicle-Stimulating Hormone (FSH), Luteinizing Hormone (LH); Human Growth Hormone (HGH); Adrenocorticotropin hormone (ACTH); Prolactin and Oxytocin	LH and FSH trigger ovulation; ACTH triggers release of corticosteroids; prolactin stimulates production of breast milk; oxytocin causes contractions of the womb
testicles (testes)	testosterone	male sex hormone
thyroid gland	Thyroxin (T4)	helps regulate metabolic rate

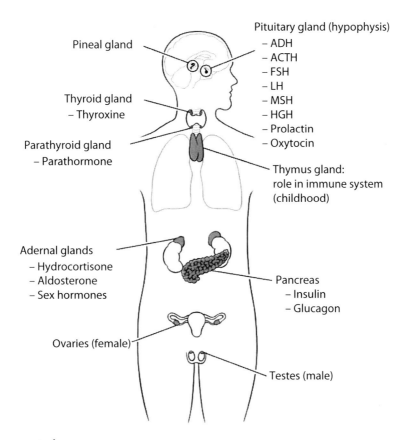

Pineal gland

Pituitary gland (hypophysis)
  – ADH
  – ACTH
  – FSH
  – LH
  – MSH
  – HGH
  – Prolactin
  – Oxytocin

Thyroid gland
  – Thyroxine

Parathyroid gland
  – Parathormone

Thymus gland:
role in immune system
(childhood)

Adernal glands
  – Hydrocortisone
  – Aldosterone
  – Sex hormones

Pancreas
  – Insulin
  – Glucagon

Ovaries (female)

Testes (male)

Figure 25.1. Endocrine system

3.   Health professionals

Endocrinologist – Doctor specializing in complaints involving the endocrine (hormone) system.
Diabetes nurse educator – Registered Nurse specializing in educating patients with diabetes about managing their symptoms, checking blood sugar levels, administering insulin and so on.

4.   Disorders of the endocrine system

Endocrine disorders are affected and influenced by the hormone involved and on whether there is too much or too little of this hormone. Some of the most common disorders are listed below.

5. Pituitary Gland

1. *Dwarfism* – Adult stature of less than 4 ft 10 in or 147 cm.

Causes: Dwarfism can be due to more than 200 different medical conditions, with achondroplasia the most common, followed by growth hormone deficiency (pituitary dwarfism) where the pituitary gland does not produce enough growth hormone.

Symptoms: In achondroplasia limbs are proportionately shorter than trunk, head is larger than average.

Investigations: Physical examination; growth chart; X-rays.

Treatment: Human Growth Hormone (HGH); sometimes surgery to increase height; shoe lifts.

2. *Gigantism* – Massive growth before the growth plates have closed.

Causes: Abnormality (often pituitary adenoma) in pituitary gland resulting in over-production of HGH.

Symptoms: Abnormally rapid growth.

Investigations: Brain scan; blood tests.

Treatment: Removing pituitary adenoma (benign tumor); radiotherapy.

3. *Acromegaly* – Developing big hands, feet, chins and nose in adulthood.

Causes: Abnormality in pituitary gland (often pituitary adenoma) resulting in over-production of HGH.

Symptoms: Very gradual increase in size of hands, etc.

Investigations: Brain scan; blood tests.

Treatment: As for gigantism.

4. *(Central) Diabetes insipidus* – The pituitary gland does not produce enough ADH, so the body cannot retain enough sodium and water.

Causes: Inadequate release of anti-diuretic hormone (ADH).

Symptoms: Excessive urination and thirst.

Investigations: Blood tests.

Treatment: Synthetic form of ADH.

6. Thyroid gland

5. *Cretinism* – Severe hypothyroidism (see below) in young children, leading to a combination of growth failure and mental retardation. Sometimes symptoms are related to thyroid gland failure due to autoimmune disease.

Causes: Lack of thyroid hormone in womb or in infancy.

Symptoms: Growth failure and mental retardation.

Investigations: Blood tests.

Treatment: Thyroid hormone. Prevented through the use of iodized salt.

6. *Hypothyroidism* (*underactive thyroid*) – Thyroid gland does not produce enough thyroxin and the persons metabolic rate slows down. Common in women >50 and men >65.

Causes: Lack of thyroid hormone.

Symptoms: My*xedema,* water retention with puffy, cheesy face; hair loss; brittle nails; memory loss; lack of concentration; fatigue (in spite of sleeping enough); lack of energy; depression.

Investigations: Check levels of thyroid hormone (T3 and T4) and of TSH. If TSH levels are high, the thyroid may in fact be struggling to maintain normal thyroid function.

Treatment: Thyroxine (hormone replacement).

7. *Hyperthyroidism* – An overactive thyroid where the thyroid gland produces too much T3 and T4 and the persons metabolic rate is increased.

Causes: Overproduction of thyroid hormone.

Symptoms: Weight loss; lots of nervous energy; increase in body temperature and sweating; feeling ravenously hungry all the time; sometimes bulging eyes and goiter (swelling around thyroid gland).

Investigations: Blood tests; scan.

Treatment: Medication; radioactive iodine to destroy thyroid hormone producing cells; subtotal thyroidectomy or hemi-thyroidectomy (partial removal of the thyroid gland).

7.   Parathyroid gland

8.   *Hypoparathryoidism* – Underactive parathyroid gland.

Causes: Not enough Parathyroid hormone (PTH) is released leading to a drop in blood calcium levels.

Symptoms: Muscle twitches; spasms; convulsions; abdominal pain; cataracts.

Investigations: Blood tests.

Treatment: Calcium; Vitamin D.

9.   *Hyperparathyroidism* – Overactive parathyroid gland.

Causes: Too much parathyroid hormone (PTH) is released resulting to a rise in blood calcium levels.

Symptoms: High blood calcium levels; unspecific symptoms.

Investigations: Blood tests.

Treatment: Remove gland.

8.   Adrenals or adrenal glands

10.   Addison's Disease – Form of adrenal gland failure.

Causes: Adrenal glands do not produce enough steroid hormones.

Symptoms: Low blood sugar; muscle weakness; fatigue; weight loss. Note people with Addison's disease can go into a 'crisis' during surgery or pregnancy and need to wear Medic Alert bracelets.

Investigations: Blood tests.

Treatment: Replacing steroid hormones.

11.   *Cushing's Syndrome* – High levels of cortisol.

Causes: High levels of cortisiol produced by adrenal glands; or person taking corticosteroid medication; or pituitary gland tumor resulting in too much Adrenocorticotropin hormone (ACTH).

Symptoms: High blood sugars leading to redistribution of fat, especially a buffalo hump and moon face; easy bruising; poor wound healing.

Investigations: Blood tests.

Treatment: Depending on the cause; tapering off corticosteroids if necessary.

9. Pancreas

12.   *Diabetes* – High levels of sugar (glucose) in the blood. Sugar is unable to enter the body's cells to be used for energy because there is a problem with the hormone insulin (which helps glucose enter the cells). There are two main types of diabetes. Type I diabetes is relatively rare (10% of patients) while Type II diabetes is by far the most common (90% of patients).

Causes: Type I diabetes is an autoimmune disease in which the pancreas quite suddenly stops producing insulin. More common in persons under 30 years of age

     In Type II diabetes the pancreas either does not produce (enough) insulin, or the insulin receptors on the body's cells are no longer 'receptive' to insulin (insulin resistance) meaning cells do not 'open up' to absorb sugar from the blood stream [see Figure 25.2]. Traditionally found in persons 45 years plus of age, however with the number of overweight people increasing around the world, a growing number of children and young people are now developing Type II diabetes.

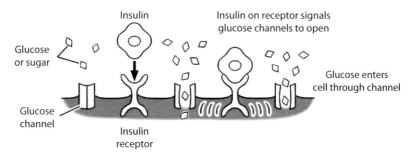

Figure 25.2. Insulin resistance

Symptoms: Sugar is needed in the cells for energy. Without sugar in the cells, the person feels tired, and listless. Eventually, the body will start to burn off fat for energy, resulting in *ketones* in the urine (*acetone* smell on breath or skin).

If diabetes is undiagnosed and untreated, sugar will remain in the bloodstream and blood sugar levels will become (very) high. In Type II diabetes, insulin levels may also be very high, because the insulin receptors are not responding to it. High insulin levels disturb fat metabolism and make arteries more likely to clog.

In many cases, people with Type II diabetes may walk around undiagnosed for a long time. They may develop symptoms very gradually and therefore get used to not feeling 'the best'.

Diabetes can lead to complications such as hypoglycemia (note this can only occur in people who use insulin or other diabetes medication); hyperglycemia and problems with nerves (diabetic neuropathy) and blood vessels (summarized below).

Hypoglycemia occurs when there is not enough sugar in the blood stream because insulin has allowed all sugar to leave the bloodstream and enter the cells. This results in the brain cells not receiving enough sugar which can lead to aggression, confusion, loss of consciousness and potentially a hypoglycemic coma.

Hyperglycemia happens when the kidneys allow sugar overload into the urine. This very sweet urine attracts more fluid from the body, leading to polyuria (too much urine produced) and the person becoming very thirsty (polydypsia). A very high blood sugar may lead to a diabetic coma, as can academia (blood is too acidic); dehydration and electrolyte imbalances.

Symptoms of diabetes can include excessive thirst and urination; weight loss; tiredness, fatigue, weakness (can be extreme); blurred vision; frequent and persistent skin and bacterial infections; slow healing and itching; numbness, pain and tingling in hands or feet and leg cramp.

Diabetes can also lead to nerve and circulation disorders affecting every part of the body, specifically eyes (blindness; eyesight problems); feet (small wounds don't heal leading to necrosis (tissue dying off) and amputation; chronic leg ulcers; brain (CVAs); heart (heart attacks); kidneys (renal failure or diabetic nephropathy); nerve damage (loss of sensation in fingertips and toes).

Symptoms of hypoglycemia can include trembling; sweating; ravenous hunger; palpitations of the heart; headache; tingling of fingers and lips; disturbances of concentration; abnormal speech; confusion; aggressive behavior and blurred vision Note hypoglycemic patients have been mistaken for drunks and thrown into a police cell!

Investigations: Blood glucose level, which may be tested in different ways including:

-   fasting blood sugar (FBS)
-   two-hr postprandial blood sugar test (2-h PPBS) – 2 hours after meal
-   oral glucose tolerance test (OGTT) – after drinking sugary drink (also called oral glucose challenge test)
-   random blood sugar (RBS)

- Patient monitoring own blood sugar levels using a small cardlike blood glucose meter or a Continuous glucose monitor, with a sensor under the skin
- A1c Test (or HbA1c – glycated hemoglobin or glycosylated hemoglobin) – indicates somebody's average blood glucose level over the past few months

A person without diabetes will have a normal blood glucose of between 4 and 7 mmol per litre or 65 to 105 mg/dL (glucose 1 mmol/L is equivalent to glucose 18mg/dL) and a A1c of less than 5%.

Treatment: Type I – Insulin injections; insulin pump (attached to abdomen); low fat diet; careful balance between diet (timing, carbohydrates and amount), insulin (timing and amount) and exercise. Type II – Drugs to help the pancreas produce more insulin; insulin injections; low fat diet; careful balance between diet (timing, carbohydrates, amount), insulin (timing and amount) and exercise. Some diabetes patients have been able to reduce their medication following gastric bypass (or gastric banding) surgery.

10. The Glycemic index (GI)

Researchers think that a low Glycemic Index (low GI) diet may help prevent type II diabetes. Food containing carbohydrates that break down quickly have a high GI and rapidly increase blood glucose levels. Foods with carbohydrates that break down more slowly have a low GI and release glucose into the bloodstream gradually. Sugar is the standard measure which has a GI of 100. An example of GI can be found in comparing different types of rice, where jasmine rice has a very high GI, while basmati rice has a medium GI, hence a low GI diet should not include jasmine rice.

Another way of describing food is using the Glycemic Load (GL). Similarly to GI, GL is a number that describes how quickly blood glucose levels go up after consuming certain foods. One unit of GL reflects the effect of consuming one gram of glucose. A low GL is <10, a high GL is >20.

Summary of main points

This chapter has given a brief overview of the encocrine system, including:

- a brief overview of various hormones and the role they play
- Latin and Greek roots
- health professionals involved
- some commonly encountered conditions relating to the endocrine system, particularly diabetes, together with common investigations and treatment methods.

Chapter 26

The digestive dystem

The digestive system is involved in the process of taking in food, breaking it down and processing it (for absorption), absorbing it into the blood stream, and eliminating the waste products created from this process from the body. Consquently the digestive system involves a range of different organs.

Different medical words are also used when talking about the digestive system. Some doctors talk about the alimentary canal (the route the food takes through the body) or the gastro-intestinal tract or GI tract (the route the food takes through stomach and bowels). The following Latin and Greek roots form the basis of many medical words to do with the digestive system.

1. Latin and Greek roots

absorb	to take in
chole	bile, gall (breaks fat globules down into smaller ones)
cholecystectomy	to cut out the gall-bladder (chole: bile; cyst: bladder)
cyst	bladder; fluid-filled sac
digest	to break down
enter	inside (entrails: bowels)
esophagus	gullet (phago: eat; eso: going to carry)
gaster/gastro	stomach
gastro-intestinal (GI)	relating to stomach and bowels
hepato	liver
intestino-	entrails, bowels
oesophagus	see esophagus
pancreas (pancreatic)	large gland (pan: all; creas: flesh/meat)
parenteral	by-passing the bowels (para: alongside)
peri	around

scopy	looking
sorb	to soak (up)
stoma	mouth; artificial opening
tomy	cut
tract	route

2. Anatomy and function of the digestive system

The gastro-intestinal tract (GI tract) consists of a range of organs and accessory glands. Figure 26.1 represents the digestive system.

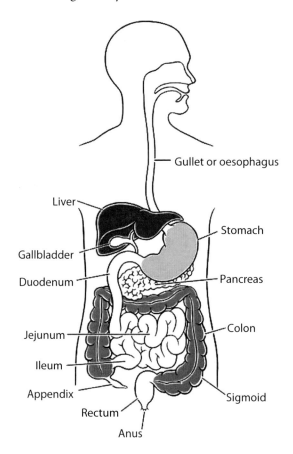

Figure 26.1. Digestive system

Table 26.1 gives an overview of the main organs and accessory organs of the digestive tract.

Table 26.1. The GI Tract

Organs	Accessory organs/glands	Role
Mouth		
	Tongue	taste buds (papillae)
	salivary glands	saliva is released when food enters → food starts to dissolve (especially white bread; rice)
	Teeth	food is broken up into small pieces and can be swallowed more easily
esophagus		gullet (tube behind the windpipe): food slides down to stomach
stomach		gastric juices to break down protein and carbohydrates
	Liver	enzymes and bile (bile breaks down fat)
	gallbladder	storage place for bile; bile is squeezed into the intestine when fatty foods come along
	pancreas	digestive enzymes; insulin; glucagon
small intestine (duodenum, jejunum, ileum)		20 feet (6.3. metres) long; intestinal juices containing digestive enzymes help break down the food into tiny particles; these are absorbed into the blood stream through the wall of the small intestine and travel to the liver for processing
	appendix	lymph tissue
large intestine (colon, sigmoid, rectum, anus)		5 feet long (1.5 metres); mainly fluid is absorbed here and stools are moved towards exit (the anus)

In short, the process of digestion involves the following:

– eating or taking in food
– moving food along the digestive tract
– digestion (breaking it down into smaller bits)
– absorption
– defecation (elimination from body)

The digestion process starts in the stomach. When food is ready, the stomach contracts and pushes the food into the bowels (usually 2–6 hours after eating). Carbohydrates are digested quickly, protein and fats are digested more slowly. Some foods and medicine are readily absorbed in the stomach (i.e. water; Vitamin B12; aspirin; whey protein shakes).

The pyloric valve is the muscular opening between the stomach and the small intestine. The pylorus opens when food is ready to leave the stomach. In some infants the pyloric valve is narrowed and food is pushed out the other way, resulting in forceful projectile vomiting (see Figure 26.2).

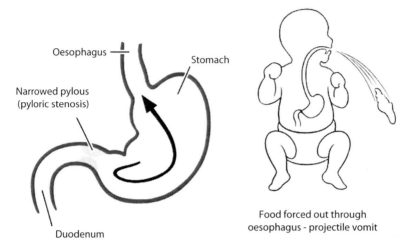

Figure 26.2. Pyloric stenosis and projectile vomiting

When food comes out of the stomach, carbohydrates and protein have been partly digested, but fats have not been digested. Glucose, fat and protein is absorbed in the small intestine, where nutrients pass into the blood which takes them to the liver for processing. Once processed the nutrients are taken to the cells or stored in the form of glycogen or fat.

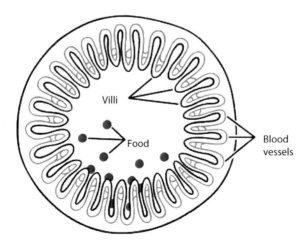

Figure 26.3. Villi in the lining of the bowel

The many functions of the liver are represented in Table 26.2.

Table 26.2. The many functions of the liver

Functions of the liver	Examples
makes plasma proteins, also heparin	
destroys old red blood cells	
liver enzymes break down poisons, making them harmless	Includes medication, e.g. paracetamol
collects nutrients	

processes nutrients	can change sugar into:
	    stored sugar (glycogen)
	    stored fat (body fat)
	
	can change glycogen:
	    back to sugar
	    to protein
	    to fat
	as required

stores nutrients	iron, copper, vitamins A, D, E, K also stores proteins which cannot be broken down (e.g. DDT) and heavy metals
makes bile (gall)	stored in gallbladder (bile breaks down fat)

3.   Peritoneum

The peritoneum is a membrane, lining the abdominal wall. It contains a lot of blood vessels and nerve endings, making it very sensitive to pain. The peritoneal cavity, is the space surrounded by the peritoneum. Some of the organs in the abdomen are inside the peritoneal cavity. The peritoneum has a rich blood supply (mesenterium). Mesenterial infarcts are very painful.

4.   Health professionals

Gastroenterologist – Physician mainly specializing in disorders affecting all parts of the digestive system i.e. stomach, liver, pancreas, small and large intestine and rectum. *Gastro-intestinologist* – Physician mainly specializing in disorders affecting small and large intestine and rectum.

5. Disorders of the digestive system

1. *Appendicitis* – Inflammation of the appendix.

Cause: Bacteria entering the appendix, usually preceded by an obstruction or infection of the gut.

Symptoms: At start: pain around belly-button; then: loss of appetite; nausea; vomiting; the pain will then shift to the right lower quadrant (RLQ) of abdomen, getting worse with coughing, sneezing, or body movements; rebound tenderness (pain gets worse when the doctor removes his hand after pushing down on the abdomen). If the appendix perforates (breaks and contents come out) this can lead to peritonitis and sepsis (bacteria overwhelming organs and the bloodstream).

Investigations: Ultrasound; CT scan; laparoscopy.

Treatment: Appendectomy; antibiotics.

2. *Cirrhosis* – Occurs when the liver is infiltrated with fibrous tissue and fat. This 'destroys' liver function i.e. the liver cannot make glycogen; cannot absorb vitamins; cannot break down bilirubin; cannot process food; cannot detoxify alcohol and drugs. Blood flow through the liver is also obstructed (like a huge backlog of traffic) and there is back flow into the GI tract resulting in hypertension in the portal vein and in the veins alongside the gullet.

Cause: Often chronic alcohol abuse; hepatitis (especially B or C).

Symptoms: Anorexia (no appetite); nausea; weight loss; more than 5 spider naevi (spider web like bloodvessels just below the surface of the skin); fatigue; ascites (fluid in the peritoneal space). Esophageal varices (weak dilated veins along the gullet) can lead to a massive hemorrhage; hepatic coma; kidney failure.

Investigations: Liver biopsies; liver function tests.

Treatment: Depends on cause.

3. *Crohn's Disease* – Inflammatory bowel disease which can affect both the small and large intestine.

Causes: Genetic predisposition where the immune system attacks harmless bowel bacteria.

Symptoms: Ongoing disease with periods of remission and flare-ups (known as *exacerbations*) which can include malabsorption (leading to malnutrition and weight loss); anal fistulas; anal fissures (small tears); perianal abscesses. Can lead to a bowel blockage (ileus).

Investigations: Colonoscopy; stool tests; CT scan.

Treatment: Meal replacements; diet (bananas); anti-diarrhea drugs, anti-inflammatory drugs; corticosteroids; immunomodulators; biologicals; anti-tumor necrosis factor (anti-TNF) drugs; occasionally surgery to remove rectum and colon (proctocolectomy); ileostomy or intestinal resection (removing diseased part of the bowel).

4.   *Dental caries* – Tooth decay

Causes: Breakdown of the tooth enamel due to acid-producing bacteria on the teeth (which destroy tooth enamel).

Symptoms: Often no symptoms; sometimes toothache or pain when eating or drinking hot or cold foods; cavities discovered during dental examination

Investigations: Dental examination; X-ray.

Treatment: Fillings; root canal treatment; crown (cap fitted over remainder of tooth).

Prevention: Good teeth hygiene (brushing, flossing); water fluoridation, dental sealants.

5.   *Diverticulitis* – Inflammation of small blind pouches (*diverticula*) in the lining of the colon.

Causes: Pressure on weak places in the wall of the colon, resulting in pouches forming.

Symptoms: Pain lower left abdomen; change in bowel habits. Can lead to complications incluing infections, tears and blockages.

Investigations: Colonoscopy.

Treatment: Surgery for blockages; high-fiber diet.

6.   *Duodenal Ulcer* – see Peptic Ulcer

7.   *Gallstones* – Solid particles that form from bile in the gallbladder

Causes: Crystallization of cholesterol (cholesterol stones) or excess bilirubin pigment stones.

Symptoms: Often no symptoms; sometimes pain after fatty meal; or pain if there is blockage and infection of the gallbladder; nausea, vomiting, jaundice, fever.

Investigations: Ultrasound scan; Endoscopic retrograde cholangiopancreatography (ERCP looking at part of the gallducts using a flexible scope); Cholescintigraphy (HIDA scan following intravenous injection of a special solution).

Treatment: Extracorporeal shockwave lithotripsy (ESWL breaking up stones using sound waves); dissolving the gallstones; (keyhole surgery) to remove the gallbladder (cholecystectomy).

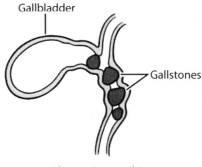

Gallbladder

Gallstones

Obstruction resulting
in colic (pain)

Figure 26.4. Gallstones

8.   *Hepatitis* – Inflammation of the liver.

Causes: Depends on the type of hepatitis (see below).

Hepatitis A and E is the result of infection through contaminated food and water. A complete recovery is possible.

Hepatitis B infections are common in Asian and Pacific Island populations, with infections possibly partly spread by eating food with shared eating utensils.

Hepatitis C and D are common in drug users, infants from infected mothers, people infected through hemodialysis or contaminated transfusions prior to the introduction of screening tests. i.e. infection occurs through contact with blood or other body fluids or transferred to infants at birth. Infection with hepatitis B, C or D virus can result in chronic hepatitis; cirrhosis; liver failure and liver cancer.

Symptoms: Tiredness; nausea; loss of appetite; jaundice (skin looks yellow); whites of the eye look yellow.

Investigations: Blood tests (to check for antibodies).

Treatment: Antiviral drugs; occasionally liver transplant.

9.   *Hemorrhoids* (also refered to as piles) – Inflammation/enlargement of veins in anus (internal or external).

Causes: Constipation may play a role as it causes pressure on the veins.

Investigations: Physical examination.

Symptoms: Bright red blood in stools; pain on defecating (passing stools).

Treatment: Local cream; surgery.

10.   *Inflammatory Bowel Disease* – see *Crohn's Disease* and *Ulcerative colitis*

11.   *Irritable Bowel syndrome* – Not a disease but a set of symptoms as a result of an abnormal functioning of the bowel.

Causes: Combination of factors, including genetics, food sensitivity and mental stress.

Symptoms: Abdominal pain; cramping; bloating; diarrhea alternating with constipation.

Investigations: Colonoscopy; stools test.

Treatment: Diet (typically avoiding certain foods).

12.   *Lactose Intolerance*

Causes: A lack of the lactase enzyme used to break down milk sugar (*lactose*).

Symptoms: Abdominal bloating.

Investigations: Stool acidity test; hydrogen breath test.

Treatments: Avoiding lactose in diet.

13.   *Pancreatitis* – Acute or chronic inflammation of the pancreas.

Causes: Alcohol abuse; gallstones.

Symptoms: Acute pain; nausea; vomiting; jaundice; diabetes symptoms.

Investigations: Imaging.

Treatment: Nil by mouth; intravenous nutrition or fluids, plus no alcohol and frequent small meals for those with chronic condition.

14.   *Peptic Ulcer* (*Gastric ulcer* or *duodenal ulcer*) – Ulcer in the stomach or duodenum.

Causes: Infection with Helicobacter Pylori (H. Pylori) bacterium; stress; aspirin, NSAIDS.

Symptoms: Intense and acute pain. Peptic ulcers may lead to perforation (a hole in the wall of the stomach), leading to a hemorrhage (severe bleed) which can result in shock; board-like stomach and death.

Investigation: Gastroscopy; breath test; stool test.

Treatment: Antibiotics against H. Pylori; medication to stop production of stomach acid.

15.   *Tumors* – Cancers can occur anywhere in the digestive tract.

Causes: Depends on type of cancer

Symptoms: Loss of appetite; weight loss; ascites (fluid); pain (usually a late symptom); jaundice.

Investigations: Gastroscopy; sigmoidoscopy; coloscopy; CT scan.

Treatment: Depends on type of cancer, see Chapter 16.

16.   *Peritonitis* – Acute inflammation of the peritoneum (membrane lining the abdominal wall). This is a very serious condition.

Causes: Infection through wounds after child-birth or through CAPD (see Chapter 27); perforation of infected organs; perforation of Fallopian tube after ectopic pregnancy. Can be prevented with antibiotics before abdominal surgery and using sterile procedures.

Symptoms: Very rigid washboard abdomen; pain; nausea and or vomiting; reduced bowel sounds/movement; fever; chills.

Investigations: Blood tests; sometimes laparotomy.

Treatment: Immediate antibiotics; surgery and lavage (washing infectious fluids out) of abdomen.

17.   *Ulcer* – see Peptic Ulcer

18.   *Ulcerative Colitis* – Type of inflammatory bowel disease in which there is ongoing inflammation and sores in the large intestine (colon) and rectum.

Causes: Genetic predisposition (immune system responds abnormally to some of the bacteria in the bowel.).

Symptoms: Periods of remission and flare-ups (known *as exacerbations*) involving fever, bloody diarrhea and cramping.

Investigations: CT scan; stool test; colonoscopy.

Treatment: Special diet; nutritional supplements; anti-inflammatory drugs; cortico-steroids; immunomodulators or anti-tumor necrosis factor (TNF) drugs; occasionally surgery to remove (part of the) colon and create a pouch by attaching the ileum to the anus; sometimes ileostomy.

6.   Some common drugs

antacids	neutralise excessive stomach acid
anti-emetics	stop vomiting
antispasmodics	calm stomach/intestinal muscles; stop cramping of smooth muscle tissue (given for colicky pains)
digestives	help digestion (breaking down of food)
emetics	to induce vomiting
laxatives	to induce bowel movements

7.   Some common investigations

- *Endoscopy* – Use of a scope (a flexible or rigid fiber-optic tubes) to look inside organs and take biopsies: eg: gastroscopy; colonoscopy
- *Contrast X-Rays*, which may include:
  Endoscopic retrograde cholangiopancreatography (ERCP) – Tube inserted into duodenum and dye injected to take X-Ray of the bile-ducts.
  Percutaneous transhepatic cholangiography (PTC) – Dye injected to take X-ray of liver and bile ducts.
  Magnetic resonance cholangiopancreatography (MRCP) – MRI used to obtain pictures of the bile ducts.

8.   Additional comments

Occasionally people are unable to take in food. For example a person with cancer in the gastro-intestinal tract which prevents food from passing through, or babies who have a heart condition which means they are unable to feed properly due to energy. In such instances, different feeding methods have to be used. These may include:

- nasogastric feeding tube (e.g. premature babies)
- PEG tube (Percutaneous endoscopic gastrostomy) tube inserted through the gastrostomy opening
- Intravenous nutrition (IVN) or total parenteral nutrition (TPN) being a mix of glucose; lipids; amino-acids; minerals; electrolytes (Na+; K+; Cl–) given directly into the bloodstream.

Similarly sometimes people are unable to defecate (pass stools/have bowel movements) due to surgical treatment for bowel cancer or very severe Crohn's Disease.

In these cases, an artificial outlet called a stoma may be created in the wall of the abdomen. Stoma is the general name given to artificial outlets for either the colon, the ileum or the ureters in the skin of the abdomen.

A colostomy is an artificial outlet for the colon (large intestine); an ileostomy is an artificial outlet for the ileum (part of the small intestine), a jejunostomy is an artificial outlet for the jejunum (part of the small intestine) and a urostomy is an artificial outlet for the ureters. While different types of stoma and stoma systems require different care, such care usually involves firstly keeping the skin around the stoma clean (shower, shallow bath, deep bath), and secondly changing the pouches (stoma bags).

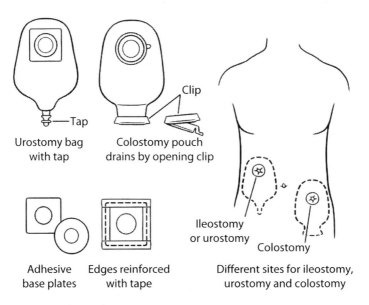

Figure 26.5. Stoma pouches and stoma sites

Summary of main points

This chapter has given a brief overview of the digestive system, including:

–   a brief overview of anatomy of the organs involved
–   Latin and Greek roots
–   health professionals involved
–   some commonly encountered conditions relating to the digestive system, together with common investigations and treatment methods.

Chapter 27

Urology and nephrology

The urinary system

The renal and the urinary system help the body get rid of certain surplus products, including wastes.

1. Latin and Greek roots

anuria	no urine production
cyst	bladder (literally a sac filled with fluid)
cystitis	inflammation of the bladder
cystoscopy	examination of the bladder through a scope passed into the urethra
dia	through
enuresis	bedwetting
glomerulus	network of capillaries where unwanted material is pushed out into the urine
glomerulonephritis	inflammation of the glomeruli and the nephrons
glomerulus	smallest element of the kidney (like very small filter)
hemo-dialysis	dialysis – rinsing out of the blood
hemofiltration	filtering the blood
-itis	inflammation of –
lysis	loosening; dissolving
nephritis	inflammation of the kidneys
nephron	smallest functional unit in the kidney
oliguria	passing very little urine
peritoneum	lining of the abdomen
peritoneal dialysis	dialysis through the peritoneum
polyuria	passing a lot of urine

renal	to do with the kidneys
tract	route; canal
uremia	(high levels of) urea in the blood (urea is a breakdown product of protein which makes skin dark and itchy)

2.   Anatomy of the urinary system

In a healthy person the urinary system is made up of:

– two kidneys
– the urinary tract, which consists of two ureters, the bladder and the urethra

3.   The kidneys

Kidneys are the filtering and cleaning organs of the urinary system and are vital in maintaining the body's internal balance by regulating a person's state of hydration. If a person is dehydrated (dry), the kidneys will act to conserve water, so that normal body functions are maintained (i.e. blood pressure; concentration of blood nutrients; healthy acid base balance and hormonal functions). Any urine passed will be dark in colour (as it is quite concentrated) and passed in smaller amounts.

In a well-hydrated person, the kidneys do not need to conserve water to maintain normal body functions. This means that a healthy person cannot become overloaded with fluid. Urine passed will be light in colour and passed in larger volumes. When the kidney(s) becomes diseased, they cannot carry out some or all of these functions.

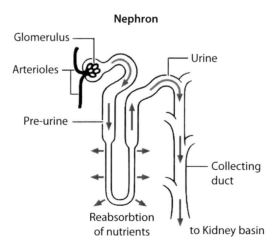

Figure 27.1. Nephron and glomerulus in the kidney

4. The urinary tract

Provides the drainage system for the body's waste water and starts with the ureters (the two tubes leading down from the kidneys). Filtered urine drains via the renal pelvis (the central urine collecting area of each kidney) into the ureters, flowing down into the bladder (a small reservoir that collects urine from the two kidneys). As the bladder fills it sends signals to the brain about the amount of stretch in the bladder wall, and the person will realize that they need to empty their bladder. The emptying of the bladder can be controlled at will and the urine will then flow out through the urethra (a drainage tube leading from the bladder to outside the body).

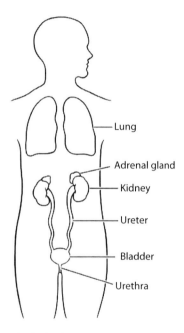

Figure 27.2. Position of kidneys in the body

5. Function of the urinary system

The kidneys

1. regulate the fluid environment within the body by
    –   maintaining the circulating blood volume
    –   maintaining concentration of blood constituents at a physiologically safe level
    –   maintaining acidity within safe limits together on a long term basis (*Please note:* The respiratory system also regulates acidity in the body, but does this on a moment-by-moment basis)

2. remove waste products from the blood through filtering
3. selectively reabsorb body constituents that need to be regulated according to the body's needs at the time
4. provide a barrier against loss of large molecules such as proteins (e.g. blood cells and plasma proteins) that should not be passed out in the urine
5. hormonal functions:
    –   the kidneys produce a hormone that is important in the production of red blood cells in the body (erythropoietin)
    –   the adrenal glands produce corticosteroids in response to body needs
6. have an integral role in the regulation of calcium and phosphate balance, which is essential for the maintenance of healthy bones (amongst other things)

6.   Health professionals

Nephrologist – Doctor who specializes in disorders of the kidneys and the urinary system.
Urologist – Doctor who specializes in disorders of the urinary system in both males and females, plus disorders of the male reproductive system.

7.   Disorders of the urinary system

1. *Kidney failure* (or *renal failure*) – Occurs when kidney function is less than 15%. Kidney failure is very common and relates very closely to kidney function.
     There are two forms of kidney failure. The first, acute kidney failure, is a life-threatening event that happens as a consequence to a major illness or trauma to the body, such as severe burns, which cause a large loss of fluid, or multiple major organ failure due to overwhelming infection (sepsis). The second, chronic kidney failure, involves a slow deterioration (worsening) of kidney function due to ongoing disease, which becomes so severe that the person requires dialysis or a kidney transplant to stay alive.

Causes: Diabetes; high blood pressure (hypertension); Nephritis (an infective or non-infective inflammation of the kidney); blockage or obstruction of the urinary tract; genetically linked problems such as *polycystic kidney disease.*

Symptoms: May include uremia which relates to an excess of urea (a waste-product of protein breakdown) in the blood.

Investigations: Creatinine Clearance Rate (CCR); Glomerular Filtration Rate (GFR)) to check how well the kidneys are working; Urine albumen test; Blood urea nitrogen (BUN)

Treatment: There are three main modes of treatment for kidney failure:
- Hemodialysis – cleaning/filtering of the blood by means of a dialysis machine. The blood is pumped from the artery and through the tubes to one side of the membrane. The other side of the membrane is washed with a dialyzing solution. The blood that passes through the artificial kidney is treated with an anticoagulant.
- Continuous Ambulatory Peritoneal dialysis (CAPD) – a method of dialysis done by the patient themselves, whereby a permanent tube is implanted in the patient's abdominal wall and four to five times a day the patient lets the dialysis fluid run into the peritoneal cavity, where it 'dwells' for some time before being drained out again.
- Kidney transplantation – the kidney of another person is placed inside the body of a person with kidney failure. Kidney transplantation will involve taking anti-rejection medication (immunosuppressants) for the rest of the person's life.

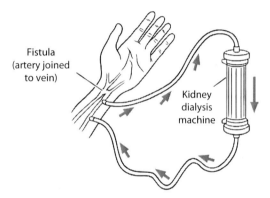

Figure 27.3. Haemodialysis

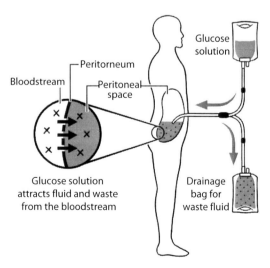

Figure 27.4. CAPD

2. *Acute and chronic glomerulonephritis*: – Glomeruli becomes inflamed, swollen, full of blood.

Causes: May be caused by bacteria, but may be due to an auto-immune reaction (e.g. in IgA nephropathy).

Symptoms: Blood and protein in urine; low blood protein; edema.
Acute glomerulonephritis: Symptoms only last 2 to 3 weeks. *Chronic glomerulonephritis*: permanent damage to nephrons which may lead to edema, coma, death.

Investigations: Blood and urine tests.

Treatment: Depending on cause: antibiotics or immunosuppressants.

3. *Kidney Stones* – Chemicals in urine can crystallize into stones (e.g. calcium, oxalate, phosphate).

Causes: Suspected genetic predisposition in some people; high protein/high salt diet.

Symptoms: Extreme cramping pain; blood or pus in urine.

Investigatons: Imaging; urine tests.

Treatment: Lithotrypsy for smaller stones (stone is crushed by high-frequency sound waves); larger stones may need to be surgically removed.

4. *Gout* – Pain and inflammation in joint (usually big toe) caused by high levels of (uric) acid (hyperuricemia).

Causes: Hereditary factors; high intake of alcohol, meat, seafood; joint injury; some medications.

Symptoms: Acute joint pain.

Investigations: Blood tests.

Treatment: Anti-inflammatory drugs.

5. *Pyelonephritis* – inflammation of the kidney pelvis which may be acute pyelonephritis (sudden onset) or chronic pyelonephritis (slow onset).

Causes: Bacteria comes up from the bladder resulting in the ureters becoming blocked (e.g. a kidney stone), so the urine cannot drain out and bacteria start to multiply.

Symptoms: Fever; chills; pain in the lower back; painful urination; nausea.

Investigations: Urine tests.

Treatment: Antibiotics; treating cause of blockage.

6. *Cystitis* (or urinary tract infection (UTI)) – Bacterial infection of the bladder lining.

Causes: Bacterial infection (often E-Coli); Risk factors include sexual intercourse ('alarm bells' in young children, warranting investigation into potential sexual abuse) and female anatomy.

Symptoms: Sharp, burning sensation when passing urine; frequent urge to pass urine.

Investigations: Urine tests.

Treatment: Antibiotics; alkalinizer sachets.

7. *Nephrotic syndrome* – A set of symptoms which can be due to illness or a disorder in itself (primary nephrotic syndrome).

Causes: Underlying illnesses may include: other form of kidney disease (e.g. glomerulonephrosis), cancer, diabetes, SLE (Systemic Lupus Erythematosus), immune disorders.

Symptoms: Protein in the urine, low levels of protein in the blood; edema around eyes, mouth, ankles.

Investigations: Biopsy; blood and urine tests; imaging.

Treatment: Depending on underlying cause, may include corticosteroids; albumen; ACE inhibitors (see Chapter 18).

8. *Polycystic disease* – Cysts form in the kidneys (inherited) which gradually squeeze out normal kidney tissue leading to kidney failure.

Causes: Inherited.

Symptoms: High blood pressure; pain in lower back.

Investigations: Blood tests; urine tests; imaging.

Treatment: Anti-hypertensive drugs; dialysis.

8.   Some common drugs

diuretics	stimulate the flow of urine; used to manage heart failure or hypertension or edema (swelling)
immunosuppressants	used to suppress the body's rejection of a kidney implant
erythropoietin	helps production of red blood cells
Potassium Chloride (KCl)	used to compensate for loss of Potassium as a result of the use of diuretics

Summary of main points

This chapter has given a brief overview of the urological system, including:

–   A brief overview of anatomy of the kidneys and their important role
–   Latin and Greek roots
–   Health professionals involved
–   Some commonly encountered conditions relating to the kidneys, together with common investigations and treatment methods.

Chapter 28

The reproductive system

This chapter is divided into two sections. Section 1 covers disorders of both male and female reproductive systems, and fertility and infertility, while Section 2 looks at complications of pregnancy.

1. Latin and Greek roots

benign	good (not cancerous)
brachytherapy	treatment delivered from a short distance: inserting radioactive material inside a tumor
HDR	High Dose Radiation
hyperplasia	overgrowth
in vitro	'in glass' i.e. in the laboratory in a test tube or specimen dish
LDR	Low Dose Radiation
malignant	literally: bad (cancerous)
vas deferens	literally: a vessel leading out

2. Section 1: Male and female reproductive systems

2.1 Anatomy of the male reproductive system

The male reproductive system consists of:

- **two testes (testicles)** – male sperm-producing glands, in the scrotum, hanging from the spermatic cord
- **epididymis** – one of two long, tightly coiled ducts which store sperm and take it from the testes to the vas deferens
- **vas deferens** – the canal that connects the testes with the urethra and takes the sperm away from the epididymis
- **prostate gland** – gland situated directly below the bladder; the prostate gland produces a fluid that helps sperm survive

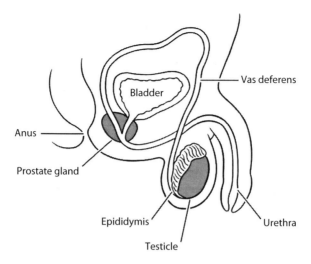

Figure 28.1. Male reproductive system

2.2 Disorders of the male reproductive system

1. *Prostatic Hypertrophy* (also referred to as B*enign Prostatic Hyperplasia (BPH)* or *Enlarged prostate*) – occurs when the prostate gland is enlarged and presses on the urethra.

Cause: The prostate gland keeps growing very gradually from around age 40 onwards.

Symptoms: Problems with urination (dribbling, leaking, frequency) and urine retention. Can lead to bladder stones and damage to bladder and kidneys.

Investigations: Rectal examination; Prostate Specific Antigen (PSA) blood test to check for inflammation or cancer; imaging.

Treatment: Watchful waiting; medication; avoiding coffee, alcohol, certain drugs.

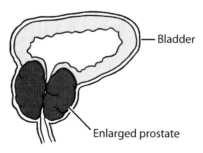

Figure 28.2. Enlarged prostate

2. *Prostate cancer*
See Chapter 16, Page 162

3.   *Prostatitis* – Inflammation of the prostate. Can be acute or chronic.

Causes: These include bacterial infection; autoimmune response; injury and many others.

Symptoms: Acute prostatitis: Fever; chills; painful urination; swollen, tender prostate. Chronic prostatitis can occur with or without symptoms.

Investigations: Urine tests; imaging.

Treatment: Rest; increased fluid intake; antibiotics.

4.   *Sexual function problems*

4a.   *Infertility/Sterility* – Please see fertility/infertility, Page 287

4b.   *Impotence* (also called *Erectile dysfunction*) – An inability to hold an erection long enough for normal intercourse.

Causes: Circulation (vascular) disorders (diabetes and smoking may be factors); neurological disorders; psychological factors; drug side-effects; hormonal problems.

Symptoms: Inability to hold erection long enough.

Investigations: History; blood and urine tests.

Treatment: Medication; self-injection.

5.   *Testicular cancer* (see Chapter 16).

6.   *Undescended Testes* (also refered to as *cryptorchidism*) – Either one or both testes have not come down into the scrotum.

Causes: Congenital condition.

Symptoms: Testes need to be in the scrotum because they need to be slightly below body temperature; undescended testes carry an increased risk of infertility and of testicular cancer.

Investigations: Physical examination

Treatment: Orchidopexy or Orchiopexy (operation to bring testis into the scrotum).

2.3   Health professionals

Fertility specialist – Doctor specializing in managing male and female infertility problems.
Urologist – see Chapter 27

2.4 Anatomy of the female reproductive system

The female reproductive system consists of:

- two ovaries, one on either side of the womb. The ovaries are the female equivalent of the testes
- two Fallopian tubes, one on either side of the womb
- womb or uterus
- cervix (the neck of the womb)
- vagina
- external genitals: vulva (containing the labia); the clitoris and its foreskin, and the openings of the vagina and the urethra (urine duct)

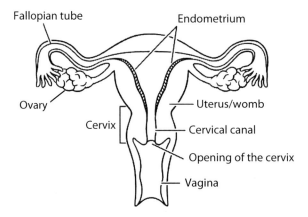

Figure 28.3. Female reproductive system

A woman's eggs mature in her ovaries. The pituitary gland in the brain produces two hormones, called Follicle Stimulating Hormone (FSH) and Luteinizing Hormone (LH). The egg develops in a follicle on the surface of the ovary under the influence of FSH and LH. Once a month, ovulation takes place and an egg is pushed away from the ovary and into the Fallopian tube, where it starts travelling towards the womb. If the egg meets sperm on its way to the womb, it may be fertilized and travel on to the womb where it may imbed itself into the lining. At this stage it is called an embryo, while in later stages of its development, it is referred to as a fetus. The lining starts producing a hormone called Human Chorionic Gonadotropin (HCG) and a pregnancy test comes up as positive (positive test for HCG in the urine or in the blood).

If the egg does not meet up with any sperm, the lining of the womb which had been prepared for a possible pregnancy, is shed and the woman has her menstrual period, usually approximately 14 days after the day on which she ovulated.

The ovarian follicle produces estrogen and progesterone, two hormones which regulate the woman's menstrual periods. When a woman goes through menopause, her ovaries stop functioning and producing these hormones. When this happens some women choose Hormone Replacement Therapy (HRT) where estrogen and/or progesterone (in either their bio-identical i.e. identical to body's natural hormones or pharmaceutical form) are taken in order to combat menopausal symptoms such as hot flashes/flushes, irritability and fatigue. Hormone replacement therapy may also be prescribed to prevent osteoporosis and cardiovascular disease, both of which may affect women after menopause.

2.5   Health professionals

Fertility specialist – Doctor specializing in managing male and female infertility problems.
Gynecologist – see Chapter 12.

2.6   Disorders of the female reproductive system

1.   *Cervical cancer* (refer Chapter 16, Page 160)

2.   *Endometrial cancer* – Cancer of the endometrium or inner lining of the womb, also referred to as *uterine cancer*.
See Chapter 16, Page 163.

3.   *Endometriosis* – Endometrial tissue (i.e. cells from the inner lining of the womb), is found outside of the womb, where it swells up and bleeds during every menstrual cycle. Common in women from puberty to menopause.

Cause: There are various theories, including that of retrograde (backwards) menstrua-tion' where bits of tissue from the womb travel up into the Fallopian tubes during a period. Other theories involve certain immune system abnormalities, cells on the outside of the ovaries changing into endometrial cells, or endometrial cells travelling through the lymph system as endometrial tissue has also been found further away from the womb.

Symptoms: Painful periods; pain during intercourse; ovulation pain; back pain; fatigue. Can lead to complications including scar tissue and adhesions (fibrous bands of scar tissue in the lower abdomen, causing organs to stick together) and infertility.

Investigations: Laparoscopy.

Treatment: Removal of endometrial tissue (e.g. by laparoscopy); hormonal treatment.

4. *Ovarian cancer* (refer Chapter 16, Page 161)

5. *Ovarian cyst* – A sac filled with fluid or with half-solid material develops in or on the ovary. Different types of cysts exist, depending on their origins. A Follicular cyst is the most common. It is benign and usually disappears by itself. A Dermoid cyst is formed from cells which produce eggs and can contain bone, teeth or hair. Corpus luteum cysts consist of yellowish tissue which grows on the ovary after ovulation and produces progesterone. Normally these 'waste away' after the period.

Causes: Ovarian cysts can be normal and may disappear by themselves; some can be malignant.

Symptoms: Constipation; frequent urination; irregular periods; abdominal pain; pain during intercourse.

Investigations: Ultrasound scan; laparoscopy; CA-125 blood test.

Treatment: Oral contraceptives (follicular cysts); surgical removal.

6. *Pelvic Inflammatory Disease* (*PID*) – An infection which starts in the neck of the womb and then moves to the tube(s) or spreads further into the abdomen.

Cause: Usually a bacterial infection, typically a sexually transmitted disease (STD) such as Chlamydia or gonorrhea.

Symptoms: Foul-smelling discharge; pain in lower belly; abnormal bleeding or spotting between periods; pain during intercourse; burning sensation when passing urine. Can lead to abscess, septicemia and infertility (due to scarring of the Fallopian tubes).

Investigations: Endocervical swabs (taken from inside the cervix).

Treatment: Painkillers; antibiotics; tracing of (sexual) contacts.

7. *Polycystic Ovaries* – Lots of small cysts develop on the ovary which may cause the affected ovary to double in size.

Cause: Hormonal imbalance: high levels of testosterone, LH and oestrogen; low levels of FSH; may be caused by problems with the adrenal glands or the pituitary gland; sometimes associated with insulin resistance.

Symptoms: No ovulation; no menstrual periods; infertility; masculine-type hair growth; low voice; weight gain.

Investigations: Blood tests; imaging.

Treatment: Often hormonal treatment; sometimes removal of part of one or both ovaries; oral diabetes medication; losing weight.

3.   Fertility and infertility

3.1   Infertility

Infertility is the inability for a couple to conceive (have a baby) and affects approximately 10% of all couples. Treatment is based on the cause of the infertility and both partners must be investigated. The American Congress of Obstetricians and Gynecologists (ACOG) and the American Society for Reproductive Medicine (ASRM) both recommend that women under age 30 try to conceive for 12 months before seeking treatment, and that women over age 30 try for six months before seeking help from a fertility specialist. However, more recent studies suggest that couples should wait no more than 6 months of trying to conceive before seeking help.

Many conditions may lower a couple's chance of conceiving. These can include:

- decrease in the number and motility of sperm
- disorder of the vaginal mucus
- problems with the transport of sperm/eggs
- disorders of ovulation
- older parents, especially over 40 years
- sexual dysfunction
- psychological disorder
- medical conditions
- endocrine disorders
- genetic factors
- infections – pelvic inflammatory disease
- trauma to the genitals
- radiation which may have destroyed eggs or sperm
- certain drugs may interfere with ovulation
- immunological incompatibility – antibodies to sperm

Treatment: Identifying the problem; outlining the options. Treatment may include emotional counselling; coital timing (timing of sexual intercourse); donor insemination (in case of semen problems); induced ovulation and or surgery or In Vitro Fertilization (IVF) in the case of tubal disease.

3.2   Men

In most cases male infertility is due to a low sperm count or poor sperm function.

Causes: Degenerative changes of the testicles through, for instance, x-rays, infection, malnutrition; sperm unable to get through due to a blockage; no or not enough viable (able to live) spermatozoa.

Symptoms: No physical symptoms.

Investigations: Semen Analysis is the main test, whereby three semen samples are analysed over the course of several weeks where sperm count, sperm motility (sperm movement 4 hours after ejaculation) and sperm normality (counting percentage of abnormal sperm, must be < 20%) are checked. The second is Post-coital test where a vaginal mucus specimen from the man's partner is examined (within 6 hours of intercourse). This test is done to analysis the penetration of mucus by the sperm and the quality of the mucus.

Treatment: Combine the few healthy sperm with the egg via IVF; donor insemination (placement of (donor) sperm within the cervix or uterus at ovulation).

3.3   Women

Causes: Failure to ovulate; blocked Fallopian tubes; fibroids or polyps in the womb inhibit the egg imbedding itself in the lining of the womb; congenital abnormalities of the genital tract; unfavourable secretions; cervical or vaginal problems which make it difficult for sperm to get through. Tubal Pelvic Inflammatory Disease is a major cause of tubal disease. Tubal damage may also follow peritonitis and pelvic adhesions after surgery. Endometriosis may also cause pelvic damage similar to tubal disease (uterine tissue growing outside of uterus). In a number of cases no cause can be found for the infertility.

Symptoms: Failure to conceive after repeated attempts.

Investigations: Analysis of cervical mucus (should be clear and there should be lots of it and it should be 'stretchy' at ovulation time); a urine test (an ovulation predictor kit which reveals whether the woman is ovulating or not); Ultrasound (detects a ripening egg); hormonal blood tests (done throughout the cycle to show variations in different hormone levels); Laparoscopy to check whether the tubes are still open as well as for any adhesions or pelvic inflammatory disease or endometriosis. Involves a coloured dye being injected into the tubes.

Treatment: Ovulation failure is treated with hormonal medication. Donor eggs are used if women suffer premature ovarian failure. Tubal damage treatment involves surgery to remove adhesions, and/or IVF. If a woman is infertile due to endometriosis, IVF may be the only option.

3.4   Artificial reproduction

Artificial reproduction means that artificial means are used in order to achieve a pregnancy. This may include the following:

1. *Artificial Insemination by Husband (AIH)*

Situations in which this may be done: Problems with the cervix; mechanical problems, such as a spinal (back) injury or a physical disability; a very low sperm count; semen stored (frozen) before chemotherapy or radiotherapy.

Method: Intra-uterine insemination whereby sperm is put inside the uterus through the cervix using a very fine catheter (narrow tube).

2. *Artificial Insemination by Donor (AID/DI)*

Situations in which this may be done: No sperm count or a very low sperm count; abnormal sperm; risk of hereditary diseases being passed on; woman has no male partner.

Method: Speculum and syringe used to bathe the cervix in semen. Success rates are the same as for normal conception.

3. *In vitro fertilization (IVF)*

Situations in which this may be done: Damaged tubes; low sperm count; poor movement of sperm; presence of anti-sperm antibodies; problems with the cervix; endometriosis; unexplained infertility.

Method: The woman takes drugs which stimulate (multiple) ovulation. The eggs are removed from the woman's body using ultrasound. Eggs and sperm are treated separately then brought together outside of the body (*in vitro*). Two to three days after fertilization, a maximum of three embryos are placed inside the uterus. Any additional healthy embryo's are frozen in case further attempts at fertilization are necessary in the future.

4. *Gamete Intra-Fallopian Transfer (GIFT)*

Situations in which this may be done: May be done if there is a 'cervical barrier' to conception (problem with the cervix).

Method: The the eggs are collected as for IVF and are placed into a catheter (fine tube) with fresh sperm; they are then placed in the Fallopian tube, allowing fertilization to take place.

5. *Ovum Donation*

Situations in which this may be done: When the woman does not ovulate (i.e. does not produce any eggs).

Method: Eggs are donated by women (usually women who are undergoing IVF themselves). The eggs are fertilized outside of the womb (*in vitro*) using sperm from the woman's partner. The embryo's which result are then placed inside her womb.

3.5 Contraception

Different types of contraception (methods for preventing pregnancy, sometimes referred to as family planning) exist, including the following:

1. *Natural family planning*
This involves abstinence from intercourse during the time of the month when the woman is fertile. Under ideal circumstances, this may be almost just as effective as the pill, or condoms and diaphragms, if the woman has a regular menstrual period. However, determining the fertile period may be very difficult.

2. *Condoms*
Thin, strong sheaths of rubber or similar material worn by the man, to stop the sperm from entering the vagina. Condoms may fail if they tear or if they slip off after climax. If the condom is used consistently and correctly, it is as effective as the diaphragm.

3. *Diaphragm*
A flexible rubber dome used with spermicidal cream or jelly. It is inserted into the vagina to cover the cervix and stops the sperm from getting past (barrier to sperm). The diaphragm must be left in place for at least 6 hours after intercourse and may be left in place as long as 24 hours. The diaphragm must be fitted by a specialist and must be refitted every two years or after each pregnancy. The diaphragm offers a high level of protection (failure rate is 2–3 pregnancies per 100 women). Failure may be caused by incorrect insertion or by the diaphragm being moved out of place during sexual intercourse.

4. *Intra-Uterine Contraceptive Device (IUCD).*
A small object shaped like a loop, spiral or ring, made of plastic or stainless steel. It has to be placed inside the womb by a specialist and may be left there indefinitely. Some women cannot use an IUCD, because the womb expels it, or because they have bleeding or discomfort. The IUCD is not recommended for women who have not had a child, as the womb is too small and the cervical canal too narrow. Sometimes, insertion of the IUCD may lead to inflammation of the pelvic organs.

5. *Spermicidals*
Sperm-killing chemicals inserted into the vagina to cover the surface of the vagina and the opening of the cervix. Quite effective on their own, but thought to be more effective when used together with either a diaphragm or a condom.

6. *Oral contraceptives* (taken by females)
Sometimes known as 'the pill'. Contraceptives may be taken orally or given by implant or by injection. Oral contraceptives are the most effective method of contraception (apart from total abstinence or surgical sterilization). They may have some side-effects, including nausea, light bleeding (spotting) between periods, breast tenderness

or enlargement, fluid retention, and weight gain. They should not be used by women who are prone to developing thrombosis.

7. *Vasectomy*
Procedure involving the cutting of the 'vas', the tube which carries the sperm. Some doctors carry out 'no-scalpel' vasectomies.

8. *Tubal ligation*
Abdominal surgery to tie the tubes so that eggs can no longer travel from the ovary to the womb.

4. Pregnancy

This Section will look at some of of the complications which may occur in the course of a pregnancy, including gestational diabetes and pre-eclampsia. Please refer to Chapter 12 for general information on pregnancy and antenatal checkups.

A 40-week pregnancy is divided into three 3-monthly periods called *trimesters* of 13–14 weeks each. In the first trimester (conception to 13 weeks) there is rapid growth. All major organs of the fetus develop. The mother experiences major changes which affect her hormone levels, circulation, metabolism, and emotions. Mothers need folic acid to prevent neural tube defects.

In the second trimester all organs of the baby are working independently. The baby continues to grow. If born just after 24 weeks, there is a slim chance of survival but possibly impaired quality of life.

In the third trimester the baby is fully developed and preparing for birth. It is laying down fat, iron and immunity reserves. Mothers commonly experience anemia and need good nutrition, rest and relaxation.

4.1   Latin and Greek roots

antenatal	before birth
cardio-toco-graphy or CTG	Cardio: heart; toco: contraction; graphy: recording
cervix	neck (of womb) (adjective: cervical)
ectopic	out of place
extra-uterine	outside the womb
fetus	developing baby in the womb (adjective: fetal)
gestation	pregnancy (literally growing and developing)
gravid	pregnant (heavy with child)
gravidarum	belonging to pregnant women

hyster	womb
hysterectomy	removal of the womb
intrauterine	Inside the womb
menses/menstrual periods	monthly (bleeds)
natal	related to birth
partum	child birth
postnatal	after birth
prenatal	before birth
term	between 37 and 42 weeks gestation (i.e. ready to be born)
uterus	womb (Latin)
ovary	gland producing female hormones; eggs develop in the ovary
ovulation	egg 'jumps' out of the ovary, into the Fallopian tube
ovum	egg (compare: ovaries)

4.2   Health professionals

Gynecologist – See Chapter 12.
Midwife – Health professional specialized in the care of women during pregnancy and childbirth, as well as immediately after childbirth.

4.3   Complications of pregnancy

Minor

Nausea and vomiting – The so-called morning sickness (which can in fact last all day), usually lasts between 4–16 weeks.

Heartburn – Pain caused by gastric juices coming up into the gullet caused by hormone changes to cardiac sphincter (cardia is top of the stomach). Worse from week 30 to 40.

Breast changes – Tingling, discomfort, feeling of fullness.

Constipation – Due to hormonal relaxation and slowing of gut.

Frequently passing urine – Due to pressure from enlarging uterus plus increased blood flow to the bladder.

Cramp and backache

Leukorrhea – White, non-irritant vaginal discharge.

Fainting – May happen more often due to vasodilation (widening of blood vessels) of extremities (arms and legs).

Varicose veins – Due to hormonal relaxing of blood vessel walls in lower legs and vulva.

Skin changes:

Linea nigra – Pigmentation line from umbilicus to top of pubic hair line.

Chloasma – Mask of pregnancy: Pigmentation of face, which will fade after childbirth.

Itching of skin (urticaria): Mostly over abdomen and breasts, buttocks and upper thighs – due to liver response to pregnancy

Carpal tunnel syndrome – Numbness with pins and needles in woman's hands and fingers, due to fluid retention in the wrist, leading to pressure on the nerve in the wrist. This may require physiotherapy and splints.

Insomnia – Not being able to sleep – may be caused by anxiety.

More serious

Every checkup will involve a urine test for sugar, ketones and protein. Protein in the urine may indicate pre-eclampsia, while the presence of sugar may indicate gestational diabetes. The practitioner will take the woman's blood pressure and weight to check for pre-eclampsia and will check the baby's heart tones and movements to make sure it is developing normally. The height of the fundus (top) of the uterus is checked to see if pregnancy and baby are developing normally.

1. *Abdominal pain in pregnancy*

Causes: In early weeks this may be caused by an abortion or an ectopic pregnancy (pregnancy within Fallopian tube)

Fibroids – benign mass in uterus

Placental abruption – see later

Stretching of round ligaments – not serious

Symptoms: Pain in abdomen.

Investigations: Ultrasound scan.

Treatments: Depending on cause.

2. *Abortion* – May be spontaneous or induced. Spontaneous abortion is known as a miscarriage. A missed abortion occurs when the baby has died inside the womb, but the woman continues to feel pregnant. This is also known as intrauterine fetal demise or IUFD.

Causes (*spontaneous abortion*): Often: blighted fetus (something wrong with the fetus, incompatible with life); occasionally: accidental use of teratogenic drugs (drugs which may harm or kills the fetus).

Symptoms: Usually vaginal blood loss; no fetal heartbeat.

Investigations: Ultrasound scan.

Treatment: Observation; occasionally a spontaneous abortion may not proceed and the pregnancy may continue; if miscarriage is in progress, medical staff will need to do a D&C (see Page 82) to ensure there are no products of conception left inside the womb, as this may lead to infection, bleeding or to the growth of a rare tumor. *Please note: An induced abortion is also referred to as a termination of pregnancy.*

3.   An*tepartum hemorrhage* (*APH*) (see vaginal bleeding during pregnancy).

4.   *Ectopic pregnancy* or *extra-uterine pregnancy* – This is a medical emergency and occurs when the fertilized egg implants itself outside of the womb, mostly in the fallopian tube. As the embryo grows bigger, the tube cannot stretch to contain the egg and ruptures, causing life-threatening intra-abdominal bleeding.

Causes: Pelvic inflammatory disease (PID); damage to the tube (e.g. tubal ligation); smoking.

Symptoms: Blood loss; cramping; pain; vaginal bleeding; uterus enlarged; early breast changes; sometimes symptoms of shock.

Investigations: Ultrasound scan; blood tests.

Treatment: Methotrexate® if diagnosed early; removal of pregnancy (salpingostomy) or removal of tube (salpingectomy).

5.   *Fetal alcohol syndrome* – see Chapter 12, Page 133.

6.   *Gestational diabetes* (also refered to as *pregnancy diabetes*) – Diabetes is a medical condition which can seriously complicate pregnancy. The mother may have diabetes prior to pregnancy or develop it during pregnancy (*gestational diabetes mellitus*).

Causes: In pregnancy diabetes the pancreas (temporarily) does not produce enough insulin or the body may not respond to it (insulin resistance – see Chapter 25). Risk factors include being overweight, having a family history of diabetes or having had pregnancy diabetes previously.

Symptoms: Excessive thirst; large volume of urine passed; weight loss; thrush; urinary tract infections.

Investigations: Sugary drink test (usually between 24 and 28 weeks of pregnancy) to see if body can process the sugar (take it out of the bloodstream).

Treatment
During Pregnancy
Good control of sugar levels; delivery of baby at hospital – with a Special Care Baby Unit (SCBU) available. Oral anti-diabetes medication is not used in pregnancy as it is considered teratogenic (can lead to fetal death). Good fetal monitoring including a kick chart (chart on which mother records baby's movements) and CTG; ultrasound scans and placental function tests.

During Labor
IV fluids with glucose and insulin and ongoing blood glucose monitoring.

Postnatal period
Monitoring blood sugar levels for both mother and baby for 48 hours. Glucose Tolerance Test (GTT) for mother 6 weeks after birth.

Maternal Complications of Diabetes
Higher incidence of pre-eclampsia, urinary tract infections, thrush, polyhydramnion (too much amniotic fluid); long-term diabetes after pregnancy; reduced fertility; increased risk of spontaneous abortion.

Fetal complications
Large baby; intra-uterine death; fetal abnormalities; respiratory distress at birth; rebound hypoglycemia (baby has low blood sugar levels after birth); birth trauma due to increased risk of operative delivery; premature labor.

7.   *Hyperemesis gravidarum* – Severe and almost continuous vomiting.

Causes: These may include high levels of HCG and estrogen; many other risk factors have been studied.

Symptoms: Severe vomiting; severe dehydration and ketosis (body using protein stores instead of fat stores).

Investigations: Fluid balance chart.

Treatment: Intravenous (IV) rehydration; sometimes TPN or nasogastric feeding.

8.   *Intraturerine Growth Retardation (IUGR)* – A slowing down of fetal growth leading to a baby who is small for gestational age. IUGR may lead to low birth weight babies.
      There are two types of IUGR. Asymmetrical growth retardation is due to malnutrition in the womb, with normal growth until the third trimester, head circumference within normal limits, but low birth weight. There is a lack of body fat and the babies head appears large when compared to the wasted appearance of body and limbs. Symmetrical (global) growth retardation is growth retardation which has occured since early pregnancy. Head circumference is in proportion to overall size and weight; outlook not so good; may involve neurological damage.

Causes: Anything that leads to placenta not functioning well; smoking, essential hypertension; multiple pregnancy, mother weighing less than 100 pounds/45kgs; poor nutrition (e.g. dieting or junk food); problems with umbilical cord; severe anemia, pre-eclampsia; threatened abortion; prolonged pregnancy; APH; certain drugs (including corticosteroids, anti-convulsants); opiates; chromosome abnormality; fetal alcohol syndrome.

Symptoms: Growth delay on scan.

Investigations: Imaging

Treatment: Bedrest; aspirin (up to 20 weeks); fetal monitoring.

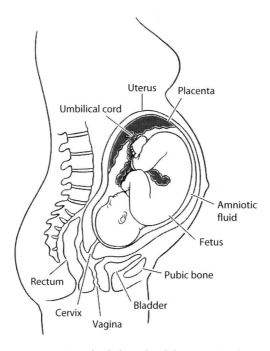

Figure 28.4. Pregnant woman at 40 weeks (baby in head down position)

9.   *Malpresentation* – Any presentation other than the vertex (back of baby's head). In all malpresentations the part of the baby that presents (is ready to come out) does not fit the opening of the birthcanal well. Types include breech (complete, incomplete); face; shoulder; brow. (Breech is where the baby's buttocks lie lowermost in the uterus. A complete breech is when the baby is sitting crosslegged with its feet next to its bottom. A frank breech is when the baby's bottom is down, and legs are extended up, with feet next to baby's ears). Early in pregnancy babies may lie in breech position, but most turn by 34 weeks, so in preterm labor, it is quite common for baby to be breech. Other malpresentations include transverse presentation or shoulder presentation when the baby lies sideways, or when the shoulder is the presenting part.

Cause: Often associated with early rupture of membranes (uneven pressure on bag of waters) and increased risk of cord prolapsed (when the umbilical cord falls out and is in danger of being squashed, depriving baby of oxygen). A breech may involve a uterus of abnormal shape; not enough water around baby; there is a mass in the uterus (e.g. a fibroid); fetal abnormality such as hydrocephalus; twins; many previous pregnancies have led to muscles around the womb being very lax; polyhydramnion (too much fluid) allowing baby to move freely.

Symptoms: Baby's heart rate may be too fast or too slow. Labor may be prolonged and can be dangerous and risky for the baby due to a lack of oxygen to the baby (both inside and outside of the womb); intra-cranial hemorrhage (bleed into baby's brain); bone breaks and bone dislocations; rupture of abdominal organs.

Investigations: Imaging; physical examination.

Treatment: Turning the baby inside the womb; Cesarean section.

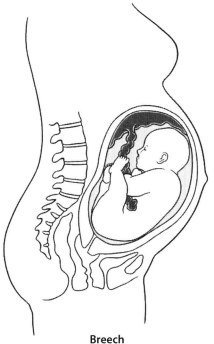

Breech
Baby's buttocks lie lower-most in the uterus

Figure 28.5. Pregnant woman at 40 weeks (baby in breech birth position)

10.   *Miscarriage* – Products of conception (baby and placenta) come away from the womb before 24 weeks. Spontaneous abortion most often occurs between 9 and 11 weeks.

Causes: Fetal chromosomal abnormalities are involved in 60% of spontaneous abortions.

Can also be due to the mother acquiring diseases i.e. Rubella; severe fever; drug overdoses; industrial chemicals; ABO (Blood Group) incompatibilities; thalassemia (see Chapter 20; retroverted uterus (womb is tipped backwards); bicornate uterus (abnormally shaped womb with two *horns*); cervical incompetence (cervix will not stay closed due to placental abruption or placenta previa).

11.   *Multiple Pregnancy* – The development of more than one fetus in the uterus. Twins may be mono-zygotic (one egg and one sperm; two amniotic sacs; one placenta; connection of circulation; same sex) or di-zygotic (two eggs and two sperm; two amniotic sacs; two placenta; no connection circulation, may be different sex).

Causes: Unknown; sometimes the result of fertility treatment.

Symptoms: All minor disorders of pregnancy, i.e. nausea, heartburn, may be worse; anemia due to greater demands on iron and folic acid; hypertension more common; polyhydramnion (more amniotic fluid than usual) is common, especially with mono-zygotic twins; more pressure symptoms caused by the increased weight and size of the uterus. Pressure symptoms includes varicose veins and swelling of legs, backache; breathlessness and indigestion. Can lead to further complications such as Polyhydramnion; premature rupture of membranes; fetal abnormality; prolapse of cord; malpresentations; prolonged labor; post-partum hemorrhage; delay in birth of second twin. Labor is often early due to overstretching of uterus.

Investigations: Ultrasound; uterus feels larger than expected for gestation; size of baby is small, which means there may be more than one baby.

Treatment: Careful monitoring of both babies is important, if there are any signs of fetal distress (baby/babies in trouble) doctors need to do an emergency Caesarean section.

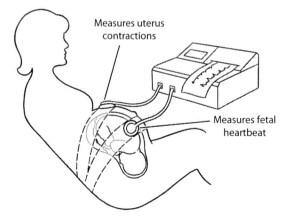

Figure 28.6. Cardiotocography

12.   *Placental abruption* – Placenta comes away from the womb after 28 weeks. Occurs in approximately 2% of pregnancies. Abruption can be mild, moderate or severe.

Causes: No cause found (very common); sometimes due to eclampsia, diffuse intravascular coagulation (or DIC); essential hypertension; fall, blow, accident; polyhydramnion with ruptured membranes.

Symptoms: Pain and visible bleeding may or may not occur.

Investigations: Ultrasound scan (if there is time).

Treatment: Depends on severity. If mild then hospitalization: observation, monitoring baby's condition. Moderate cases will include an assessment of the baby's condition; if not good, mother must be induced (induction of labor) OR Emergency Caesarean Section if fetus is still alive; blood transfusions for mother.

13.   *Placenta previa* – Painless bleeding from separation of an abnormally situated placenta. The placenta lies partly or wholly in the lower uterine segment.

There are 4 grades of severity. Grade 1 and 2 is where the placenta partly covers the neck of the womb (os); vaginal delivery may be tried. Grades 3 and 4 is where the placenta covers the neck of the womb in front of the baby: Caesarean Section required.

Symptoms: Often first sign of placenta previa is bleeding (if not detected by ultrasound).

Bleeding may occur at rest and may vary from very light to extremely heavy, causing a serious threat to baby and mother.

Investigations: Ultrasound scan (USS).

Treatment: Regular scans to check the position of placenta; hospitalization for check-ups and rest; plan of delivery; monitoring baby's movement. No vaginal examinations.

14.   *Pre-eclampsia (also known as pregnancy induced-hypertension (PIH) or toxemia or Gestational Proteinuria Hypertension or GPH)*

Cause: Not fully known, but may involve problem with blood vessels in the placenta, so blood pressure rises to ensure the developing child receives enough blood (oxygen and nutrients). Other factors may include (family) history of diabetes; high blood pressure; kidney problems; autoimmune disorders; diet; first pregnancy; multiple pregnancy; age (>35) and obesity.

Mainly occurs after 20 weeks and disappears after delivery. Between 6–7% of all pregnancies are complicated by hypertension (Fleming et al. 2005) and in 80% of these cases pre-eclampsia occurs.

Symptoms: Hypertension; swelling in hands, neck, face; protein in the urine (kidneys leaking protein into urine); sudden weight gain (>2 pounds or >1kg a week). Can lead on to eclampsia, a very serious state where convulsions occur and where the placenta may come away from the womb, leading to the child's death; bleeding inside blood vessels; drop in platelets; major organs damaged (lungs, kidneys, liver); capillaries in eye may be damaged, resulting in blindness.

Investigations: Women rarely have any symptoms until the condition has already become advanced. Therefore antenatal checkups (should) always include blood pressure, weight and urine checks.

Professionals look for a change in blood pressure of 15–20 mm Hg above the normal reading (e.g. if blood pressure is normally 120/70, it may now be 135/85 or 140/90); Proteinuria (protein in the urine) without any signs of a urinary infection; swelling and rapid weight gain, which may mean the body is retaining fluid.

Treatment: Careful monitoring of fetus and symptoms; may need hospitalization, careful monitoring and bed-rest; lying on left side. Sometimes it is necessary to deliver the baby prematurely if symptoms worsen. Mother may be given corticosteroids to help baby's lungs develop more quickly (see Chapter 12.1).

15.   *Rhesus disease* (See Chapter 28) – Health professionals are worried about mothers who are Rhesus negative (Rh^{-ve}), because if the baby is Rhesus positive (Rh^{+ve}) and there is any mixing of blood between mother and baby, the mother can form antibodies. During further pregnancies, antibodies in the mother's bloodstream may cross the placenta and destroy the baby's red blood cells if those babies too are Rhesus positive.

The first pregnancy is usually not affected, because at that stage the mother has not yet formed antibodies (unless the mother has had a blood transfusion with Rhesus Positive blood and formed antibodies then).

Causes: The blood groups of mother and baby may mix due to hypertension; placental abruption; trauma to placenta during amniocentesis; external cephalic version (turning a breech baby); placenta previa; previous blood transfusion to mother of Rhesus positive blood.

Symptoms: Baby's blood will flow more quickly because it will be thinner, due to hemolysis and anemia (see Chapter 20).

Investigations: Doppler sound test of baby's blood circulation.

Treatment: Mother is given $Rh_0(D)$ Immunoglobulin to prevent her blood from making anti-bodies, thus preventing Rhesus disease in following pregnancies.

16. *Vaginal bleeding in pregnancy*

Any vaginal blood loss during pregnancy should always be investigated. Bleeding can be due to:

–   *Abortion or miscarriage* (see above)
–   *Cervical Incompetence* – The cervix opens, causing a spontaneous abortion, usually between 16 and 22 weeks. Congenital condition (born with it). Factors may include damage/injury during previous termination of pregnancy; lacerations (damage) during previous childbirth. A purse string suture is put in the cervix (to keep it closed) and taken out at 38 weeks.
–   *Cervical lesion* – Changes in the lining of the cervix, can be benign or cancerous.
–   *Ectopic pregnancy* (see above)
–   *Implantation bleeding* – Bleeding caused by embryo implanting in the lining of the womb. Usually occurs on the 7th day after fertilization; may last 3–4 days. Sometimes mistaken for a menstrual period.
–   *Increased blood supply in pregnancy* – Bleeding may occur especially after intercourse, this does not affect the pregnancy.
–   *Placenta previa* (see above).

4.4   Some common investigations

Please refer to Chapter 12.

5.   Sexual Health

Please see Pages 282 and 284 for an overview of the anatomy of the male and female reproductive systems.

Common problems include what is referred to as sexual risk-taking behavior which may result in:

–   Increased prevalence in HIV infection (see Chapter 24)
–   Increased prevalence of unwanted pregnancies resulting in abortions
–   Increased prevalence of sexually transmitted diseases (STDs), which are also referred to as sexually transmitted infections or STIs

Having repeated abortions (terminations of pregnancy) may result in problems maintaining a pregnancy once the woman has reached a stage in her life where she does wish to have children. Repeated terminations may result in scarring of the inner lining of the uterus (endometrium) making implantation of the embryo problematic.

Repeated terminations may also lead to what is sometimes referred to as an incompetent cervix or weakened cervix, where the cervix opens too soon during the later stages of pregnancy. Please note that a weakened cervix may also be due to other causes, including previous cervical surgery, damage to the cervix during a difficult birth, or to congenital malformations.

5.1 Most common STIs

1. *Chlamydia* – one of the most common STIs in many countries

Causes: Sexually transmitted infection with the Chlamydia trachomatis bacteria.

Symptoms: Burning sensation when passing urine; discharge from penis, vagina or rectum; in females symptoms of pelvic inflammatory disease (PID), salpingitis (inflammation of the Fallopian tubes) or hepatitis (inflammation of the liver). Please note: Chlamydia may lead to infertility in females, mainly due to scarring of the Fallopian tubes; up to 25% of infected males may not experience any symptoms. When someone is diagnosed with chlamydia, they should also be checked for other STIs including gonorrhea and syphilis.

Investigations: Antibody tests or culture of samples of discharge from penis, vagina or rectum.

Treatment: Antibiotics, tetracyclines.

2. *Genital warts* – may also be referred to as condyloma acuminate or venereal warts.

Causes: Infection by specific strains of the Human Papilloma Virus or HPV, usually strains 6 and 11.
Please note: Other *specific* strains of HPV (e.g. strains 16, 18, 31 and 45) have been linked to cervical cancer.

Symptoms: Grey or flesh-coloured warts, usually in genital areas. NB if found in children, this may be suspicious for sexual abuse.

Investigations: Applying acetic acid solution; colposcopy; cervical smear test.

Treatment: Cryotherapy; laser treatment; electrodesiccation (using electric current to destroy the warts).

3. *Gonorrhea* – common STD, also referred to as clap or the drip.

Causes: Sexually transmitted infection with the Neisseria gonorrhoeae bacteria.

Symptoms: Burning sensation when passing urine; white, yellow or green discharge from penis, vagina or rectum; pain in the testicles in males; females may have symptoms of pelvic inflammatory disease (PID), salpingitis (inflammation of the Fallopian tubes); fever, rash and joint pain if the infection spreads through the bloodstream.

Symptoms usually appear within 2 to 5 days after the infection, but may take up to 1 month to appear in some men.

Please note: Gonorrhea may lead to infertility in females, mainly due to scarring of the Fallopian tubes. When someone is diagnosed with chlamydia, they should also be checked for other STIs including chlamydia, HPV and syphilis.

Investigations: Cultures of samples of the discharge (fluid) or blood culture.

Treatment: Antibiotics; if relevant: vaccinations against Hepatitis B and HPV; the person's sexual contacts should be traced and also checked for the infection.

4.   *Syphilis* (see Chapter 17, Page 176).

Summary of main points

This chapter has covered disorders of the male and female reproductive systems including:

–   a brief overview of anatomy of the organs involved
–   Latin and Greek roots
–   health professionals involved
–   fertility and infertility
–   complications of pregnancy
–   sexual health, some common consequences of sexual risktaking behaviours

Appendix

Some common investigations

Blood tests:

Blood culture	Page 125
Blood gases	Page 125
Blood grouping	Page 210
Chromosome study	Page 125
Cholesterol	Page 212
Clotting time	Page 211
CPR	C-Reactive protein, Page 224
Electrolytes	Page 125
ESR	Erythrocyte Sedimentation Rate, Page 224
Full blood count	Also: Complete Blood Count, Page 125
Genetic study	Page 125
Glucose	Pages 125, 258, 259
Groups and Coombs test	Page 125
PKU (phenylketonuria)	Page 125
PSA	Pages 156, 282
SBR	Serum Bilirubin, Page 125
Thyroid function tests	Page 125
Urea,Creatinine	Page 125
Enzymes	Elevated liver enzymes may be found in blood in case of a liver condition; elevated cardiac enzymes may be found in the blood after a heart attack
INR	regular test to monitor patient on blood-thinning medication (such as warfarin)

Biopsies	**some living material taken for testing (e.g. for cancer)**
Bone marrow aspiration	biopsy of bone marrow
hook wire biopsy	deep biopsy of breast tissue
fine needle biopsy	biopsy using fine hollow needle and local anesthetic
smear test	checking cervical cells
liver biopsy	checking for liver disease, liver cancer or liver secondaries

Imaging
Radiological tests

Abdominal X-Ray	Page 125
Chest X-Ray	Pages 49, 125, 203

Contrast X-rays:

Angiogram/angiography	Page 211
Barium meal/barium swallow	Page 162
Barium enema	Page 159
Cholangiogram	contrast X-Ray of gall-ducts
IVP	contrast X-Ray of kidneys and ureters
Myelogram	contrast X-Ray of space around the spinal cord

Ultrasonography: examinations by sound waves

Cranial ultrasound	Page 126
Echo or echocardiogram	Page 126
Renal ultrasound	Page 126

Urine tests

culture microscopy and sensitivity	Checking if bacteria grow on urine sample in the lab, and what antibiotics they are sensitive to
Early Morning Urine (EMU)	

Respiratory investigations

Acid Fast Bacilli Tests	Page 203
Bronchoscopy	Page 203
Lung function test	Page 203
Mantoux test	Page 203
Oxygen saturation	Page 203
Peak flow meter	Page 203
Pulse oxymetry	Pages 98, *104*
Spirometry	lung function test, Page 203
Sputum specimen	Page 203
Transbronchial biopsies	Page 203
Ziehl-Neelsen (Zn) stain test	Page 203

Endoscopies: looking inside an organ through a (flexible) fibre-optic tube

Arthroscopy	(looking inside a joint, e.g. knee joint)
Bronchoscopy	Page 203
Cystoscopy	looking inside the bladder, Pages 157, 273
Gastroscopy (Stomach)	looking inside the stomach, Page 157

Hysteroscopy	looking inside the uterus, Page 157
Laparoscopy (Abdomen)	looking inside the abdomen, Page 157
Oesophagoscopy	looking inside the gullet, Page 157 (also esophagoscopy)
Colposcopy	viewing cervix and vagina, Page 157

Scanning

CT scan	*Computerized tomography,* Pages 177, 203
MRI scan	Magnetic Resonance Imaging, Page 177
PET scan	Positron Emission Tomography – scan using radio-active material to monitor areas of high activity (high cell turnover) in the body
Radionuclide (Nuclear) Scan	imaging using small amounts of radioactive material
VQ scan	ventilation perfusion scan of the lungs

Electrical tests

EEG	ElectroEncephaloGram (testing brain activity), Page 174
EMG	ElectroMyoGram (testing muscle activity), Page 226
ECG	ElectroCardioGram (testing heart activity), Page 191

Other investigations

Audiometry	hearing test
Bleeding time	Page 210
CTG (CardioTocoGraphy)	Pages 291, *298*
D & C (Dilatation and Curettage)	Page 82
Doppler scanning	ultrasound scanning of a moving structure, such as blood flowing through an area
Endotracheal aspirate culture	keeping a specimen taken from an endotracheal tube in the lab to see if it grows any bacteria
Exercise Tolerance Test	ECG whilst patient is on the treadmill, Page 191
Fertility Tests	Pages 287, 288
Gastric aspirate	Page 126
Heart Catheterization	catheter (narrow tube) inserted in artery in arm or groin and guided through to the heart; contrast dye injected into coronary
Holter monitor	monitoring ECG for a longer time, using a portable tape, recorder, whilst patient carries on normal everyday activities

Lumbar puncture	Page 177
PTCA	see Heart Catheterization, Page 190
Radio-Active Iodine	
Uptake Test	patient swallows radio-active iodine tablet/liquid; 6–24 hours later radio-active activity in the thyroid is measured.
Spinal Tap	Page 177 (see lumbar puncture)
Telemetry	Monitoring ECG from a distance, using a portable transmitter
TORCH study	Page 126
Viral study	Page 126
Visual Acuity	Eyesight test, Page 202

References

Adams, F.M., & Osgood, C.E. (1973). A cross-cultural study of the affective meanings of color. *Journal of Cross-Cultural Psychology, 4*(2), 135–156.

Angelelli, C. (2008). The role of the interpreter in the healthcare setting: A plea for a dialogue between research and practice. In Valero Garcés, C. & Martin A. (Eds.), *Building bridges: The controversial role of the community interpreter*, pp. 139–152. Amsterdam, the Netherlands: John Benjamins.

Angelelli, C. (2004). *Medical interpreting and cross-cultural communication*. Cambridge, England: Cambridge University Press.

Bancroft, M. (2013). http://www.volinterpreting.org

Battle, D. (Ed.) (2002). *Communication disorders in multicultural populations* (3rd ed). London, England: Butterworth.

Bolden, G. (2000). Toward understanding practices of medical interpreting: Interpreters' involvement in history taking. *Discourse Studies, 2*, 387–419.

Bontempo, K., & Napier, J. (2011). Evaluating emotional stability as a predictor of interpreter competence and aptitude for interpreting. *Interpreting, 13*(1), 85–105.

Bot, H. (2007). Gespreksvoering met behulp van een tolk. *De Psycholoog* 42: 362–367

Bot, H. (2005). Dialogue Interpreting as a specific case of reported speech. *Interpreting* 7(2), 237–261.

Bowe, H. & Martin, K. (2007). *Communication across cultures. Mutual understanding in a global world*. Melbourne, Australia: Cambridge University Press.

California Healthcare Interpreters Association (n.d.). *California standards for healthcare interpreters: Ethical principles, protocols, and guidance on roles and intervention*. Los Angeles, CA: California Healthcare Interpreters Association.

Cambridge, J. (1999). Information loss in bilingual medical interviews through untrained interpreters." *The Translator* 5 (2), 201–219.

Camplin-Welch, V. (2007). Cross-Cultural Resource for Health Practitioners working with Culturally And Linguistically Diverse (CALD) Clients. Auckland, New Zealand: Waitemata District Health Board and Refugees As Survivors New Zealand Trust.

Candlin, C. & Gotti, M. (Eds). (2004a). *Intercultural aspects of specialized communication*. Bern, Switzerland: Peter Lang.

Candlin, C. & Gotti, M. (Eds). (2004b). *Intercultural discourse in domain-specific English*. Special issue of *Textus* 17/1, Genoa, Italy: Tilgher.

Candlin, C. & S. Candlin (2003). Health care communication: A problematic site for applied linguistics research. *Annual Review of Applied Linguistics* 23, 134–154.

Chabner, D.E. (2011). *The language of medicine. Ninth Edition*. Philadelphia, PA: Elsevier/Saunders.

Chen, A. (2003). *In the right words: Addressing language and culture in providing health care*, Asian and Pacific Islander American health forum, remarks at Grantmakers in Health Issue Dialogue. San Francisco, CA.

Chesher, T. (1997) Rhetoric and reality: Two decades of community interpreting and translating in Australia. In S.E.Carr, R. Roberts, A. Dufour and D. Steyn (Eds.). *The Critical Link: Interpreters in the community,* pp. 277–289. Amsterdam, the Netherlands & Philadelphia, PA: John Benjamins.

Clifford, A. (2005). Healthcare interpreting and informed consent: What is the interpreter's role in treatment decision-making. TTR: Traduction, terminologie, redaction, 18, 2, 225–247.

Coney, S. (1988). *The unfortunate experiment. The full story behind the inquiry into cervical cancer treatment*. Auckland, New Zealand: Penguin Books.

Crezee, I. (2003). Health interpreting: The cultural divide. In L. Brunette, G. Bastin, G., I. Hemlin & H. Clarke (Eds.), *The Critical Link 3. Interpreters in the community*, pp. 249–259. Amsterdam, the Netherlands & Philadelphia, PA: John Benjamins.

Crezee, I. (2009a). The development of the interpreting profession. In D. Clark and C. McGrath (Eds.), *Interpreting in New Zealand: The pathway forward* (pp. 75–80). Wellington: Crown.

Crezee, I. (2009b). Interpreting and the New Zealand healthcare system. In D. Clark and C. McGrath (Eds.), *Interpreting in New Zealand: The pathway forward* (pp. 102–107). Wellington: Crown.

Crezee, I. and Grant, L. (2013). Missing the plot? Idiomatic language in interpreter education. *International Journal of Interpreter Education, 5*(1), 17–34.

Crezee, I. and Sachtleben, A. (2012) Teaching health interpreting in multilingual and muliticultural classrooms: Towards developing special pedagogies. Paper delivered at the AUSIT Jubilation Conference, Sydney, Australia: 1–3 December 2012.

Crezee, I., Julich, S. & Hayward, M. (2013). Issues for interpreters and professionals working in refugee settings. *Journal of Applied Linguistics and Professional Practice, 8*(3), 254–273.

Department of Health (2007). *Departmental Report 2007*. London, England: Department of Health.

Dijk, T. van. (1977). *Text and context. Explorations in the semantics and pragmatics of discourse*. London, England: Longman. doi:10.1111/j.1398–9995.2009.02244.x.

Dysart-Gale, D. (2007). Clinicians and medical interpreters: Negotiating culturally appropriate care for patients with limited English ability. *Family & Community Health, 30*(3), 237–246.

Faden, R. & Beauchamp, T. (1986). *A history and theory of informed consent*. New York, NY: Oxford University Press.

Ferner, S., & Liu, H. (2009). Comprehensive strategy towards delivering better communications and better health care to non-English speaking New Zealanders? *Journal of the New Zealand Medical Association, 122*(1304).

Fischbach, H. (Ed.) (1998). *Translation and medicine*. American Translators Association Scholarly Monograph Series. Volume X 1998. Philadelphia, PA: John Benjamins.

Flores G. (2006). Language barriers to health care in the United States. *New England Journal of Medicine, 355*(3):229–31.

Flores G. (2005). The impact of medical interpreter services on the quality of health care: a systematic review. *Medical Care Research and Review, 62*(3):255–99.

Flores, G., Barton Laws, M. & Mayo, S., (2003). Errors in medical interpretation and their potential clinical consequences in paediatric encounters. *Pediatrics*, 111 (1), 6–14.

Gentile, A., Ozolins, U. & Vasilakakos, M. (1996). *Liaison interpreting: A handbook*. Melbourne, Australia: Melbourne University Press.

Gile, D. (1995). *Basic concepts and models for interpreter and translator training*. Amsterdam, the Netherlands & Philadelphia, PA: John Benjamins.

Gill, P, Shankar, A, Quirke, T. & Fremantle, N. (2009).Access to interpreting services in England: secondary analysis of national data. *BMC Public Health, 9*(1), 12. doi:10.1186/1471-2458-9-12

Ginori L. & E. Scimone, (1995), *Introduction to interpreting*, Sydney, Australia: Lantern Press.

Gonzalez Davies, M. (2004). *Multiple voices in the translation classroom: Activities, tasks and projects*. Amsterdam, the Netherlands & Philadelphia, PA: John Benjamins.

Gonzalez Davies, M. (1998). Student assessment by medical specialists. In H. Fischbach (Ed.). *Translation and medicine*. American Translators' Association Scholarly Monograph Series. Volum X 1998, pp. 93–102. Amsterdam, the Netherlands & Philadelphia, MA: John Benjamins.

Gray, B. Hilders, J. & Stubbe, M. (2012). How to use interpreters in general practice: the development of a New Zealand toolkit. *Journal of Primary Health Care, 4*(1):52–61.

Grice, P. (1975). Logic and conversation. In P. Cole & J. Morgan (eds.), *Syntax and Semantics, 3: Speech Acts*, pp. 41–58. New York, NY: Academic Press.

Hale, S. (2012). Are we there yet? Taking stock of where we are up to and where we are heading. Jill Blewett Memorial Lecture delivered at the AUSIT Jubilation Conference, Sydney, Australia: 1–2 December 2012.

Hale, S. (2008) Controversies over the role of the court interpreter. In C. Valero-Garcés & A. Martin (Eds.). *Crossing borders in community interpreting. Definitions and dilemmas*, pp. 99–122. Amsterdam, the Netherlands & Philadelphia, PA: John Benjamins.

Hale, S. (2007). *Community interpreting. research and practice in Applied Linguistics*. Basingstoke, England: Palgrave Macmillan.

Hale, S. (2005). The Interpreter's identity crisis, In J. House, J.R. Martín Ruano & N. Baumgarten (Eds.), *Translation and the construction of identity. IATIS Yearbook 2005*, pp. 14–29. Manchester/Northampton, MA: St Jerome.

Hale, S. (2004). *The Discourse of court interpreting: Discourse practices of the law, the witness and the interpreter*. Amsterdam, the Netherlands & Philadelphia, PA: John Benjamins.

Hale, S. (1996). Pragmatic considerations in court interpreting. *The Australian Review of Applied Linguistics, 19* (1), 61–72.

Hammell, K.W. (2009). Self-care, productivity, and leisure, or dimensions of occupational experience? Rethinking occupational "categories". *Canadian Journal of Occupational Therapy, 76*(2), 107–114.

Health Media (1988). *Counselling with interpreters sexual Assault interviews*. Sydney, Australia: Department of Health NSW. (Video resource).

Helman, C. (1990). *Culture, health and illness 2*. Oxford, England: Butterworth-Heinemann.

Hermann, A. (2002). Interpreting in antiquity. (Translated by Ruth Morris). In F. Pöchhacker & M. Shlesinger, M. (Eds.) (2002). *The interpreting studies reader*, pp. 15–22. London, England: Routledge.

Hofstede, G. (1980). *Culture's consequences: International differences in work-related values (cross cultural research and methodology)*. London, England: Sage Publications.

Hofstede, G. (2003). *Culture's consequences, comparing values, behaviors, institutions, and organizations across nations*. London, England: Sage Publications.

Holt, R., Crezee, I. & Rasalingam, N. (2003). *The communication gap: Immigrant healthcare in Aotearoa New Zealand*. Auckland, New Zealand: Auckland University of Technology School of Languages and the New Zealand Federation of Ethnic Councils.

Hunt, L.M. & Voogd, K.B. (2007). Are good intentions good enough? Informed consent without trained interpreters. Journal of General Internal Medicine, 22 (5), 598–605.

Jackson, K. (2006). *Fate, spirits and curses: Mental health and traditional beliefs in some refugee communities*. Auckland, New Zealand: Rampart.

Johnston, T. & Napier, J. (2010). Medical Signbank—bringing deaf people and linguists together in the process of language development. *Sign Language Studies, 10*(2), 258–275.

Kaufert, J. & Putsch, R. (1997). Communication through interpreters in healthcare: ethical dilemmas arising from differences in class, culture, language, and power. *Journal of Clinical Ethics, 8*(1):71–87.

Keesing, R. (1981). *Cultural Anthropology: A contemporary perspective*. New York, NY: Holt, Rinehart and Winston.

Kübler-Ross, E. & Kessler, D. (2008). *On grief and grieving: Finding the meaning of grief through the five stages of loss*. New York, NY: Simon and Schuster.

Kübler-Ross, E. (1969). *On death and dying.* NewYork, NY: Macmillan.

Labov, W. & Fanshell, D. (1977). *Therapeutic discourse.* New York, NY: Academic Press.

Langdon, H. (2002). *Interpreters and translators in communication disorders; A practitioner's handbook.* Eau Clair, WI: Thinking Publications.

Langdon H. & Li-Rong L. (2002). *Collaborating with interpreters and translators.* Eau Clair, WI; Thinking Publications

Lave, J. (1996). Teaching, as learning, in practice. *Mind, culture, and activity, 3*(3), 149–164.

Lave, J. (1991). Situated Learning in Communities of Practice. In L. B. Resnick, J.M. Levine & S. D. Teasley (Eds.), *Perspectives on Socially Shared Cognition,* pp. 64 -82. Pittsburgh, PA: Learning Research and Development Center, University of Pitts-burgh/American Psychological Association.

Lave, J. (1990). Views of the classroom: Implications for math and science learning research. In J. W. Stigler,R. A. Schweder & G. Herdt (Eds), *CulturalPsychology: Essays on Comparative Human Development,* pp. 309–27. Cambridge, England: Cambridge UniversityPress.

Lave, J. & Wenger, E. (1991). *Situated learning: Legitimate peripheral participation.* Cambridge, England: Cambridge University Press.

Lee, T., Lansbury, G. & Sullivan, G. (2005). Health care interpreters: A physiotherapy perspective. *Australian Journal of Physiotherap 51,* 161–165.

Lim, S., Mortensen, A., Feng, K., Ryu, G. & Cui, C. (2012). Waitemata DHB cultural responsiveness to its Asian, migrant and refugee populations – cultural competence concepts and initiatives. Paper presented to the Growing Pacific Solutions Conference, Auckland, New Zealand, April 2012.

Mairs, R. (2011). Translator traditor:the interpreter as traitor in classical tradition. *Greece & Rome, 58,* 1. doi:10.1017/S0017383510000537.

Major, G., Napier, J., Ferrara, L., & Johnston, T. (2012). Exploring lexical gaps in Australian Sign Language for the purposes of health communication. *Communication & Medicine, 9*(1), 7–47.

Mason, I. (2004). Conduits, mediators, spokespersons: Investigating translator/interpreter. In Schäffner, C. (Ed.), *Translation research and interpreting research. Traditions, gaps and synergies,* pp. 88–87. Clevedon, Oh.: Multilingual Matters:

Mason, I. (1999). Dialogue interpreting: A selective bibliography of research. The Translator, Special issue. Dialogue interpreting, *5*(2) 381–385.

Meador, H.E., & Zazove, P. (2005). Health care interactions with deaf culture. *The Journal of the American Board of Family Practice, 18*(3), 218–222.

McMorrow, L. (1998). Breaking the Greco-Roman mold in medical writing: the many languages of 20th century medicine. In H. Fischbach (Ed.). *American Translators Association Series: Transla-tion and medicine,* pp. 13–18. Amsterdam, the Netherlands and Philadelphia, PA: John Benjamins.

Merlini, R. & Favaron, R. (2005). Examining the "voice of interpreting" in speech pathology. *Interpreting 7*(2), 263–302.

Meyer, B. (2000). Medizinische Aufklärungsgespräche: Struktur und Zwecksetzung aus dis-kursanalytischer Sicht. University of Hamburg, Germany: Sonderforschungsbereich 538 (Mehrsprachigkeit – Working Papers on Multilingualism).

Meyer, B. (2001). How untrained interpreters handle medical terms. In I. Mason (Ed.), *Triadic exchanges: Studies in dialogue interpreting,* pp. 87–106. Manchester/Northampton, MA: st. Jerome.

Meyer, B., Apfelbaum, B, Pöchhacker, F. & Bischoff, A. (2003). Analysing interpreted doctor-patient communication from the perspectives of linguistics, interpreting studies and health sciences. In L. Brunette, G. Bastin, G., I. Hemlin & H. Clarke (Eds.), *The Critical Link 3. Interpreters in the community,*pp. 67–80. Amsterdam, the Netherlands & Philadelphia, PA: John Benjamins.

Morris, R. (1999). The gum syndrome: Predicaments in court interpreting. *Forensic Linguistics* 6(1), 6–29.

Muller, F. & Thiel, J.H. (1969). *Beknopt Grieks-Nederlands woordenbroek*, (11th ed., edited by W. den Boer). Groningen, the Netherlands: Wolters-Noordhoff.

Muller, F. & Renkema, E.H. (1970). *Beknopt Latijns-Nederlands woordenboek*, (12th ed. edited by A. D. Leeman). Groningen, the Netherlands: Wolters-Noordhoff.

Napier, J. (2010). An historical overview of signed language interpreting research: Featuring high-lights of personal research, *Cadernos de Tradução, 2*(26), 63–97. doi: 10.5007/2175–7968.2010 v2n26p63.

Napier, J. (2011). If a tree falls in a forest and no one is there to hear it, does it make a noise? *Advances in Interpreting Research: Inquiry in Action*, *99*, 121.

Napier, J., Major, G., & Ferrara, L. (2011). Medical Signbank: A cure-all for the aches and pains of medical sign language interpreting? In L. Leeson, S. Wurm & M. Vermeerbergen (Eds.), *Signed Language Interpreting: Preparation, practice and performance* (pp. 110–137). Manchester, England: St Jerome.

National Center for State Courts (NCSC). (2011). *Guide to translation of legal materials.* Retrieved from http://www.ncsc.org/Topics/Access-and-Fairness/Language-Access/Resource-Guide.aspx

National Council on Interpreting in Health Care. (2005). *National standards of practice for interpreters in health care.* San Francisco, Ca: NCICH.

O'Neill, M. (1998). Who makes a better medical translator: The medically knowledgeable linguist or the linguistically knowledgeable medical professional? A physician's perspective. In H. Fischbach (Ed.). *American Translators Association Series: Translation and medicine*, pp. 69–80. Amsterdam, the Netherlands and Philadelphia, PA: John Benjamins.

Ozolins, U. (2010). Factors that determine the provision of Public Service Interpreting: Comparative perspectives on government motivation and language service implementation. *The Journal of Specialised Translation*, *14*, 194–215.

Ozolins, U. & Hale, S. (2009). Introduction: Quality in Interpreting – A shared responsibility. In S. Hale, U. Ozolins & L. Stern (Eds). *The Critical Link 5: Quality in Interpreting – a shared responsibility*, pp. 1–10. Amsterdam, the Netherlands & Philadephia, PA: John Benjamins.

Pan American Health Organization (September 2005): Regional Declaration on the New Orienta-tions of Primary Health Care. Retrieved from http://new.paho.org

Phelan, M. (2001). *The interpreter's resource.* Clevedon, Oh.: Multilingual Matters.

Pöchhacker, F. (2004). *Introducing interpreting studies.* London, England: Routledge.

Pöchhacker, F. & Shlesinger, M. (2007). *Healthcare interpreting: Discourse and interaction.* Amsterdam, the Netherlands & Philadelphia, PA: John Benjamins.

Pöchhacker, F. & Shlesinger, M. (Eds.) (2002). *The interpreting studies reader.* London, England: Routledge.

Pourahmad, J. (2010). History of medical sciences in Iran. *Iranian Journal of Pharmaceutical Research*, *7*(2), 93–99.

Prendergast, A.V. (1991). *Medical terminology: A text/workbook*, (3rd ed.). Redwood City, Ca: Addison-Wesley Nursing.

Pym, A., Shlesinger, M., & Jettmarová, Z. (2006). *Sociocultural aspects of translating and interpreting.* Amsterdam, the Netherlands & Philadelphia, PA: John Benjamins.

Risse, G.B. (1999). *Mending bodies, saving souls: a history of hospitals.* Oxford, England and New York, NY: Oxford University Press.

Roat C. (2000). Healthcare interpreting: An emerging discipline. *ATA Chronicle, 29*(3), 18–21.

Roat C. (1999a). Certifying medical interpreters: Some lessons from Washington State. *ATA Chronicle, 28*(5), 23–26.

Roat, C. (1999b). *Bridging the gap: A basic training for medical interpreters. Seattle, WA:* The Cross Cultural Health Care Program, 1995, 1999.

Roberts-Smith, L., Frey, R. & Bessell-Browne, S. (1990), *Working with interpreters in law, health & social work.* Sydney, Australia: National Accreditation Authority for Translators and Interpreters.

Roy, C. (2002). The problem with definitions, descriptions and the role metaphors of interpreters. In F. Pöchhacker & M. Shlesinger, M. (Eds.), *The interpreting studies reader,* pp. 344–353. London, England: Routledge.

Roy, C. (2000). *Interpreting as a discourse process.* New York, NY: Oxford University Press.

Rudvin, M. (2007). Professionalism and ethics in community interpreting: The impact of individualist versus collective group identity. *Interpreting, 9*(1), 47–69.

Rudvin, M. (2004). Professionalism and contradictions in the interpreter's role. Paper delivered at the Critical Link 4 Conference in Stockholm, 20–23 May 2004.

Sarangi, S. (2004). Towards a communicative mentality in medical and healthcare practice. *Communication & Medicine, 1* (1), 1–11.

Scollon, R. & Scollon, S. (2001). *Intercultural communication: A discourse approach.* Malden, MA: Blackwell Publishing.

Searle, J. (1969). *Speech Acts.* Cambridge, England: Cambridge University Press.

Searle, J. (1975). Indirect speech acts. In P. Cole & J. Morgan (eds.), *Syntax and Semantics, 3: Speech Acts,* pp. 59–82. New York, NY: Academic Press.

Segura, J. (1998). Some thoughts on the Spanish language in medicine. In H. Fischbach (Ed.). *American Translators Association Series: Translation and medicine,* pp. 37–48. Amsterdam, the Netherlands and Philadelphia, PA: John Benjamins.

Simon, C.M., Zyzanski, S.J., & Durand, E. (2006). Interpreter accuracy and informed consent among Spanish-speaking families with cancer. *Journal of Health Communication, 11*(5), 509–522.

Stewart, M.A. (1995). Effective physician-patient communication and health outcomes: A review. *CMAJ: Canadian Medical Association Journal, 152*(9), 1423.

Strengthening Access to Primary Healthcare (SAPHC). (2006). Literature Review: Examining Spanish-speaking patients' satisfaction with interpersonal aspects of care. *Medical Care Research and Review, 62* (3), 255–299.

Sultz, H.A. & Young, K.M. (2006). *Health care USA: Understanding its organization and delivery.* Sudbury, MA: Jones and Bartlett.

Swabey, L., & Nicodemus, B. (2011). Bimodal bilingual interpreting in the US healthcare system. *Advances in Interpreting Research: Inquiry in Action, 99,* 241.

Tate, G. & Turner, G.H. (2002). The code and the culture. Sign language interpreting – in search of the new breed's ethics. In F. Pöchhacker & M. Shlesinger, M. (Eds.) (2002). *The interpreting studies reader,* pp. 372–383. London, England: Routledge.

Tebble, H. (2004). Discourse analysis and its relevance to ethical performance in medical interpreting. In C. Wadensjö, B. Dimitrova & A.L. Nilsson, (Eds.), *Critical Link 4: Professionalisation of interpreting in the community:* 4th *International Conference on Interpreting in Legal, Health and Social Service Settings,* p. 57. Amsterdam, the Netherlands & Philadelphia, PA: John Benjamins.

Tebble. H. (2003). Training doctors to work effectively with interpreters. In L. Brunette, G. Bastin, I. Hemlin & H. Clarke (Eds.), *The Critical Link 3. Interpreters in the community. Selected papers in legal, health and social service settings,* pp. 81–98. Amsterdam, the Netherlands & Philadelphia, PA: John Benjamins.

Tebble, H. (1998). *Medical interpreting: improving communication with your patients.* Canberra and Geelong, Australia: Deakin University.

Tellechea Sánchez, M.T. (2005). El intérprete como obstáculo: Fortalecimiento y emancipación del usuario y para superarlo. C. Valero Garcés (ed.). *Traducción como mediación entre lenguas culturas,* pp. 114–122. Alcalá de Henares, Spain: Universidad de Alcalá de Henares.

Thierer, N. & Breitbard, L. (2006). *Medical terminology: Language for health care* (2nd ed.). New York, NY: McGraw-Hill.

Tylor, E.G., (1871). *Primitive culture.* New York, NY: J.P. Putnam's Sons.

U.S. Census Bureau http://www.census.gov). Accessed 9 August 2012.

US Census Bureau. (2011). State and County Quick Facts. Retrieved from: http://quickfacts.census.gov/qfd/states/00000.html

Valero-Garcés, C. & Martin, A. (Eds.) (2008). *Crossing borders in community interpreting: Definitions and dilemmas.* Amsterdam, the Netherlands & Philadelphia, PA: John Benjamins.

van Dijk, T. (1977). Discourse as social interaction. Discourse studies: A multidisciplinary introduction, Vol. 2. London, England: Sage.

Van Hoof, H. (1998a). A contribution to the history of medical translation in Japan. In H. Fischbach (Ed.). American Translators Association Series: Translation and medicine, pp. 29–36. Amsterdam, the Netherlands and Philadelphia, PA: John Benjamins.

Van Hoof, H. (1998b). The language of medicine. A comparative ministudy of English and French. In H. Fischbach (Ed.). *American Translators Association Series: Translation and medicine,* pp. 49–65. Amsterdam, the Netherlands and Philadelphia, PA: John Benjamins.

Vazquez, C. & Javier, R. (1991). The problem with interpreters: Communications with Spanish-speaking patients. *Hospital and Community Psychiatry, 42,* 163–165.

Venuti, L. (Ed.) (2000). *The translation studies reader.* London, England: Routledge.

Wadensjö, C. (2002). The double role of a dialogue interpreter. In F. Pöchhacker & M. Shlesinger, M. (Eds.), *The interpreting studies reader,* pp. 354–370. London, England: Routledge.

Wadensjö, C. (1998). *Interpreting as interaction.* London, England & New York, NY: Longman.

Waitemata District Health Board (WDHB), Asian Health Support Services (AHSS) (2012). *CALD 9: Working with Asian clients in mental health.* Auckland: Waitemata DHB. Retrieved from http://www.caldresources.org.nz/info/Home.php

Walker, S.M., Wood, M., & Nicol, J. (2013). *Mastering medical terminology: Australia and New Zealand.* Chatswood, Australia: Elsevier.

Wall, B.M. (n.d.) History of hospitals. Retrieved from http://www.nursing.upenn.edu/nhhc/Welcome%20Page%20Content/History%20of%20Hospitals.pdf

Suggested further readings for Parts II and III

Aberg, J.A., Kaplan, J.E., Libman, H., Emmanuel, P., Anderson, J.R., Stone, V.E., … & Gallant, J.E. (2009). Primary care guidelines for the management of persons infected with human immunodeficiency virus: 2009 update by the HIV medicine Association of the Infectious Diseases Society of America. *Clinical infectious diseases, 49*(5), 651–681.

Abraham, D, Cabral, N. & Tancredi, A. (eds.) (2004). *A handbook for trainers: language interpreting in the healthcare sector.* Toronto, Canada: Healthcare Interpretation Network.

Alberti, K.G.M.M., & Gries, F.A. (2009). Management of non-insulin-dependent diabetes mellitus in Europe: A concensus view. *Diabetic Medicine, 5*(3), 275–281.

Allman, K., & Wilson, I. (Eds.). (2011). *Oxford handbook of anaesthesia.* Oxford, England: Oxford University Press.

American Nurses Association. (2006). *Nursing facts: Today's Registered Nurse – Numbers and demographics*. Washington, D.C.: American Nurses Association.

American Psychiatric Association (2013). *Diagnostic and Statistical Manual of Mental Disorders* (Fifth ed.). Arlington, VA: American Psychiatric Publishing.

Anandan C., Nurmatov U., van Schayck O. & Sheikh A. (2010). Is the prevalence of asthma declining? Systematic review of epidemiological studies. *Allergy 65* (2), 152–67.

Anatomical Chart Company. *The world's best anatomical charts*. Third Edition. Philadelphia, PA: Lippincott Williams & Wilkins.

Apgar, V. (1953). A proposal for a new method of evaluation of the newborn infant. *Current Research in Anesthesia and Analgesia, 32* (4): 260–267.

Atkinson, F., Foster-Powell, K. & Brand-Miller, J. (2008). International tables of Glycemic Index and Glycemic Load values. *Diabetes Care, 31*, 12, 2281–2283. doi:10.2337/dc08-1239.

Bancroft, M. (2013). The voice of love. http://www.volinterpreting.org

Beers, M. & R. Berkow (Eds). (2000). *The Merck Manual of Geriatrics* (3rd ed). New York, NY: John Wiley & Sons.

Bhattacharya, V. (2011). *Postgraduate vascular surgery The candidate's guide to the FRCS*. Leiden, the Netherlands: Cambridge University Press.

Biggs W., Bieck A., Pugno P. & Crosley P. (2011). Results of the 2011 National Resident Matching Program: Family medicine. *Family Medicine 43*(9):619–24.

Bisno A. & Stevens D. (2009). *Streptococcus pyogenes*. In: G. Mandell, J. Bennett & R. Dolin (Eds.), *Principles and practice of infectious diseases* (7th ed). Philadelphia, PA: Elsevier Churchill Livingstone.

Braddom, R.L. (2010). *Physical medicine and rehabilitation (4th ed.)*. Edition. Philadelphia, PA: Elsevier/Saunders.

Burgers, J.S., Fervers, B., Haugh, M., Brouwers, M., Browman, G., Philip, T., & Cluzeau, F.A. (2004). International assessment of the quality of clinical practice guidelines in oncology using the Appraisal of Guidelines and Research and Evaluation Instrument. *Journal of Clinical Oncology, 22*(10), 2000–2007.

Camargo, C.A., Rachelefsky, G., & Schatz, M. (2009). Managing Asthma Exacerbations in the Emergency Department Summary of the National Asthma Education and Prevention Program Expert Panel Report 3 Guidelines for the Management of Asthma Exacerbations. *Proceedings of the American Thoracic Society, 6*(4), 357–366.

Camm, A.J., Kirchhof, P., Lip, G.Y., Schotten, U., Savelieva, I., Ernst, S., ... & Folliguet, T. (2010). Guidelines for the management of atrial fibrillation The Task Force for the Management of Atrial Fibrillation of the European Society of Cardiology (ESC). *Europace, 12*(10), 1360–1420.

Christian, S., Kraas, J., Conway, W. (2007). Musculoskeletal Infections. *Seminars in Roentgenology 42*, 92–101.

Chung, J.H., Phibbs, C.S., Boscardin, W.J., Kominski, G.F., Ortega, A.N., & Needleman, J. (2010). The effect of neonatal intensive care level and hospital volume on mortality of very low birth weight infants. *Medical care, 48*(7), 635–644.

Cieza, A., & Stucki, G. (2005). Understanding functioning, disability, and health in rheumatoid arthritis: the basis for rehabilitation care. *Current opinion in rheumatology, 17*(2), 183–189.

Cloherty, J.P., Eichenwald, E.C., Hansen, A.R. & Stark, A.R. (2012). *Manual of neonatal care*. Philadelphia, PA: Lippincott Williams & Wilkins.

Colledge, N., Walker, B. & Ralston, S. (Eds.). (2010). *Davidson's principles and practice of medicine*, (21st ed.). Edinburg, Scotland: Churchill Livingstone.

Craig, D.I. (2008). Medial tibial stress syndrome: Evidence-based prevention. *Journal of Athletic Training, 43*(3), 316–318.

Crezee J., Van Haaren P., Westendorp H., De Greef, M., Kok H., Wiersma J., Van Stam G., Sijbrands J., Zum Vörde Sive Vörding P., Van Dijk, J., Hulshof M. & Bel A. (2009). Improving locoregional hyperthermia delivery using the 3-D controlled AMC-8 phased array hyperthermia system: a preclinical study. *International Journal of Hyperthermia, 25*(7), 581–92.

Davidson, J.E., Powers, K., Hedayat, K.M., Tieszen, M., Kon, A.A., Shepard, E., … & Armstrong, D. (2007). Clinical practice guidelines for support of the family in the patient-centered intensive care unit: American College of Critical Care Medicine Task Force 2004–2005. *Critical Care Medicine, 35*(2), 605–622.

Dolk, H., Loane, M., & Garne, E. (2011). Congenital heart defects in Europe: Prevalence and perinatal mortality, 2000 to 2005. *Circulation, 123*(8), 841–849.

Drake, R.L., Vogl, A.W., & Mitchell, A.W.M. (2010). *Gray's Anatomy for students.* Philadelphia, PA: Churchill Livingstone.

Eddleston, M., & Pierini, S. (2000). *Oxford handbook of tropical medicine* (Vol. 158). NewYork, NY: Oxford University Press.

Eng D. (2006). Management guidelines for motor neurone disease patients on non-invasive ventilation at home. *Palliative Medicine, 20,* 69–79.

Engstrom, P.F., Benson 3rd, A. B., Chen, Y.J., Choti, M.A., Dilawari, R.A., Enke, C.A., … & Yeatman, T.J. (2005). Colon cancer clinical practice guidelines in oncology. *Journal of the National Comprehensive Cancer Network: JNCCN, 3*(4), 468.

Faucy, A. (2006). *Harrison's rheumatology.* New York, NY: McGraw-Hill.

Finster M; Wood M. (April 2005). The Apgar score has survived the test of time. *Anesthesiology* 102 (4): 855–857. doi:10.1097/00000542-200504000-00022.

Fleisher, G.R., & Ludwig, S. (Eds.). (2010). *Textbook of pediatric emergency medicine.* Philadelphia, PA: Lippincott Williams & Wilkins.

Fleming, S.M., O'Gorman, T., Finn, J., Grimes, H., Daly, K., & Morrison, J.J. (2005). Cardiac troponin I in pre-eclampsia and gestational hypertension. *BJOG: An International Journal of Obstetrics & Gynaecology, 107*(11), 1417–1420.

Fox, G.F., Hoque, N., & Watts, T. (2010). *Oxford handbook of neonatology.* Oxford, England: Oxford University Press.

Friedman-Rhodes, E. & Hale, S. (2010). Teaching medical students to work with interpreters. *JoTrans, 14.*

Gallagher, P.F., Barry, P.J., Ryan, C., Hartigan, I., & O'Mahony, D. (2008). Inappropriate prescribing in an acutely ill population of elderly patients as determined by Beers' Criteria. *Age and Ageing, 37*(1), 96–101.

Gérvas, J., Starfield, B., & Heath, I. (2008). Is clinical prevention better than cure? *Lancet, 372,* 1997–99.

Gore, R.M., Levine, M.S., & Laufer, I. (2008). *Textbook of gastrointestinal radiology* (Vol. 1). Philadelphia, PA: Saunders/Elsevier.

Gregory, K.D., Niebyl, J.R., & Johnson, T.R. (2012). Preconception and prenatal care: Part of the continuum. *Obstetrics: Normal and Problem Pregnancies,* 101.

Griffiths, J., Austin, L., & Luker, K. (2004). Interdisciplinary teamwork in the community rehabilitation of older adults: an example of flexible working in primary care. *Primary Health Care Research and Development (5),* 228–239.

Hall, B. & Chantigian, R. (2003). *Anesthesia. A comprehensive review.* Philadelphia, PA: Mosby.

Hammer, C., Detwiler, J.S., Detwiler, J. Blood, G; Dean Qualls, C. (2004) Speech-Language Pathologists' training and confidence in serving Spanish-English Bilingual children. *Journal of Communication Disorders* 37, 2, 91–108.

Hampton, J.R., Harrison, M.J., Mitchell, J.R., Prichard, J.S., & Seymour, C. (1975). Relative contributions of history-taking, physical examination, and laboratory investigation to diagnosis and management of medical outpatients. *British Medical Journal,* 2(5969), 486.

Harris, B., Lovett, L., Newcombe, R., Read, G., Walker, R. & Riad-Fahmy, D. (1994). Maternity blues and major endocrine changes: Cardiff puerperal mood and hormone study II. *British Medical Journal,* 308:949–953.

Hart I., Sathasivam S. & Sharshar T. (2007). Immunosuppressive agents for myasthenia gravis. *Cochrane Database of Systematic Reviews,* 4. doi: 10.1002/14651858.CD005224.pub2.

Heaney R. & Rafferty K. (2001). Carbonated beverages and urinary calcium excretion. *American Journal of Clinical Nutrition,*74 (3):343–347.

Hedrick, J. (2003). Acute bacterial skin infections in pediatric medicine: current issues in presentation and treatment. *Pediatric Drugs,* 5(Supplement 1), 35–46.

Hwa-Froelich, D. & Westby, C. (2003). Considerations when working with interpreters. *Communication Disorders Quarterly* 24, 2, 78–85.

Isaac, K. (2002). *Speech pathology in cultural and linguistic diversity.* London, England: Whurr.

International Classification of Primary Care (ICPC). Retrieved from http://www.globalfamilydoctor. com/wicc/icpcstory.html

Jang, I., Gold, H., Ziskind, A., Fallon, J., Holt, R., Leinbach, R., May, J. & Collen, D. (1989). Differential sensitivity of erythrocyte-rich and platelet-rich arterial thrombitolysis with recombinant tissue-type plasminogen activator. A possible explanation for resistance to coronary thrombolysis. *Circulation,* 79(4):920–8.

Jenkins, D., Kendall, C., McKeown-Eyssen, G., Josse, R., Silverberg, J. & Booth,G. (2008). Effect of a low–glycemic index or a high–cereal fiber diet on Type 2 Diabetes. *Journal of the American Medical Association,* 300(23):2742–2753.

Jenkins, D., Wolever, T., Taylor, R., Barker, H., Fielden, H. Baldwin, J., Bowling, A, Newman, H., Jenkins, A. & Goff, D. (1981). Glycemic index of foods: a physiological basis for carbohydrate exchange. *American Journal of Clinical Nutrition 34,* 362–366.

Johnston M. (2011) Encephalopathies. In R. Kliegman, R. Behrman, H. Jenson & B. Stanton (Eds.), *Nelson Textbook of Pediatrics.* (19th ed). Philadelphia, Pa: Saunders Elsevier.

Jones, R., Hunt, C., Stevens, R., Dalrymple, J., Driscoll, R., Sleet, S., & Smith, J.B. (2009). Management of common gastrointestinal disorders: quality criteria based on patients' views and practice guidelines. *The British Journal of General Practice,* 59(563), e199.

Kaemmerer H., Meisner H., Hess J. & Perloff J. (2004). Surgical treatment of patent ductus arteriosus: a new historical perspective. *American Journal Of Cardiology,* 94(9), 1153–4.

Kambanaros, M., van Steenbrugge, W. (2004). Interpreters and language assessment: Confrontation naming and interpreting. *Advances in Speech-Language Pathology* 6, 4, 247–252.

Kauffman, T, J. Barr, M. Moran (Eds.) (2007). *Geriatric rehabilitation manual. Second edition.* Edinburgh, Scotland & New York, NJ: Churchill Livingstone Elsevier.

Kemp, C. & Rasbridge, L. (2004). *Refugee and immigrant health: A handbook for health professionals.* Cambridge, England: Cambridge University Press.

Kingsnorth, A.(2011). *Fundamentals of surgical practice: A preparation guide for the Intercollegiate MRCS Examination.* Leiden, the Netherlands: Cambridge University Press.

Kitzmiller, J.L., Wallerstein, R., Correa, A., & Kwan, S. (2010). Preconception care for women with diabetes and prevention of major congenital malformations. *Birth Defects Research Part A: Clinical and Molecular Teratology,* 88(10), 791–803.

Kussmaul, W.G. (2012). Guidelines on diagnosis and treatment of stable Ischemic Heart Disease: Keeping up with a constantly evolving evidence base. *Annals of internal medicine,* 157(10), 749–751.

Langdon, H., Quintanar-Sarellana, R. (2003). Roles and responsibilities of the interpreter in interactions with Speech-Language Pathologists, parents, and students. *Seminars in Speech and Language* 24, 3, 235–244.

Leeseberg Stamler, L. & Yiu, L. (2005). *Community health nursing: A Canadian perspective.* Upper Saddle River, NJ: Prentice Hall.

Longmore, M., Wilkinson, I., Davidson, E., Foulkes, A., & Mafi, A. (2010). *Oxford handbook of clinical medicine.* Oxford, England: Oxford University Press.

Longo, D. (2012). *Harrisons Online: Principles of internal medicine.* New York, NY: McGraw-Hill.

Mancia, G., Laurent, S., Agabiti-Rosei, E., Ambrosioni, E., Burnier, M., Caulfield, M.J., ... & Zanchetti, A. (2009). Reappraisal of European guidelines on hypertension management: a European Society of Hypertension Task Force document. *Journal of Hypertension, 27*(11), 2121–2158.

Martinez, G. (2008). Language-in-healthcare policy, interaction patterns, and unequal care on the U.S.-Mexico border. *Language Policy* 7,345–363. doi 10.1007/s10993-008-9110-y

Marx, J., Hockberger, R., & Walls, R. (2009). *Rosen's emergency medicine-concepts and clinical practice,* (7th ed.). Maryland Heights, MI: Mosby/Elsevier.

Mayo Clinic. (2012). Cholesterol levels. Retrieved 28 June 2012 from http://www.mayoclinic.com/health/cholesterol-levels/CL00001 retrieved 28 June 2012

McLatchie, G., Borley, N., & Chikwe, J. (2007). *Oxford handbook of clinical surgery.* Oxford, England: Oxford University Press.

McVary K., Roehrborn C., Avins AL, et al. (2011). Update on AUA guideline on the management of benign prostatic hyperplasia. Journal of Urology, 185(5):1793–803. Epub 2011 Mar 21.

Melman, A. & Newnham, R. (2011). A what-comes-next guide to a safe and informed recovery. New York, NY: Oxford University Press.

Miller D. & Leary S. (2007). Primary-progressive multiple sclerosis. *Lancet Neurology,* (6), 903–912.

Miller, B. (2010). *General surgical lists and reminders.* Brisbane, Australia: University of Queensland Press.

Nicodemus, B. (2009). *Prosodic markers and utterance boundaries in American Sign Language interpretation.* Washington, DC: Gallaudet University Press.

Nicolaides, K.H., Syngelaki, A., Ashoor, G., Birdir, C., & Touzet, G. (2012). Noninvasive prenatal testing for fetal trisomies in a routinely screened first-trimester population. *American Journal of Obstetrics and Gynecology,206* (2012), 322.e1–322.e15.

Nursing and Midwifery Council. (2010). *Changes to pre-registration nursing programmes: FAQs.* Nursing and Midwifery Council. Retrieved from http://nmc-uk.org

Qaseem, A., Fihn, S.D., Williams, S., Dallas, P., Owens, D.K., & Shekelle, P. (2012). Diagnosis of Stable Ischemic Heart Disease: Summary of a Clinical Practice Guideline From the American College of Physicians/American College of Cardiology Foundation/American Heart Association/American Association for Thoracic Surgery/Preventive Cardiovascular Nurses Association/Society of Thoracic Surgeons. *Annals of internal medicine, 157*(10), 729–734.

Qureshi, A. (2011). *Textbook of interventional neurology.* Leiden, the Netherlands: Cambridge University Press.

Ramos, G.A., Chopra, I.J., & Bales, S.R. (2012). Endocrine disorders in pregnancy. *Women's health review: A clinical update in Obstetrics-Gynecology (Expert Consult-Online),* 226.

Reiss, U., Zucker, M. & Hanley, J. (2002). *Natural hormone balance for women.* New York, NY: Atria Books.

Robertson, A. (1998). *Preparing for birth: Background notes for pre-natal classes.* Third edition. Glebe, Australia: Ace Graphics.

Roehrborn, C. (2011). Male lower urinary tract symptoms (LUTS) and benign prostatic hyperplasia (BPH). Medical Clinics of North America, 95(1), 87–100.

Roseberry-McKibbin, C. (2002). *Multicultural students with special language needs* (2nd ed). Oceanside, CA: Academic Associates.

Schenker, Y, Wang, F, Selig, S.J., Ng, R. & Fernandez, A. (2007). The impact of language barriers on documentation of informed consent at a hospital with on-site interpreter services. *Journal of General Internal Medicine, 22* (Suppl 2), 294–299.

Sinclair, A., & Dickinson, E. (1998). *Effective Practice in Rehabilitation: The evidence of systematic reviews.* King's Fund.

Singh J., Christensen, R., Wells, G., Suarez-Almazor, M., Buchbinder, R., Lopez-Olivo, M., Tanjong Ghogomu, E. & Tugwell, P. (2012). Update of the 2008 ACR Recommendations for use of DMARDs and biologics in the treatment of Rheumatoid Arthritis. *Arthritis Care & Research,* 625–639.

Smyth R. & Openshaw P. (2006). Bronchiolitis. *Lancet* 368 (9532): 312–22. doi:10.1016/S0140-6736 (06)69077-6.

Sobin L., Gospodarowicz M., Wittekind C. (Eds.) (2009). *TNM Classification of Malignant Tumors,* (7th ed.). Oxford, England: Wiley-Blackwell.

Soper, N. & Kaufman, D. (2011). *Northwestern handbook of surgical procedures.* Evanston, Ill.: Northwestern University.

Sperry, L. (2006). Cognitive Behavior Therapy of DSM-IV-TR Personality Disorders 2. New York, NY: Routledge.

Tanner, J.M., Whitehouse, R.H., & Hughes, P.C.R. (1976). Relative importance of growth hormone and sex steroids for the growth at puberty of trunk length, limb length, and muscle width in growth hormone-deficient children. *The Journal of pediatrics, 89*(6), 1000–1008.

Tarrant, A., Ryan, M., Hamilton, P. & Bejaminov, O. (2008). A pictorial review of hypovolaemic shock in adults. *British Journal of Radiology, 81*, 252–257.

Tasker, R.C., McClure, R.J., & Acerini, C.L. (2013). *Oxford handbook of paediatrics.* Oxford, England: Oxford University Press.

Tesio, L.U.I. G. I. (2007). Functional assessment in rehabilitative medicine: Principles and methods. *Europa medicophysica, 43*(4), 515.

Turner, S., Paton, J., Higgins, B., & Douglas, G. (2011). British guidelines on the management of asthma: What's new for 2011? *Thorax, 66*(12), 1104–1105.

Van Tulder M, Malmivaara A. & Koes B (2007). Repetitive strain injury. *Lancet* 369 (9575): 1815–22. doi:10.1016/S0140-6736(07)60820-4

Varney, H., Kriebs, J.M., & Gegor, C.L. (2004). *Varney's Midwifery* (4th ed.). Burlington, MA: Jones & Bartlett Learning.

Wiesel, S.W., & Delahay, J.N. (Eds.). (2010). *Essentials of orthopedic surgery.* New York, NY: Springer.

Wyatt, J.P., Illingworth, R.N., Graham, C.A., & Hogg, K. (2012). *Oxford handbook of emergency medicine.* Oxford, England: Oxford University Press.

Xiong, Lian. (2009). Complete lung whiteout. *Nursing Critical Care,* July 1, 2009.

Useful websites

Websites which are managed by bona fide professional bodies are an extremely useful source of information, as information tends to be continually updated and reviewed by the relevant (medical) professionals. Some recommended websites are:

American Association for Thoracic Surgery (AATS): http://www.aats.org/
American College of Cardiology: http://www.cardiosource.org/acc
American College of Emergency Physicians: http://www.acep.org/
American College of Gastroenterology: http://gi.org/
American College of Radiology: http://www.acr.org/
American College of Rheumatology: http://www.rheumatology.org/
American College of Surgeons: http://www.facs.org/
American Congress of Obstetricians and Gynecologists (ACOG): http://www.acog.org/
American Heart Association (AHA): http://www.heart.org/HEARTORG/
American Pregnancy Association: http://www.americanpregnancy.org/
American Society for Reproductive Medicine (ASRM): http://www.asrm.org/
American Translators Association (ATA): http://ata.net.org
Auslan Medical Signbank: http://www.auslan.org.au/medical/
Australian College of Midwives: New South Wales Branch: http://www.nswmidwives.com.au
Australian College of Nursing: http://www.nursing.edu.au/
Australian Government Department of Health and Ageing: http://www.health.gov.au/internet/
     main/publishing.nsf/content/health-ahca-sooph05-outs_outpatient.htm
Australian Society of Interpreters and Translators. http://www.ausit.org
Australian Nursing and Midwifery Council. http://www.anmc.org.au/
British Cardiovascular Society: http://www.bcs.com/pages/default.asp
Canadian Medical Association: http://www.cma.ca
Cancer Topics. National Cancer Institute: http://www.cancer.gov/cancertopics/
Chartered Institute of linguists (IoL): http://www.iol.org.uk
Clinical Nutrition Certification Board: http://www.cncb.org/
Graduate Medical School Admissions Test: http://www.gamsatuk.org/
Harrison's Online on Access Medicine: http://www.accessmedicine.com/public/learnmore_hol.aspx
Health Care Interpreter Network. http://www.hcin.org/
Health Resources and Services Administration. Maternal and Child health: http://mchb.hrsa.gov/
International Council of Nurses (ICN). http:// www.icn.ch/
Interpreting in health care settings: http://healthcareinterpreting.org/new/
Medical Council of New Zealand: http://www.mcnz.org.nz/
Medical Interpreting: www.medicalinterpreting.org
National Cancer Institute at the National Institutes of Health.
National Council on Interpreting in Health Care. http://www.ncihc.org/
National Digestive Diseases Information Clearinghouse (NDDIC): http://digestive.niddk.nih.gov/
National Eye Institute: http://www.nei.nih.gov/
National Kidney Disease Education Program (NKEDEP): http://www.nkdep.nih.gov
New Zealand College of Midwives: http://www.midwife.org.nz

New Zealand Society of Translators and Interpreters: http://www.nzsti.org
North American Registry of Midwives: http://www.narm.org
Nursing and Midwifery Council: http://www.nmc-uk.org
Nursing Council of New Zealand: http://www.nursingcouncil.org.nz/
PubMed MEDLINE Plus: http://www.nlm.nih.gov/medlineplus/
PubMed MEDLINEV: http://www.ncbi.nlm.nih.gov/pubmed/
Royal College of General PractitionersV http://www.rcgp.org.uk/
Royal College of PhysiciansV http://www.rcplondon.ac.uk/
Royal College of Physicians: Cardiology http://www.rcplondon.ac.uk/specialty/cardiology
Royal College of physicians and Surgeons of CanadaV http://www.royalcollege.ca/
Royal College of Midwives: http://www.rcm.org.uk/
Royal College of Nursing Australia (RCNA). http://www.rcna.org.au/
Society for Cardiovascular Angiography and Interventions (SCAI)V http://www.scai.org/Default.aspx
The American Board of Family Medicine: https://www.theabfm.org/
The Mayo Clinic: http://www.mayoclinic.com/
The Merck Manual Illustrated:. http://www.merckmanuals.com
The Royal College of Surgeons of England: http://www.rcseng.ac.uk/
U.S. Department of Health and Human Services, Centers for Medicare & Medicaid Services:
U.S. National Library of Medicine. National Institutes of Health. http://www.nlm.nih.gov/
US Centers for Disease Control and Prevention: http://www.cdc.gov/
US National Library of Medicine http://www.nlm.nih.gov.
World Health Organization (WHO): http://www.who.int
www.scottishrefugeecouncil.org.uk. Briefing: Refugees and asylum seekers – the facts. Scottish Refugee Council.

Index

endometriosis 285
endometrium 285, 301
endoscopic retrograde
cholangiopancreatography
267, 271
endoscopies 157, 306
(see also endoscopy 157, 271)
endoscopy 157, 271
(see also endoscopies 157, 306)
endotracheal 103
endotracheal aspirate culture 126
endotracheal tube 103, 120
enlarged prostate 282
ENT (also: Ear Nose
and Throat) 239
(see also ORL 239)
enter 261
Entonox 112
enuresis 273
enzymes 305
epi- 167
epididymis 281
epidural 112, 167
epidural anesthesia 95, 96
epilepsy 132, 172
epinephrine
(also: adrenaline) 252
EpiPen® 248
episiotomy 113
ER 71
(see also Emergency Room 71)
ERCP 267, 271
(see also Endoscopic
Retrograde Cholangio-
Pancreatography. 267, 271)
erectile dysfunction 283
Erythrocyte Sedimentation Rate
(also: ESR) 136, 224
erythropoietin 276, 279
esophagitis 76
esophagoscopy 157
esophagus (also: gullet)
263, 264
ESR (also: Erythrocyte
Sedimentation Rate) 136, 224
ESWL (also: Extracorporeal
shockwave lithotripsy) 267
Eustachian tube 234, 238
ex 193
exacerbations 266, 270
excimer laser 234
Exercise ECG (also: stress test or
treadmill test) 191
Expected Date of Confinement
(also: EDC) 110

Expected Date of Delivery
(also: EDD) 108
expectorants 202
expiration 194, 195
exploratory surgery 86
Expression Room 67
external fixation 222
external genitals 284
extopic pregnancy 294
(see also extra-uterine
pregnancy 294)
extracorporeal shockwave
lithotripsy (also: ESWL) 267
extra-uterine 291
extra-uterine pregnancy
(also: extopic pregnancy) 294
extremities 293
extubated 103
extubation 124
eye clinic 55

F
Fallopian tubes 284
falls 84
family doctors (also: General
Practitioners or GPs) 43
Family History 109
Family Physicians (also:
Family Doctors or General
Practitioners or GPs) 43
family planning 54, 290
farsightedness 234
FAS (also: Fetal Alcohol
Syndrome) 133
fascia 226
Fasting Blood Sugar
(also: FBS) 258
fatal 208
FBC (also Full Blood
Count) 109
FBS (also: Fasting Blood
sugar) 258
febrile convulsions 133
feeding intolerance 124
femoral 213
femoropopliteal 211, 214
fem-pop 211, 214
(see also femoropopliteal
211, 214)
femur 219
fertility specialist 283, 285
Fetal Alcohol Syndrome
(also: FAS) 133
fetal circulation 119
fetal distress 298

fetal dystocia 119
Fetal scalp electrode
(also: FSE) 112
fetus 284, 291
fibrillations 180
fibroids 293
fibula 219
filariasis 248
fine needle biopsy 305
fissures 266
fitting 172
flashes (also: flushes) 285
flow murmur 133
'fluid on the lungs' 199
flushes (also: flashes) 285
focal seizures 172
Foley catheter 99
Follicle Stimulating Hormone
(also: FSH) 252
foreign substances 243
Foundation House Officers 62
fractures 221
frank breech 296
(see also breech 296)
Front Desk 73
FSE (also: Fetal Scalp
Electrode) 112
FSH 252
full-blown AIDS 247
fundus 109, 113
fuse 205

G
GA 95 (see also General
Anesthetic or General
Anesthesia 95)
GAD 151 (see also Generalized
Anxiety Disorder 151)
gallbladder 263
gallstones 267
Gamete Intra-Fallopian
Transfer 289
(see also GIFT 289)
gas exchange 194
gas gangrene 222
gaster 261
gastric aspirate 126
gastric bypass 259
gastric carcinoma 162
gastric juices 263
gastric lavage 85
gastric ulcer 269
gastro 261
gastroenterologist 265
gastro-intestinal 261, 262